Bill Arp

The farm

Sketches of domestic life in war and peace

Bill Arp

The farm
Sketches of domestic life in war and peace

ISBN/EAN: 9783337221577

Printed in Europe, USA, Canada, Australia, Japan

Cover: Foto ©ninafisch / pixelio.de

More available books at **www.hansebooks.com**

THE

FARM AND THE FIRESIDE:

SKETCHES OF DOMESTIC LIFE
IN WAR AND IN PEACE.

WRITTEN AND PUBLISHED FOR THE ENTERTAINMENT

OF THE GOOD PEOPLE AT HOME, AND

DEDICATED ESPECIALLY TO

MOTHERS AND CHILDREN.

BY
CHAS. H. SMITH.
(BILL ARP.)

ATLANTA, GEORGIA:
THE CONSTITUTION PUBLISHING COMPANY.
1892.

Entered according to Act of Congress, in the year 1892,

BY THE CONSTITUTION PUBLISHING COMPANY,

in the Office of the Librarian of Congress, at Washington.

CONTENTS.

The Georgia Cracker and the Gander Pulling	9
The Original "Bill Arp"	18
Big John	27
The Roman Runagee	31
His Late Trials and Adventures	37
Bill Arp Addresses Artemus Ward	43
The Falling Leaves	46
Adventures on the Farm	52
Smoking the Pipe of Peace	58
The Sounds on the Front Piazza	63
Mr. Arp Feels His Inadequacy	67
A Feast in a Sycamore Grove	70
Trials and Tribulations	74
Love Affairs	78
Tells of His Wife's Birthday	82
Mrs. Arp Goes Off on a Visit	85
The Voice of Spring	90
The Love of Money	96
Cobe Talks a Little	99
The Ups and Downs of Farming	103
The Family Preparing to Receive City Cousins	108
Bad Luck in the Family	112
The Struggle for Money	117
On a Strain	126
New Years Time	130
Old Things are Passing Away	134
The Country	138

CONTENTS.

But Once a Year	142
Grandfather's Days	150
Making Sausage	157
The Old Trunk	162
The Georgia Colonel	166
On the Old Times—Alexander Stephens, etc	169
Sticking to the Old	174
A Prose Poem on Spring	178
Uncle Bart	181
Christmas on the Farm	183
Democratic Principles	187
Politics	191
Harvest Time	194
The Old and the New	197
The Old School Days	211
Old School Days	216
Roasting Ears and the Midnight Dance	221
Open House	224
The Old Tavern	228
The Old Time Darkeys	232
Owls, Snakes and Whang-Doodles	238
The Autumn Leaves	242
Uncle Tom Barker	246
Bill Arp on Josh Billings	252
The Code Duello	255
Billy in the Low Grounds	260
William Gets Left	263
Pleasures of Hope and Memory	267
Arp's Reminiscenses of Fifty Years	271
William and His Wife Visit the City	277
The Buzzard Lope	281
Up Among the Stars	285

Oh! These Women	289
The Mischievous Little Ones	293
Thoughts on Spring and Love	297
Bill Arp Plays Ring Master	301
Doctors Turned Loose	305
On Hailstones, etc	309
Runaway Negroes, Ghosts and Old-Time Darkeys	313
The Candy Pulling	318
Family Reform	322
Music	327
The Sorrel Hair	333

THE FARM AND THE FIRESIDE.

CHAPTER I.

THE GEORGIA CRACKER AND THE GANDER PULLING.

Not to go back in history further than my own time and recollections, let me venture upon some unoccupied territory and tell how Cherokee Georgia became the home of that much-maligned and misunderstood individual known as the Georgia cracker. I have lived long in his region, and am close akin to him.

There is really but little difference between the Georgia cracker and the Alabama or Tennessee cracker. They all have, or had, the same origin, and until the Appalachian range was opened up to the rest of mankind by railroads and the school-house, these crackers had ways and usages, and a language peculiarly their own.

It will be remembered that until 1835 the Cherokee Indians owned and occupied this region of Georgia—the portion lying west of the Chattahoochee and north of the Tallapoosa rivers. They were the most peaceable and civilized of all the tribes, but they were not subject to Georgia laws, and had many conflicts and disturbances with their white nabors. It seemed to be manifest destiny that they should go. "Go west, red man," was the white man's fiat. They went at the point of the bayonet, and all their beautiful country was suddenly opened to the ingress of whomsoever might come. Georgia had it surveyed and divided into lots of 40 and 160 acres, and then made a lottery and gave every man and widow and orphan child a chance in the drawing. But the cracker didn't wait for the drawing. The rude, untamed and restless people from the mountain borders of Georgia and the Carolinas flocked hither to pursue their wild and fascinating occupation of hunting and fishing for a livelihood. They came separately, but soon assimilated and shared a common interest. There are such spirits in every community. There are some right here now who would rather go up to Cohutta mountains on a bear hunt than to go to New York or Paris for pleasure. I almost would myself, and I recall the earnest cravings of my youth to go west and find a wilderness, and with my companions live in a hut and kill deer and turkeys, and sometimes a bear and a panther.

But for my town raising and old field school education I, too, would have made a very respectable cracker. This was the class of young men and middle-aged that first settled among these historic hills and valleys and climbed these mountains and fished in these streams. By and by the fortunate owners of these lands received their certificates and many of them came from all parts of the State to look up their lots and see how much gold or how much bottom land there was upon them, but gold was the principal attraction. The Indians had found gold and washed it out of the creeks and branches and traded it in small parcels to the white man, and it was believed that every stream was lined with golden sand. This proved an illusion, and so the squatters were not disturbed, or else they bought their titles for a song and then sang "sweet home" of their own. They built their cabins and cleared their lands and raised their scrub cattle, and with their old-fashioned rifles kept the family in game. Many of these settlers could read and write, but in their day there was but little to read. No newspapers, and but few books were found by the hunter's fireside. Their children grew up the same way, but what they lacked in culture they supplied in rough experiences and hair-breadth escapes and fireside talk and in the sports that were either improvised or inherited. Pony races gander pullings, shooting matches, coon hunting and quiltings had more attractions than books. How they got to using such twisted language as you'uns and we'uns and inguns and mout and gwine and all sich is not known, nor was such talk universal. When such idioms began in a family they descended and spread out among the kindred, but it was not contagious. I know one family now of very extensive connections who have a folk-lore of their own, and it can be traced back to the old ancestor who died half a century ago. But these corruptions of language are by no means peculiar to the cracker, for the English cockneys and the genuine yankee have an idiom quite as eccentric, though they do not realize it and would not admit it.

The Georgia cracker was a merry-hearted, unconcerned, independent creature, and all he asked was to be let alone by the laws and the outside world.

The justice court of his beat was quite enough limitation for him. He had far more respect for the old spectacled 'squire than for the highest court in the nation. From this home-made tribunal he never appealed until the young lawyers began to figure in it, and seduced him into the mysteries of the law and the wonderful performances of the writ of "sasherary." Nevertheless, they looked upon lawyers as suspects and parasites, and their descendants have the same opinion still. The old 'squire was specially "fornent" them, and looked upon the sasherary as an insult to his judicial capacity. Sometimes he would let two young limbs of the law argue a case before him for half an hour, and then quietly remark, "Gentlemen, I judgmenticated this case last night at home," and would proceed with his docket. That old 'squire and the preacher were quite enough to pilot these people through life and across the dark river.

A few years after they had settled down as the successors to the Indians a class of more substantial citizens began to look in upon this beautiful country. They purchased the valley lands and the river bottoms, and soon the forests began to fall before the ax of the pioneers. Some of them brought slaves with them and erected sawmills and framed houses with glass windows to live in, and the school master came along, but the crackers were in the majority and lived along in the same old primitive way. As late as 1847 they had gander pullings, and one that I witnessed that summer lasted for two hours, and the original Bill Arp was the victor. I could have seen more of them, but I did not care to, just for the same reason that a kind-hearted man does not wish to see but one hanging.

One Saturday morning when we arrived at Blue Gizzard court-ground, the clans had gathered in unusual force. As preliminary to the more important contest that was soon to come off, some of the boys were shooting at a small piece of white paper that was pinned to a distant tree. Some were gathered around the spring. Some were trying old Mother Tutten's fresh cider and ginger cakes that she offered from the hindgate of her little wagon, and some were sampling the corn whiskey that was kept in a jug in the little log courthouse hard by. We soon perceived the central and most attractive spot to be a small tree with a limb forking about ten feet from its base. A long, slender, springy pole was resting in the fork with the large end pressed to the ground and fastened with stobs crossed on either side and driven firmly in the clay. This incline raised the long end of the pole quite high in the air, and to that end was looped a plow line, and to the lower end of the line another loop was slipped over the crimson feet of a venerable gander and left him swinging, head downwards, just high enough for a horseman to reach it easily as he rode underneath. The doomed bird gave an occasional squawk, and, with wings half open and neck half bent, looked with inquisitive alarm upon the proceedings. The feathers had been stripped from its neck and a thick coat of grease put on instead. The undergrowth had been removed and a running path for the horsemen carefully cleared of all obstructions. The tournament began at 11 o'clock. Twenty sovereigns, mounted on their plow nags, ranged themselves at one end of the path and awaited the call of their names by the old 'squire, who had them written on a fly-leaf in the back of his docket. No man was allowed to ride until he had planked up a dollar. The old 'squire had contributed the gander just out of good will to the boys, he said, and he was nominated as treasurer and umpire and carried the bag, and on his decision the whole sum was to be awarded the victor. He had adjourned his court for two hours to see the fun and keep down any disturbance of the peace. Eight "whippers" were mustered in, four on each side of the running course. They were all armed with good long switches or hickorys, and their willing duty was to see to it that no man's nag moved towards the gander with less alacrity than a gallop. "Now, boys," said he, "not a lope that would keep a nag a-lopin' half an hour in the shade of a tree, but a right lively gallop, and if the critter slows up any, you must peartin him up a little—especially as he's a-nighin' towards the gander."

The boys were true sovereigns. They were not knights. They were arrayed in their home-made pants and home-made shirts and home-knit galluses. Their shoes were made at the tanners and their hats at the hatter's. Coats and vests were not in their regalia. All the naborhood were their spectators, including many women, some with infants at the breast and some with sons in the tournament.

The gathering people exchanged salutations and smiles and gave the family news and gradually drew near the place where the anserian struggle was impending.

The old squire had participated in some old-fashioned musters in his day, and so, when everything was ready he stood on a log and, raising his right hand, exclaimed: "Tention company! In the proceedings that we are about to proceed with it are expected that every man will conduct his behavior accordin' to what's far and honest—no man are to take any disadvantage of ary other man nor of the gander. Thar he are hangin' without a friend. Tote fair boys, tote fair; and put him out of misery as quick as you ken, in reason. Jack Pullum—three paces to the front—now ready—aim—charge."

As Jack stuck his heels in his pony's flank the crowd shouted: "Charge 'em Jack! Charge 'em!" But Jack's critter wasent used to charging. He rebelled at the go and the "whippers in" had to come to his support. He dashed in and out of the path wildly, but finally took the bit in his teeth and started down the line on a desperate run for freedom amid the shouts and cheers of the multitude. He steered well until he suddenly eyed the great white bird just ahead of him. He stopped as if on the brink of a precipice, but Jack went on. That capped the climax of tumultuous hilarity. The like of that was what they came for. Jack caught on his hands and feet, and was soon remounted and took another start, and his nag behaved better, but still did not come in reach of the gander, and Jack lost his chance until the second grand round. "We'uns hain't got no geese at our house," said he, "and my animal never seed one afore as I knows on."

"Samuel Swillin, to the front," called the 'squire. "Ready, aim, charge." Sam's critter was more tractable and Sam got a fair grab, but the grease was too slick for him, and as he slipped his hold the poor bird swang to and fro and flapped his wings and squawked loud and long at the terrible squeeze and the more terrible elongation of his œsophagus. Sam was congratulated on his effort. He wiped his fingers on a pine top, and said: "Yes I'll be dadburned if I wouldent have got him, but the dingd thing was so allfired slickery. I was in hopes that Jack Pullum would have got the fust grab and sleeked offen some of it."

"Rube Underwood—to the front—ready—aim—charge." Rube had a big mouth, and was freckled faced and red headed, and rode a flee-bitten gray that had been taught to dance and prance around and go sideways—"jest to show smart," as the boys said—and it took the animal sometime to be convinced that dancing and prancing wasn't in order at this particular time. A walloping lick just as he neared the goal caused him to make a fearful leap right under the bird, and as Rube had to use both hands to hold his seat, the gander's head collided square in Rube's face and some swore got in his mouth and "effen he had jest shet it he would have had the prize." He retired in good order and awaited his second turn. One by one the riders came as they were called. One after another got some of the grease and wiped it on their horses' manes, but the muscles of the gander were old and tough, and every one of the twenty had gone his round and failed, when the squire called a halt and ordered another greasing. It was evident, however, that some damage had been done the bird, for his wings hung droopy and his voice was failing him. There was a laceration of sinews going on, and but for the fresh greasing the sport would have soon ended. "'Tention, company," said the 'squire. "The proceedinses will now take a little recess. Boys, you can light and look at your saddles, and ef you want water you can go to the spring and git it, but don't wait long, for my old gander are hangin' there without a friend and sufferin'."

The tournament was soon resumed. Bill Arp was the tenth man of the second round. He was the tenth of the first, and many predicted then that he would break that gander's neck or the plow line or the pole, for his grip was like a vise and his agility notorious, but somehow the gander ducked at the critical moment and Bill grabbed his head instead of his neck and made a miscarriage.

As Bill's turn came again the crowd ejaculated : "Now, watch him boys." "Can't he ride, though?" "See how he sots on his critter." "Blamed if he ain't tarred to his nag." "Look at his eye." "No whippers for him." "He's a gwine to carry that gander's head a half a mile before he stops." "Farewell, goose, I'll preach your funeral." "Good-bye gander."

And sure enough, Bill got the right grip this time and in a trice had given the neck a double and something had to break as the pole and the line swiftly followed his motion. For a moment it seemed uncertain what would break or what had broken for the strained tendons popped like a whip as Bill's nag went on at full speed. For a little while the quivering, headless body swung backwards and forwards and was then at rest. Then came the shouts and wild hurrah. Bill was game and so was his critter, and as they came round to the front the crowd gathered round to see the gander's head that he held high in his hand—the warm blood trickling from the arteries. After the jubilee was over Bill invited the nineteen and the 'squire to old Mother Tutten's wagon, and having purchased her stock of cakes and cider and the jug in the courthouse he "gin 'em all a treat." There was not a fuss nor a fight in all the "proceedinses." In a few minutes thereafter the voice of the bailiff was heard crying "Oh yes, oh yes—the honorable court of the 825th deestrict are now met kordin' to adjournment. God save the state and the honorable court."

These rough, rude people were the original Georgia crackers. They constituted a large proportion of the population of Cherokee half a century ago. They were generally poor, but they enjoyed life more than they did money. They were sociable and they were kind. When one of their number was sick they nursed him—when he died they dug a grave and buried him, and that was the end of the chapter. There was no tombstone, no epitaph, no obituary. Their class is fast disappearing from our midst. Civilization has encroached upon them, and now their children and their children's children have assimilated with a higher grade of humanity.

It was among these untutored people that I cast my professional fortunes about 42 years ago. I had been studying law about two months and was admitted on the sly on promise of future diligence—or rather upon the idea that if anybody was fool enough to employ me it was nobody else's business. Another young man of my age was admitted at the same time and he knew less of law if possible than I did. I remember that the first case we had was up in Shake-rag district where two nabors had fallen out because one had accused the other of stealing his hog. And so he sued him in justices court for thirty dollars worth of slander. My Brother Alexander was employed for the plaintiff and I for the defendant. I dident know that a justice court had no jurisdiction over a slander case. My Brother Alexander dident know it. The jury dident know it. I rather suspect that the old 'squire knew it but he wasent the man to limit his own consequence and so we rolled up our sleeves and waded in. My Brother Alexander made a very fine speech for his maiden effort. He talked eloquently to that jury about the value of a man's character—how dear it was to him and his wife and his children and how it should be transmitted down the line from generation to generation pure and untarnished by the foul breath of slander. And he closed his speech with an extract from Shakespeare, wherein he said "He who steals my purse steals trash, but he who filches from me my good name takes that which does not enrich him but makes me poor indeed."

I was very much alarmed and very much impressed with his eloquence, and so I concluded that my very best chance was to ridicule the whole business and laugh it out of court if I could, and I told that jury in conclusion that it was impossible for my client to slander anybody for he had no character of his own to begin with, and nobody would believe anything he said whether he was on oath or off oath.

The old 'squire charged the jury to weigh all the evidence and to agree on a verdik if they could, and if they couldn't then they mout split the difference and compromise. The jury retired to a log near by and cussed and discussed the matter and joked and carried on powerful, and in about half an hour came back with this verdik, "We, the jury, find for the plaintiff two dollars and a half, onless the defendant will take back what he said."

Well, I didn't exactly know whether I had gained the case or lost it, but I took my client out doors and advised him to take it back and save the cost. He finally consented to do this, but said he had hearn that they was gwine to make him sign a lie-bill and he'd be dingnation dadburned if he would do it. So we returned to the seat of war and I stated to his honor that my client had concluded to accept the suggestion of the jury and would take back what he said. The old 'squire congratulated us on our disposition to peace and harmony, and just then my client stretched forth his hand and said: "But 'squire, if I take back what I said, I want it understood that he must bring my hog back."

The next question that came up was who should pay the cost. I contended that my client had complied with the verdict of the jury and was not bound for the costs. My Bro. Alexander contended that he complied a little too late; that he had to be sued to make him comply, and therefore he was bound for the costs. The old 'squire seemed muddled over the question, and finally said that he would leave it to the jury. So they retired to the log again, and in about five minutes came back with this verdict: "We, the jury, find that the lawyers shall pay the cost."

Well, I thought it was all right—and I think so yet. I planked up my dollar, and my Bro. Alexander paid his and we mounted our horses and rode home covered with dust and glory—and glory was all we ever received from our clients.

CHAPTER II.

The Original "Bill Arp."

Some time in the spring of 1861, when our Southern boys were hunting for a fight, and felt like they could whip all creation, Mr. Lincoln issued a proclamation ordering us all to disperse and retire within 30 days, and to quit cavorting around in a hostile and belligerent manner.

I remember writing an answer to it as though I was a good Union man and a law-abiding citizen, and was willing to disperse, if I could, but it was almost impossible, for the boys were mighty hot, and the way we made up our military companies was to send a man down the lines with a bucket of water and sprinkle the boys as he came to 'em, and if a feller sizzed like hot iron in a slack trough, we took him, and if he didn't sizz, we dident take him; but still, nevertheless, notwithstanding, and so forth, if we could possibly disperse in 30 days we would do so, but I thought he had better give us a little more time, for I had been out in old field by myself and tried to disperse myself and couldent do it.

I thought the letter was right smart, and decently sarcastic, and so I read it to Dr. Miller and Judge Underwood, and they seemed to think it was right smart, too. About that time I looked around and saw Bill Arp standing at the door with his mouth open and a merry glisten in his eye. As he came forward, says he to me: "Squire, are you gwine to print that?"

"I reckon I will, Bill," said I. "What name are you gwine to put to it?" said he. "I don't know yet," said I; "I havent thought about a name." Then he brightened up and said: "Well, 'Squire, I wish you would put mine, for them's my sentiments;" and I promised him that I would.

So I did not rob Bill Arp of his good name, but took it on request, and now, at this late day, when the moss has covered his grave, I will record some pleasant memories of a man whose notoriety was not extensive, but who filled up a gap that was open, and who brightened up the flight of many an hour in the good old times, say from 30 to 40 years ago.

He was a small, sinewy man, weighing about 130 pounds, as active as a cat, and always presenting a bright and cheerful face. He had an amiable disposition, a generous heart, and was as brave a man as nature ever makes.

He was an humble man and unlettered in books; never went to school but a month or two in his life, and could neither read nor write; but still he had more than his share of common sense; more than his share of good mother wit, and was always welcome when he came about.

Lawyers and doctors and editors, and such gentlemen of leisure who used to, in the olden time, sit around and chat and have a good time, always said, "come in Bill, and take a seat;" and Bill seemed grateful for the compliment, and with a conscious humility squatted on about half the chair and waited for questions. The bearing of the man was one of reverence for his superiors and thankfulness for their notice.

Bill Arp was a contented man—contented with his humble lot. He never grumbled or complained at anything; he had desires and ambition, but it did not trouble him. He kept a ferry for a wealthy gentleman, who lived a few miles above town, on the Etowah river, and he cultivated a small portion of his land; but the ferry was not of much consequence, and when Bill could slip off to town and hear the lawyers talk, he would turn over the boat and the poles to his wife or his children, and go. I have known him to take a back seat in the court house for a day at a time, and with a face all greedy for entertainment, listen to the learned speeches of the lawyers and charge of the court, and go home happy, and be able to tell to his admiring family what had transpired. He had the greatest reverence for Colonel Johnston, his landlord, and always said that he would about as leave belong to him as to be free; "for," said he, "Mrs. Johnston throws away enough old clothes and second-hand vittels to support my children, and they are always nigh enough to pick 'em up."

Bill Arp lived in Chulio district; we had eleven districts in the county, and they had all such names as Pop-skull, and Blue-gizzard, and Wolf-skin, and Shake-rag, and Wild-cat, and Possum-trot, but

Bill lived and reigned in Chulio. Every district had its best man in those days, and Bill was the best man in Chulio. He could out-run, out-jump, out-swim, out-rastle, out-ride, out-shoot anybody, and was so far ahead that everybody else had given it up, and Bill reigned supreme. He put on no airs about this, and his nabors were all his friends.

But there was another district adjoining, and it had its best man, too. One Ben McGinnis ruled the boys of that beat, and after awhile it began to be whispered around that Ben wasn't satisfied with his limited territory, but would like to have a small tackle with Bill Arp. Ben was a pretentious man. He weighed about 165 pounds, and was considered a regular bruiser. When Ben hit a man he meant business, and his adversary was hurt—badly hurt, and Ben was glad of it. But when Bill Arp hit a man he was sorry for him, and if he knocked him down, he would rather help him up and brush the dirt off his clothes than swell around in triumph. Fighting was not very common with either. The quicker a man whips a fight the less of it he has to do, and both Ben and Bill had settled their standing most effectually. Bill was satisfied with his honors, but Ben was not, for there was many a Ransy Sniffle who lived along the line between the districts, and carried news from the one to the other, and made up the coloring, and soon it was narrated around that Ben and Bill had to meet and settle it.

The court-grounds of that day consisted of a little log shanty and a shelf. The shanty had a dirt floor and a puncheon seat, and a slab for the 'Squire's docket, and the shelf was outside for the whiskey.

The whiskey was kept in a gallon jug, and that held just about enough for the day's business. Most every body took a dram in those days, but very few took too much, unless, indeed, a dram was too much. It was very uncommon to see a man drunk at a country court-ground. Pistols were unknown, and bowie-knives and brass-knuckles and sling-shots and all other devices that gave one man an artful advantage over another.

When Colonel Johnston, who was Bill Arp's landlord, and Major Ayer and myself got to Chulio, Bill Arp was there, and was pleasantly howdying with his nabors, when suddenly we discovered Ben McGinnis arriving upon the ground. He hitched his horse to a swinging limb and dismounted and began trampoosing around, and every

Bill Arp and Ben McGinnis.

little crowd he got to, he would lean forward in an insolent manner and say, "Anybody here got anything agin Ben McGinnis? Ef they have, I golly, I'll give 'em five dollars to hit that; I golly, I dare anybody to hit that," and he would point to his forehead with an air of insolent defiance.

Bill Arp was standing by us and I thought he looked a little more serious than I ever had seen him. Frank Ayer says to him, "Bill, I see that Ben is coming around here to pick a fight with you, and I want to say that you have got no cause of quarrel with him, and if he comes, do you just let him come and go, that's all." Col. Johnston says, "Bill, he is too big for you, and your own beat knows you, and and you havn't done anything against Ben, and so I advise you to let him pass; do you hear me?"

By this time Bill's nervous system was all in a quiver. His face had an air of rigid determination, and he replied humbly, but firmly, "Col. Johnston, I love you, and I respect you, too; but if Ben McGinnis comes up here outen his beat, and into my beat, and me not having done nothing agin him, and he dares me to hit him, I'm going to hit him, if it is the last lick I ever strike. I'm no phist puppy dog, sir, that he should come out of his deestrict to bully me."

I've seen Bill Arp in battle, and he was a hero. I've seen him when shot and shell rained around him, and he was cool and calm, and the same old smile was upon his featurrs, but I never saw him as intensely excited as he was that moment when Ben McGinnis approached us, and, addressing himself to Bill Arp, said, "I golly, I dare anybody to hit that."

As Ben straightened up, Bill let fly with his hard, bony fist right in his left eye, and followed it up with another so quick that the two blows seemed as one. I don't know how it was, and never will know; but in less than a second, Bill had him down and was on him, and his fists and his elbows and his knees seemed all at work. He afterwards said that his knees worked on Ben's bread basket, which he knew was his weakest part. Ben hollered "enough" in due time, which was considered honorable to do when a feller had enough, and Bill helped him up and brushed the dirt off his clothes, and said, "Now, Ben, is it all over betwixt us, is you and me all right?" And Ben said, "It's all right 'twixt you and me, Bill; and you are much of a gentleman."

Bill invited all hands up to the shelf, and they took a drink, and he and Ben were friends.

This is enough of Bill Arp—the original, the simon pure. He was a good soldier in war. He was the wit and the wag of the camp-fires, and made many a homesick youth laugh away his melancholy. He was a good citizen in peace. When told that his son was killed he looked no surprise, but simply said: "Major, did he die all right?" When assured that he did, Bill wiped away a falling tear and said, "I only wanted to tell his mother."

You may talk about heroes and heroines; I have seen all sorts, and so has most everybody who was in the war, but I never saw a more devoted heroine than Bill Arp's wife. She was a very humble woman, very, and she loved her husband with a love that was passing strange. I have seen that woman in town, three miles from her home, hunting around by night for her husband, going from one saloon to another, and in her kind, loving voice inquiring "is William here?" Blessings on that poor woman; I have almost cried for her many a time. Poor William, how she loved him. How tenderly would she take him, when she found him, and lead him home, and bathe his head and put him to bed. She always looked pleased and thankful when asked about him, and would say, "he is a good little man, but you know he has his failings." She loved Bill and he loved her; he was weak and she was strong. There are some such women now, I reckon. I know there are some such men.

BIG JOHN LAMENTS THE WAR.

CHAPTER III.

"BIG JOHN."

"Big John" was one of the earliest settlers of Rome, and one of her most notable men. For several years he was known by his proper name of John Underwood, but when another John Underwood moved there, the old settler had to be identified by his superior size, and gradually lost his surname, and was known far and near as "Big John." The new comer was a man of large frame, weighing about 225 pounds, but Big John pulled down the scales at a hundred pounds more. He had shorter arms and shorter legs, but his circumference was correspondingly immense. He was notable for his humor and his good humor. The best town jokes came from his jolly, fertile fancy, and his comments on men and things were always original, and as terse and vigorous as ever came from the brain of Dr. Johnson. He was a diamond in the rough. He had lived a pioneer among the Indians of Cherokee, and it was said fell in love with an Indian maid, the daughter of old Tustenuggee, a limited chief, and never married because he could not marry her. But if his disappointment preyed upon his heart, it did not prey long upon the region that enclosed it, for he continued to expand his proportions. He was a good talker and an earnest laugher—whether he laughed and grew fat, or grew fat and laughed, the doctors could not tell which was cause and which was effect, and it is still in doubt, but I have heard wise men affirm that laughing was the fat man's safety-valve, that if he did not laugh and shake and vibrate frequently, he would grow fatter and fatter, until his epidermic cuticle could not contain his oleaginous corporosity.

Big John had no patience with the war, and when he looked upon the boys strutting around in uniform, and fixing up their canteens and haversacks, he seemed as much astonished as disgusted. He sat in his big chair on the sidewalk, and would remark, "I don't see any fun in the like of that. Somebody is going to be hurt, and fighting don't prove anything. Some of our best people in this town are kin to them fellers up North, and I don't see any sense in tearing up families by a fight." He rarely looked serious or solemn, but the impending strife seemed to settle him. "Boys," said he, "I hope to God this thing will be fixed up without a fight, for fighting is a mighty bad business, and I never knowed it to do any good."

Big John had had a little war experience—that is, he had volunteered in a company to assist in the forcible removal of the Cherokees to the far west in 1835. It was said that he was no beligerent then, but wanted to see the maiden that he loved a safe transit, and so he escorted the old chief and his clan as far as Tuscumbia, and then broke down and returned to Ross Landing on the Tennessee river. He was too heavy to march, and when he arrived at the Landing, a prisoner was put in his charge for safe keeping. Ross Landing is Chattanooga now, and John Ross lived there, and was one of the chiefs of the Cherokees. The prisoner was his guest, and his name was John Howard Payne. He was suspected of trying to instigate the Cherokees to revolt and fight, and not leave their beautiful forest homes on the Tennessee and Coosa and Oostanaula and the Etowah and Connasauga rivers. He brought Payne back as far as New Echota, or New Town, as it was called, an Indian settlement on the Coosawattee, a few miles east of Calhoun, as now known. There he kept the author of "Home, Sweet Home" under guard, or on his parol of honor, for three weeks, and night after night slept with him in his tent, and listened to his music upon the violin, and heard him sing his own sad songs until orders came for his discharge, and Payne was sent under escort to Washington.

Many a time have I heard Big John recite his sad adventures. "It was a most distressive business," said he. "Them Injuns was heartbroken; I always knowd an Injun loved his hunting-ground and his rivers, but I never knowd how much they loved 'em before. You know they killed Ridge for consentin' to the treaty. They killed him on the first day's march and they wouldent bury him. We soldiers had to stop and dig a grave and put him away. John Ross and John Ridge were the sons of two Scotchmen, who came over here when they were young men and mixed up with these tribes and got their good will. These two boys were splendid looking men, tall and handsome, with long auburn hair, and they were active and strong, and could shoot a bow equal to the best bowman of the tribe, and they beat 'em all to pieces on the cross-bow. They married the daughters of the old chiefs, and when the old chiefs died they just fell into line and succeeded to the old chiefs' places, and the tribes liked 'em mighty well, for they were good men and made good chiefs. Well, you see Ross dident like the treaty. He said it wasent fair and that the price of the territory was too low, and the fact is he dident want to go at all. There are the ruins of his old home now over there in DeSoto, close to Rome, and I tell you he was a king. His word was the law of the Injun nations, and he had their love and their respect. His half-breed children were the purtiest things I ever saw in my life. Well, Ridge lived up the Oostanaula river about a mile, and he was a good man, too. Ross and Ridge always consulted about everything for the good of the tribes, but Ridge was a more milder man than Ross, and was more easily persuaded to sign the treaty that gave the lands to the State and to take other lands away out to the Mississippi.

"Well, it took us a month to get 'em all together and begin the march to the Mississippi, and they wouldn't march then. The women would go out of line and set down in the woods and go to grieving, and you may believe it or not, but I'll tell you what is a fact, we started with 14,000, and 4,000 of 'em died before we got to Tuscumbia. They died on the side of the road; they died of broken hearts; they died of starvation, for they wouldn't eat a thing; they just died all along the way. We didn't make more than five miles a day on the march, and my company didn't do much but dig graves and bury Injuns all the way to Tuscumbia. They died of grief and broken hearts, and no mistake. An Indian's heart is tender, and his love is strong; it's his nature. I'd rather risk an Injun for a true friend than a white man. He is the best friend in the world, and the worst enemy. He has got more gratitude and more revenge in him than "anybody."

Big John's special comfort was a circus. He never missed one, and it was a good part of the show to see him laugh and shake and spread his magnificent face.

He took no pleasure in the quarrels of mankind, and never backed a man in a fight; but when two dogs locked teeth, or two bulls locked horns, or two game chickens locked spurs, he always liked to be about. "It is their nature to fight," said he, "and let 'em fight." He took delight in watching dogs and commenting on their sense and dispositions. He compared them to the men about town, and drew some humorous analogies. "There is Jimmy Jones," said he, "who ripped and splurged around because Georgia wouldn't secede in a minute and a half, and he swore he was going over to South Carolina to fight; and when Georgia did secede shore enough, he didn't join the army at all, and always had some cussed excuse, and when conscription came along, he got on a detail to make potash, con-ding him, and when that played out he got him a couple of track dogs and got detailed to catch runaway prisoners. Just so I've seen dogs run up and down the palings like they was dying to get to one another, and so one day I picked up my dog by the nap of the neck and dropped him over on the outside. I never knowed he could jump that fence before, but he bounced back like an Indian rubber ball, and the other dog streaked it down the sidewalk like the dickens was after him. Dogs are like folks, and folks are like dogs, and a heap of 'em want the palings between. Jack Bogin used to strut round and whip the boys in his beat, and kick 'em around, because he knew he could do it, for he had the most muscle; but he couldn't look a brave man in the eye, muscle or no muscle, and I've seen him shut up quick when he met one. A man has got to be right to be brave, and I had rather see a bully get a licking than to eat sugar."

CHAPTER IV.

THE ROMAN RUNAGEE.

ATLANTA, GA., May 22, 1864.

MR. EDITOR: "Remote, unfriended, melancholy, slow," as somebody said, I am seeking a log in some vast wilderness, a lonely roost in some Okeefenokee swamp, where the foul invaders cannot travel nor their pontoon bridges float. If Mr. Shakespeare were correct when he wrote that "sweet are the juices of adversity," then it is reasonable to suppose that me and my folks, and many others, must have some sweetening to spare. When a man is aroused in the dead of night, and smells the approach of the foul invader; when he feels constrained to change his base and become a runagee from his home, leaving behind him all those ususary things, which hold body and soul together; when he looks, perhaps the last time, upon his lovely home where he has been for many delightful years raising children and chickens, strawberries and peas, lye soap and onions, and all such luxuries of this sublunary life; when he imagines every unusual sound to be the crack of his earthly doom; when from such influences he begins a dignified retreat, but soon is constrained to leave the dignity behind, and get away without regard to the order of his going—if there is any sweet juice in the like of that, I haven't been able to see it. No, Mr. Editor, such scenes never happened in Bill Shakspeare's day, or he wouldn't have written that line.

I don't know that the lovely inhabitants of your beautiful city need any forewarnings, to make 'em avoid the breakers upon which our vessel was wrecked; but for fear they should some day shake their gory locks at me, I will make public a brief allusion to some of the painful circumstances which lately occurred in the eternal city.

Not many days ago the everlasting Yankees (may they live always when the devil gets 'em,) made a valiant assault upon the city of the hills—the eternal city, where for a hundred years the Indian rivers have been blending their waters peacefully together—where the Cherokee children built their flutter mills, and toyed with frogs and tadpoles whilst these majestic streams were but little spring branches babbling along their sandy beds. For three days and nights our valiant troops had beat back the foul invader, and saved our pullets from their devouring jaws. For three days and nights we bade farewell to every fear, luxuriating upon the triumph of our arms, and the sweet juices of our strawberries and cream. For three days and nights fresh troops from the South poured into our streets with shouts that made the welkin ring, and the turkey bumps rise all over the flesh of our people. We felt that Rome was safe—secure against the assault of the world, the flesh and the devil, which last individual is supposed to be that horde of foul invaders who are seeking to flank us out of both bread and existence.

But alas for human hopes! Man that is born of woman (and there is no other sort that I know of) has but a few days that is not full of trouble. Although the troops did shout; although their brass band music swelled upon the gale; although the turkey bumps rose as the welkin rung; although the commanding general assured us that Rome was to be held at every hazard, and that on to-morrow the big battle was to be fought, and the foul invaders hurled all howling and bleeding to the shores of the Ohio, yet it transpired somehow that on Tuesday night the military evacuation of our city was peremptorily ordered. No note of warning—no whisper of alarm—no hint of the morrow came from the muzzled lips of him who had lifted our hopes so high. Calmly and coolly we smoked our killikinick, and surveyed the embarkation of troops, construing it to be some grand manœuvre of military strategy. About ten o'clock we retired to rest, to dream of to-morrow's victory. Sleep soon overpowered us like the fog that covered the earth, but nary bright dream had come, nary vision of freedom and glory. On the contrary, our rest was uneasy—strawberries and cream seemed to be holding secession meetings within our corporate limits, when suddenly, in the twinkling of an eye, a friend aroused us from our slumber and put a new phase upon the "situation." General Johnston was retreating, and the foul invaders were to pollute our sacred soil the next morning. Then came the tug of war. With hot and feverish haste we started out in search of transportation, but nary transport could be had. Time-honored friendship, past favors shown, everlasting gratitude, numerous small and lovely children, Confederate currency, new issues, bank bills, black bottles, and all influences were urged and used to secure a corner in a car but nary corner—too late—too late—the pressure for time was fearful and tremendous—the steady clock moved on—no Joshua about to lengthen out the night, no rolling stock, no steer, no mule. With reluctant and hasty steps, we prepared to make good our exit by that overland line which railroads do not control, nor A. Q. Ms impress.

With our families and a little clothing, we crossed the Etowah bridge about the break of day on Wednesday, the 17th of May, 1864, exactly a year and two weeks from the time when General Forrest marched in triumph through our streets. By and by the bright rays of the morning sun dispersed the heavy fog, which like a pall of death had overspread all nature. Then were exhibited to our afflicted gaze a highway crowded with wagons and teams, cattle and hogs, niggers and dogs, women and children, all moving in disheveled haste to parts unknown. Mules were braying, cattle were lowing, hogs were squealing, sheep were blating, children were crying, wagoners were cursing, whips were popping, and horses stalling, but still the grand caravan moved on. Everybody was continually looking behind, and driving before—everybody wanted to know everything, and nobody knew anything. Ten thousand wild rumors filled the circumambient air. The everlasting cavalry was there, and as they dashed to and fro, gave false alarms of the enemy being in hot pursuit.

About this most critical juncture of affairs, some philanthropic friend passed by with the welcome news that the bridge was burnt, and the danger all over. Then ceased the panic; then came the peaceful calm of heroes after the strife of war is over—then exclaimed Frank Ralls, my demoralized friend, "Thank the good Lord for that. Bill, let's return thanks and stop and rest—boys let me get out and lie down. I'm as humble as a dead nigger—I tell you the truth—I sung the long metre doxology as I crossed the Etowah bridge, and I expected to be a dead man in fifteen minutes. Be thankful, fellows, let's all be thankful—the bridge is burnt, and the river is three miles deep. Good sakes, do you reckon those Yankees can swim? Get up, boys—let's drive ahead and keep moving—I tell you there's no accounting for anything with blue clothes on these days—ding'd if I ain't afraid of a blue-tailed fly."

With a most distressing flow of language, he continued his rhapsody of random remarks.

Then there was that trump of good fellows, Big John—as clever as he is fat, and as fat as old Falstaff—with indefatigable diligence he had secured, as a last resort, a one-horse steer spring wagon, with a low, flat body sitting on two rickety springs. Being mounted thereon, he was urging a more speedy locomotion by laying on to the carcass of the poor old steer with a thrash-pole ten feet long. Having stopped at a house, he procured a two-inch auger, and boring a hole through the dashboard, pulled the steer's tail through and tied up the end in a knot. "My running gear is weak," said he, "but I don't intend to be stuck in the mud. If the body holds good, and the steer don't pull out his tail, why, Bill, I am safe." "My friend," said I, "will you please to inform me what port you are bound for, and when you expect to reach it?" "No port at all, Bill," said he, "I am going dead strait to the big Stone Mountain. I am going to get on the top and roll rocks down upon all mankind. I now forewarn every living thing not to come there until this everlasting foolishness is over." He was then but three miles from town, and had been traveling the livelong night. Ah, my big friend, thought I, when wilt thou arrive at thy journey's end? In the language of Patrick Henry, will it be the next week or the next year? Oh, that I could write a poem, I would embalm thy honest face in epic verse. But I was in a right smart hurry myself, and only had time to drop his memory a passing rhyme.

> Farewell, Big John, Farewell!
> 'Twas painful to my heart
> To see thy chances of escape,
> Was that old steer and cart.
>
> Methinks I see thee now,
> With axletrees all broke,
> And wheels with nary hub at all,
> And hubs with nary spoke.
>
> But though the mud is deep,
> Thy wits will never fail;
> That faithful steer will pull thee out,
> If he don't pull out his tail.

Mr. Editor, under such variegated scenes we reported progress, and in course of time arrived under the shadow of thy city's wings, abounding in gratitude and joy.

Big John Makes Haste Slowly.

With sweet and patient sadness, the tender hearts of our wives and daughters beat mournfully as we moved along. Often, alas, how often was the tear seen swimming in the eye, and the lips quivering with emotion, as memory lingered around deserted homes, and thoughts dwelt upon past enjoyments and future desolation. We plucked the wild flowers as we passed, sang songs of merriment, exchanged our wit with children—smothering, by every means, the sorrow of our fate. These things, together with the comic events that occurred by the way, were the safety-valves that saved the poor heart from bursting. But for these our heads would have been fountains and our hearts a river of tears. Oh, if some kind friend would set our retreat to music, it would be greatly appreciated indeed. It should be a plaintiff tune, interspersed with occasional comic notes, and frequent fuges scattered promiscuously along.

Our retreat was conducted in excellent good order, *after the bridge was burnt.* If there was any straggling at all, they straggled ahead. It would have delighted General Johnston to have seen the alacrity of our movements.

But I must close this melancholy narrative, and hasten to subscribe myself   Your runagee,   BILL ARP.

P. S.—Tip is still faithful unto the end. He says the old turkey we left behind has been setting for fourteen weeks, and the fowl invaders are welcome to *her.* Furthermore, that he threw a dead cat into the well, and they are welcome to that.   B. A.

HIS LATE TRIALS AND ADVENTURES.

Some frog-eating Frenchman has written a book, and called it "Lee's Miserables," or some other such name, which I suppose contains the misfortunes of poor refugees in the wake of the Virginny army. General Hood had also got a few miserables in the suburbs of his fighting-ground, and if any man given to romance would like a fit subject for a weeping narrative, we are now ready to furnish the mournful material.

As the Yankees remarked at Bull Run, "these are the times that try men's soles," and I suppose my interesting family is now prepared to show stone bruises and blisters with anybody. It is a long story, Mr. Editor, and cannot possibly be embraced in a single column of your wandering newspaper; but I will condense it as briefly as possible, smoothing over the most affecting parts, so as not to occasion too great a diffusion of sympathetic tears.

After our hasty flight from the eternal city, we became converted over to the doctrine of squatter sovereignty, and pitched our tents in the piney woods. Afar off in those fields of illimitable space, we roamed through the abstruse regions of the philosophic world. There no unfriendly soldier was perusing around and asking for papers. There the melancholy mind was soothed. There the lonely runagee could contemplate the sandy roads, the wire-grass woods, and the millions of majestic pines that stood like ten-pins in an alley, awaiting some huge cannon-ball to come along and knock 'em down. The mountain scenery in this romantic country was grand, gloomy and peculiar, consisting in numberless gopher-hills, spewed up in promiscuous beauty as far as the eye could reach. All around us the swamp frogs were warbling their musical notes. All above us the pines were sighing and singing their mournful tunes. Dame Nature has spread herself there in showing her lavish hand, and wasting timber along those endless glades. Truly, we were treading on classic ground, for we pitched our tents in a blackberry patch, and morning, noon and night, luxuriated in peace upon the delicious fruit which everywhere adorned the sandy earth.

But those piney woods to which we fled, did not, by any means, agree with our ideas of future comfort. After it had rained some forty days and forty nights without a recess, the corn crop had pretty well died out, and General Starvation seemed about to assume command of the region round about.

We felt constrained to depart from those coasts, and seek an Egypt somewhere in a rounder and more rolling country. So we took the train for Atlanta and designed to take roundance from there and find a retreat away up the Chattahoochee river where Mrs. Arp's father lived.

All along the line, at every station, pretty women get on and get off. When they leave us, an affectionate man like myself unconsciously whispers, "Depart in peace, ye treasures of delight." Casting a longing, lingering look behind, I exclaimed in the beautiful language of Mr. Shakespeare, 'I have thee not, but yet I see thee still.' Farewell, sweet darlings, until I come again. But woman is sometimes very variegated and peculiar in the way she does. I am just reminded how, on a late occasion, I found but one vacant seat in the car after I located my numerous and interesting family. A luxurious lady, with some aggravating curls, had occupied nearly all of a seat spreading herself like a setting-hen, all over the velvet cushion. "Madam, can I share this seat with you?" said I. "Certainly, sir," and she closed in her skirts some several inches. In a short space of time she became affected with drowsiness. Her neck became as limber as a greasy rag. Leaning on my shoulder, she seemed wonderfully affectionate, as her head kept bobbing around, and I felt very peculiar at such times as she would subside into my palpitating bosom. About this critical juncture, I ventured to turn my astonished gaze towards Mrs. Arp, and seeing that she was waiting for some remark, I observed, "Hadn't I better remove my seat? Do you think I can endure the like of this?"

"I do not, William," said she. "You had better stand up awhile, and when you get tired some of the children will relieve you." The glance of her eye and the manner in which she spoke brought me up standing, and gave me a correct view of the situation. Immediately I assumed a perpendicular attitude, and the curly head was left without a prop. I assure you, Mr. Editor, a man's wife is the best judge of such peculiar things; and as for me, I am always governed by it.

We arrived in Atlanta about the time the first big shells commenced scattering their unfeeling contents among the suburbs of that devoted city. Then came the big panics; then shrieked the man-eater; then howled the wild hyena among the hills of Babylon.

All sorts of people seemed moving in all sorts of ways, with an accelerated motion. They gained ground on their shadows as they leaned forward on the run, and their legs grew longer at every step. With me it was the second ringing of the first bell. I had sorter got used to the thing, and set myself down to take observations. "How many miles to Milybright?" said I. But no response came, for their legs were as long as light, and every bursting shell was an old witch on the road. Cars was the all in all. Depots were the center of space, converging lines from every point of the compass made tracks to the offices of railroad superintendents. These functionaries very prudently vamoosed the ranch to avoid their too numerous friends, leaving positive orders to their subordinates. The passenger depot was thronged with anxious seekers of transportation. "Won't you let these boxes go as baggage?" "No, madam, it is impossible." Just then somebody's family trunk as big as a nitre bureau was shoved in, and the poor woman got desperate. "All I've got ain't as heavy as that," said she; "I am a poor widow, and my husband was killed in the army. I've got five children, and three of them cutting teeth, and my things have got to go." We took up her boxes and shoved them in. Another good woman asked very anxiously for the Macon train. "There it is, madam," said I. She shook her head mournfully and remarked, "You are mistaken, sir, don't you see the engine is headed right up the State road, towards the Yankees? I sha'nt take any train with the engine at that end of it. No, sir, that ain't the Macon train." Everywhere was hurrying to and fro at a lively tune. "What's to-day, nigger," said a female darkey, with a hoop-skirt on her arm. "'Taint no day, honey, dat eber I seed. Yesterday was Sunday, and I recokon to-day is Runday from de way de white folks are movin' about. Yah, yah; ain't afeered of Yankees myself, but dem sizzin bum-shells kills a nigger quicker dan you can lick your tongue out. Gwine to get away from here—I is."

I went into a doctor's shop, and found my friend packing up his vials and poisons and copiva and such like. Various excited individuals came in, looked at a big map on the wall, and pointed out the roads to McDonough and Eatonton and Jasper, and soon their proposed lines of travel were easily and greasily visible from the impression of their perspiring fingers. An old skeleton, with but one leg, was swinging from the ceiling looking like a mournful emblem of the fate of the troubled city. "You are going to leave him to stand guard, doctor?" said I. "I suppose I will," said he; "got no transportation for him." "Take the screw out of his skull," said I, "and give him a crutch, maybe he will travel; all flesh is moving and I think the bones will catch the contagion soon."

A few doors further, and a venerable auctioneer was surveying the rushing, running crowd, and every now and then he would raise his arm with a seesaw motion and exclaim, "Going—going—gone! Who's the bidder?" "Old Daddy Time," said I, "he'll get them all before long." The door of an old friend's residence swung open to my gaze, and I walked in. Various gentlemen of my acquaintance were discussing their evidences of propriety over a jug of departing spirits. "I believe I'll unpack," said one, "dinged if I'm afraid of a bluetailed fly; I'm going to sit down and be easy. "In a horn," said I. Just then a sizzing, singing, crazy shell sung a short-metre hymn right over the house. "Jake, has the dray come?" he said, bouncing to his feet: "confound that dray—blame my skin if I'll ever get a dray to move these things—boys, let's take another drink." After which, another friend remarked, "Boys, lets all stay; durned if it don't look cowardly to run! Boys, here's to—who shall we drink to?" "Here's to Cassabianca," said I. "Good, good," they all shouted. "Here's to Cabysianka. Let me speak it for you, boys," said our host; "I've spoken it a thousand times." He mounted the seat of a broken sofa, and spreading himself, declaimed:

"The boy stood on the burning deck,
When all had fled but him."

"That's me," said one. "It's me exactly," said another. "I'm Cabysianka myself—dog my cat if I don't be the last one to leave this ship." Another shell sizzed, and bursted a few yards off, "Boys let's take another drink and leave the town—dod rot the Yankees." "Here's to—the—the 'Last of the Mohikans,'" said I. "Exactly—that's so. I'm him myself. I'm the mast of the Lobikens; durned if I'll leave these diggins as long as—as long as——" "As the State road," said I, "which is now about four inches and a half." "That's it; that's so," said my friends. "Here's to the State road and Dr. Brown and Joe Phillips, as long as four inches and a half."

By and by the shells fell as thick as Governor Brown's proclamations, causing a more speedy locomotion in the excited throng who hurried by the door, but my friends inside had passed the Rubicon, and one by one retired to dream of Bozarris and his Suliote band. Vacant rooms and long corridors echoed with their snores, and they appeared like sleeping heroes in the halls of the Montezumas.

Contageous diseases are said to be catching and the Atlanta big panics brought the Atlanta folks to an active perpendicular quicker than all the physic ever seen in a city drug store. It certainly has a tendancy to arouse the dormant energies of feeble invalids. Weak backs and lame legs, old chronics and rheumatics, in fact, all the internal diseases which honest fear of powder and ball had developed since the war began, were now forgotten in the general flight; and the examining boards could have seen many a discharge invalidated, and a *living, moving lie* given to their certificates.

All day and all night long the iron horses were snorting to the echoing breeze. Train after train of goods and chattels moved down the road, leaving hundreds of anxious faces waiting their return. There was no method in this madness. All kinds of plunder was tumbled in promiscuously. A huge parlor mirror, some six feet by eight, all bound in elegant gold, with a brass buzzard spreading his wings on top, was set up at the end of the car and reflected a beautiful assortment of parlor furniture to match, such as pots, kettles, baskets, bags, barrels, kegs, bacon and bedsteads piled up together. Government officials had the preference and government officials all have friends. Any clever man with a charming wife or a pretty sister could secure a corner in more cars than one, and I will privately mention to you, Mr. Editor, that I have found a heap of civility on this account myself. Indeed, I have always thought that no man is excusable who has not either one or the other.

CHAPTER V.

BILL ARP ADDRESSES ARTEMUS WARD.

ROME, GA., September 1, 1865.

MR. ARTEMUS WARD, *Showman*—

SIR: The reason I write to you in perticler, is because you are about the only man I know in all "God's country," *so-called*. For some several weeks I have been wantin' to say sumthin'. For some several years we rebs, *so-called*, but now late of said country deceased, have been tryin' mighty hard to do somethin'. We didn't quite do it, and now it's very painful, I assure you, to dry up all of a sudden, and make out like we wasn't there.

My friend, I want to say somethin'. I suppose there is no law agin thinkin', but thinkin' don't help me. It don't let down my thermometer. I must explode myself generally so as to feel better. You see, I'm tryin' to harmonize. I'm tryin' to soften down my feelin's. I'm endeavoring to subjugate myself to the level of surroundin' circumstances, *so-called*. But I can't do it until I am allowed to say somethin'. I want to quarrel with somebody and then make friends. I ain't no giant-killer. I ain't no Norwegian bar. I ain't no boar-constrickter, but I'll be hornswaggled if the talkin' and writin' and slanderin' has got to be all done on one side any longer. Sum of your folks have got to dry up or turn our folks loose. It's a blamed outrage, *so-called*. Ain't you editors got nothin' else to do but peck at us, and squib at us, and crow over us? Is every man what can write a paragraph to consider us bars in a cage, and be always a-jobbin' at us to hear us growl? Now, you see, my friend, that's what's disharmonious, and do you jest tell 'em, one and all, e pluribus unum, *so-called*, that if they don't stop it at once or turn us loose to say what we please, why we rebs, *so-called*, have unanimously and jointly and severally resolved to—to—to—think very hard of it—if not harder.

That's the way to talk it. I ain't agoin' to commit myself. I know when to put on the breaks. I ain't goin' to say *all* I think. Nary time. No, sir. But I'll jest tell you, Artemus, and you may tell it to your show. If we ain't allowed to express our sentiments, we can take it out in *hatin'*; and hatin' runs heavy in my family, sure. I hated a man once so bad that all the hair cum off my head, and the man drowned himself in a hog-waller that night. I could do it agin, but you see I'm tryin' to harmonize, to acquiess, to becum calm and sereen.

Now, I suppose that, poetically speakin',

"In Dixie's fall,
We sinned all."

But talkin' the way I see it, a big feller and a little feller, *so-called*, got into a fite, and they fout and fout a long time, and everybody all 'round kept hollerin', "hands off," but helpin' the big feller, until finally the little feller caved in and hollered enuf. He made a bully fite, I tell you. Well, what did the big feller do? Take him by the hand and help him up, and brush the dirt off his clothes? Nary time! No, sur! But he kicked him arter he was down, and throwed mud on him, and drugged him about and rubbed sand in his eyes, and now he's gwine about huntin' up his poor little property. Wants to confiscate it, *so-called*. Blame my jacket if it ain't enuf to make your head swim.

But *I'm* a good Union man, *so-called*. *I* ain't agwine to fight no more. *I* shan't vote for the next war. *I* ain't no gurrilla. I've done tuk the oath, and I'm gwine to keep it, but as for my bein' subjugated, and humilyated, and amalgamated, and enervated, as Mr. Chase says, it ain't so—nary time. I ain't ashamed of nuthin' neither—ain't repentin'—ain't axin' for no one-horse, short-winded pardon. Nobody needn't be playin' priest around me. I ain't got no twenty thousand dollars. Wish I had; I'd give it to these poor widders and orfins. I'd fatten my own numerous and interestin' offspring in about two minutes and a half. They shouldn't eat roots and drink branch-water no longer. Poor unfortunate things! to cum into this subloonary world at sich a time. There's four or five of them that never saw a sirkis or a monkey-show—never had a pocket-knife, nor a piece of chees, nor a reesin. There's Bull Run Arp, and Harper's Ferry Arp, and Chicahominy Arp, that never saw the pikters in a spellin' book. I tell you, my friend, we are the poorest people on the face of the earth—but we are poor and proud. We made a bully fite, and the whole American nation ought to feel proud of it. It shows what

Americans can do when they think they are imposed upon. Didn't our four fathers fight, bleed and die about a little tax on tea, when not one in a thousand drunk it? Bekaus they succeeded, wasn't it glory? But if they hadn't, I suppose it would have been treason, and they would have been bowin' and scrapin' round King George for pardon. So it goes, Artemus, and to my mind, if the whole thing was stewed down it would make about half a pint of humbug. We had good men, great men, Christian men, who thought we was right, and many of them have gone to the undiscovered country, and have got a pardon as is a pardon. When I die I am mighty willing to risk myself under the shadow of their wings, whether the climate be hot or cold. So mote it be.

Well, maybe I've said enough. But I don't feel easy yet. I'm a good Union man, certain and sure. I've had my breeches died *blue*, and I've bot a *blue* bucket, and I very often feel *blue* and about twice in a while I go to the doggery and git *blue*, and then I look up at the *blue* cerulean heavens and sing the melancholy chorus of the *Blue-tailed Fly*. I'm doin' my durndest to harmonize, and think I could succeed if it wasn't for sum things.

I don't want much. I ain't ambitious, as I used to was. You all have got your shows and monkeys and sircusses and brass bands and organs, and can play on the patrolyum and the harp of a thousand strings, and so on, but I've only got one favor to ax you. I want enough powder to kill a big yaller stumptail dog that prowls around my premises at night. Pon my honor, I won't shoot at anything blue or black or mulatter. Will you send it? Are you and your folks so skeered of me and my folks that you won't let us have any ammunition? Are the squirrels and crows and black racoons to eat up our poor little corn-patches? Are the wild turkeys to gobble all around with impunity? If a mad dog takes the hiderphoby, is the whole community to run itself to death to get out of the way? I golly! it looks like your people had all took the rebelfoby for good, and was never gwine to get over it. See here, my friend, you must send me a little powder and a ticket to your show, and me and you will harmonize sertin.

With these few remarks I think I feel better, and I hope I han't made nobody fitin' mad, for I'm not on that line at this time.

I am truly your friend, all present or accounted for.

CHAPTER VI.

The Falling Leaves.

The blackgum leaves are turning red,
The sycamores are turning yellow,
The farmer feels serene and glad,
For everything is ripe and mellow.

The nights are getting cool, and the days are getting shorter. The fodder is all pulled and safely stowed away in the barn loft.

If facts are stubborn things, then pulling fodder in the low grounds is a fact. There ain't a redeeming circumstance about it. Its working on a continual strain to pull it, and there's no fun in tyeing it up, and I reckon that the toting of it two or three hundred yards to the wagon road, ten bundles at a time, stepping like a blind horse over corn-stalks bent down, and tripping up in tangled morning glories, and every now and then losing your holt and having to load up again, and all the time smothered up so that you can't see where you are going, and not a breath of refreshing air to cool you, is about the meanest business I have ever experienced. It's all fact—solemn fact—no romance, no poetry, no joke. But that ain't all of it. Its got to be hauled and then thrown up in the barn loft and stacked away, and if there's any hotter place to work in than a barn loft, I don't know it, and I've been considerin' that after its all done you can't sell it for more than a dollar a hundred, and right now, in my present frame of mind, if I had any to sell and some fellow without any soul was to offer me 90 cents I should hit him if it was the last lick I ever struck. They may jew me on corn and wheat and cotton and potatoes, but I won't be jewed on my fodder by nobody. It does seem to me that all this sort of work ought to be done by machinery or not to be done at all.

I've been diggin' my taters. Me and the children have been looking forward to this interesting side-show to the farming business with pleasant anticipations. I always did love to follow after the plow

SPLITTING THE MIDDLES.

and see 'em roll out and tumble up, and pick up the big ones and feel the weight of them, but I didn't calculate on having to make a full hand. For two whole days my boys pressed me into service, and I got awful tired of picking up and toting off in the baskets to the end of the rows where the vines would be handy to cover them up. My farmer boy stripped the vines with a horse-rake of his own invention, and it done it better and cleaner than I ever saw done with a plow. Then he run a one-horse twister on each side, and me and the little chaps kept up pretty well, and when he split op·n the middles and throws 'em up right and left we all had to move up lively, I tell you. My legs are all right, but I don't believe my back is as limber as it used to be. I got awful tired, and the plow business seemed to go 'long so smooth and easy I ventured to exchange work for awhile. I could run round the rows pretty well, but when I come to splitting open the middles the plagued thing seemed to get cranky, and would run out and run in, first on one side and then on the other, and the furrows I left behind looked like the track of a crazy snake. I used to could plow, but *it looks like I have lost the lick.* *My boys was a-lookin' at me* and smotherin' their fun, and about the time I was willin' to quit I observed Mrs. Arp and the girls a-perusin' me through the crack of the fence. They was mighty nigh dead from laughing, which I didn't enjoy, but the sympathizin' woman suddenly composed herself and remarked that I was workin' too hard considerin' my age and infirmity. "You are all over in a sweat of perspiration," said she, "and I thought you had a touch of St. Vitus dance, as you was following that plow. Let the boys do it, and come to the house and rest." But I wouldent. I'm not going to give it up yet by no means. I'm not going to get old before she does—nary time. So I stuck to the patch until the job was done and I got the sticky turpentine juice that milks out of the yams all over my hands, and the stain died my fingers an Injun red, and it wouldn't wash off nor scour off, but it's all honest, and is a sign of work. I tell you what, hard work and the sweat of the face is the curse of that original sin put on us, but it was tempered down in mercy, and there is a comfort that follows it that folks who don't try it don't know anything about. The law of compensation comes into everything in this life, and the poor can be about as happy as the rich, if they have a mind to, and don't spend their time in grumblin' and complainin' about their hard lot in this subloonary life.

Hard work is the best antidote for grumbling. It won't do to stop. If I can't plow I can do something else; I can tote water for a rest.

Grease the wagon, oil the machinery, lubricate the energies with a little recreation. Don't run in the old ruts too long. Dig a while and then try another tool. My good old father used to say, "William, when you get tired hoeing potatoes you may weed the onions for a rest." Chop wood, shell corn, go to mill, and it won't hurt to take a little tramp after squirrels and ducks and partridges or pursue the social 'possum on a moonlight night. Variety is the spice of life. It helps a man in body and mind, but the poor women can't do such things to any great extent—tho' my girls do sometimes go 'possum huntin' with me and the boys and blow the melodious cows' horns and scream at a booger in every bush. One day the boys said it was too wet to plow and they were going down on the creek to hunt rabbits, so I concluded to go along and tote the game. Mrs. Arp said she knew we wouldn't kill anything, and we asked her if she would cook all we brought home, and she said, "Yes, and dress it, too." About the time we got started the two little chaps came up and begged me so sweetly to let them go I couldn't refuse, and so there were six of us in all, and two guns and two dogs, and in about an hour we had jumped six rabbits, and killed five of them, and they were getting awful heavy, when suddenly one of the boys looked up in an elm tree that was in the middle of a canebrake and said, "I thought them things up there were squirrels' nests, but I do believe I saw one of 'em move." We all stopped and looked, and sure enuf it did move, and the other one moved and we knew they were coons. I never saw boys get excited so quick. They called the dogs and made for the canebrake. The creek was to cross and nary log in sight, so they just waded through and surrounded the tree and held the dogs fast while one of the boys got ready to fire. By this time I was getting ready to be a boy again myself, and I hollered to them to wait, and I pulled the little chaps through the cane till I found a log and got them across, and was soon on the battle-ground. Bang went a gun and down came a wounded coon, the biggest old fellow I ever saw, and I never saw such a fight in my life. He wasn't hurt much with the small shot and he did fight and growl and screech most amazin'. First one dog and then the other backed out with a howl and then set in on him again, until finally old Zip surrendered and gave up the ghost. Bang went another gun and the other coon let go and fell into a fork, and there he lay for dead for about fifteen minutes, when one of the boys said he was going to have him anyhow. So he climbed the tree, and when he had got about fifty feet up the coon straightened up in the fork and looked savagely at him and gave a growl. I wish you could have seen that boy slide. He came down that tree like a fireman comes down a scaling ladder. He left his hat and right smart of his breeches on the bark and grapevines. Well, of course they shot him again, and that tumbled him, and then we had another fight, and the boys say they never had as much fun, and they feel sorry for your town boys who don't have any sport and are penned up within brick walls and the best they can do is to waste a few dollars on a French actress, and not know a word she said, and then go home and say, bully for Sara. Well, I shouldered the biggest coon, and I think he weighed about twenty pounds when we started and about forty when I got home, and I laid him down suddenly in Mrs. Arp's lap and said, "Skin him and cook him, if you please?" I oughtent to have done that. It was premature, and not altogether calculated to promote our conjugal felicity. Mrs. Arp is a stately, deliberate woman, but I think she got up a little quicker than I had ever observed her. If I were to kill a thousand coons I wouldn't try that little joke again. It didn't pay.

But we had lots of fun out of the coons, and the time spent in the hunt was not wasted, for the sport renewed our energies and made us feel all the more like work.

And so we go, mixing in with our daily labor any fun that comes to hand.

CHAPTER VII.

ADVENTURES ON THE FARM.

Variety is the spice of life; and if a man can get any fun out of trouble he had better do it. Farming is an ever-changing employment. There is something new turns up nearly every day, something unexpected and out of the general run. It aint so with storekeepers, nor carpentering, nor any mechanical business, for with those pursuits one day is pretty much like another, and that is why I like farming. There is more play for a man's ingenuity and contrivance and more gratification in his success. If a farmer contrives a good gate or a good stall for the stables, or makes a good wagon tongue, or a single-tree, or plow stock, he is proud of his labors and thinks more of himself.

I have been mighty busy of late fixing up fences. Fences are a big thing in these parts, and if a man aint careful it will take about half he makes on his farm to keep 'em mule high and bull strong and pig tight. I had about a mile to build this spring, and timber was too scarce to make it all of rails, so I went to work and cut down a lot of pines for stock; and borrowed a carrylog and began to haul 'em to the saw mill. The pines were on the side of a rocky ridge, and the steers were sorter bull-headed and took all sorts of roads to get down, and run over saplings, and against stumps, and my old darkey couldn't do much with 'em, and the iron dogs would come out of the logs when the hind end rolled over a rock, and the log would stop and the steers go on, and it took all hands to head 'em with sticks and thrash poles and make 'em turn around and go back and straddle the log again—we had to swing one big log five times before we got down to the road—and it was "gee Dick," and "haw Tom," and "come back here," and "whar you gwine" a hundred times, and the key come out of the bow, and the bow dropped down, and old Tom thought he was loose and started for home, and we had a time of it all around. After awhile I noticed that the dogs were too straight and didn't

BILL TRIES THE CARRY-LOG.

swell around the log as they ought to, so I sent 'em to the shop and bent 'em, and after that we could drive 'em in deeper, and we had no more trouble on that line. When we got all the stocks down to the big road, we began to haul 'em to the mill, and there was a right smart hill to go up, which was the only hill on the way. Old Tom is a mean old steer. He is just like some folks, he has fits of pulling and fits of not pulling and when he does pull he wants to pull as hard as he can. He took a notion that the hill was too much for him, so he wouldn't go worth a cent; we hawd him, and gee'd him and whipped him, and hollered at him and twisted his tail, but he got sullen and got down on his knees and played off, and we fooled away half a day without moving a stock. Then I sent after the mules and a double tree, and fifth chain, and hitched the mules in front and all hands hollered "get up there," and I cracked the long whip and old Tom come down to his work, for he saw he had help, and the way we jerked those logs up the hill was a cortion. We had no more trouble after that, until the time to go home, and I concluded a ride on the carrylog tongue would suit me pretty well, for Ralph, my fourteen year old boy, said it was good riding, and so I mounted on the little plank seat, and took the lines and the whip and give the words of command, and suddenly old Tom took a notion to run away for amusement. It was down a gentle grade for a quarter of a mile, and there were deep little ruts in the road, and pine roots crossing it ever and anon and some turnouts around the bad places, and so I began to pull on the lines and holler, "wo, wo, wo, I tell you; wo Tom, wo Dick," but they paid no more attention to me than if I was a big hog in the road. They just went a kiting, and didn't miss a big stump half an inch, and the ruts and the roots bumped me up and down like a churn dasher. I never was scared so bad in my life. The darkey and Ralph come a running as fast as they could to get ahead of the brutes, and that made 'em worse. I didn't dare to jump off for fear the big wheels would get me, and then there was those confounded iron dogs with their big hooks hanging down and I expected every minute to be jolted off, and have 'em catch me in the slack of my pants, or somewhere else, and drag me home a mangled and lifeless carcass. I dropped the long whip and let the lines go, when suddenly a turn in the road brought the infernal beasts right square up against a wagon that was coming, and they stopped. I left that tongue before you could say Jack Robinson, and sat down on a log to be thankful.

Driving steers is not my forte, and I shall hereafter let all such foolishness alone. The folks have not got done laughing at me yet. Carl drew a picture on his slate of a carrylog and steers and two big hooks a hanging down, and a man hugging the tongue, and when I came into the room Jesse was a cackling and the girls a giggling, and Mrs. Arp laughing like she had found a circus; but I can't see any more fun in it than a last year's bird's nest.

I am building a fence now, a good fence, and a cheap fence. We got one hundred chestnut posts, six feet long, in one day, and hauled 'em home. I put 'em twenty-two inches in the ground and twelve feet apart; my plank is twelve feet long. The base is ten inches wide, and the next three six inches wide, and then comes the barbed wire two inches below the top of the post, and this makes the fence just four feet high. There is a strip of six-inch plank nailed up and down in the middle of every panel, which is nearly as good as if there was a post in the middle. This strip keeps the plank in line and keeps them from warping. The nails should not be driven in straight, but a little slanting to make 'em hold better. I built a half mile of this kind of fence two years ago, and can find no fault with it. The wind can't blow it down, and stock never try to jump it. My lumber cost me five dollars a thousand for sawing; my wire cost me half a cent a foot, and that makes the fence cost twenty-eight cents a rod besides my labor, and a rail fence can't be built much cheaper, considering the value of timber. Fences are generally made too high and too top-heavy, and the wind rocks 'em about, and the posts get loose, and the rain drips in and rots 'em. Gates are most always made too heavy—a gate should be made wide, say nine feet, and very light. Use bolts instead of nails at the corner and in the middle of the brace. Don't let the gate swing when it is shut. Let the bottom of the latch post rest on a piece of scantling, bevel the scantling a little and let the gate slide upon it as it shuts. An iron roller put in like one is put in a bed-post is a good thing, for then the gate will roll up instead of slide up. A gate is open very little compared with the time it is shut, and if it rests on something when shut it will never swag when open. A gate should be no higher than the fence, but I make my farm gates with the hinge post three feet higher, and run a brace across that one from the other two corners. Pack post well at the bottom, especially on the front and back. The plank will hold 'em the other way. I think I know a right smart about gates and about fencing, but I don't know how to drive steers, and I don't want to learn.

CHAPTER VIII.

SMOKING THE PIPE OF PEACE.

REFLECTIONS AND DEDUCTIONS—BUGS AND THINGS—THE RISE AND FALL OF PRESIDENTS AND PREACHERS—A HIGH-MINDED MULE—A LITTLE POLITICAL DISCOURSE—SOLDIERS OF THE CAMP AND SOLDIERS OF THE CROSS.

I love to meet a nabor and hear him say, "how's craps?" I continue to like farmin'. I like it better and better, except that the wheat is sumwhat doubtful about making a crop. A little long bug with a tail at both ends has got in the joints and sucked the sap out, and it's fallin' down in patches. Looks like there is always somthin' preyin on somthin', and nothin' is safe from disaster in this subloonary world. Flies and bugs and rust prey on the green wheat. Weevils eat it up when it's cut and put away. Rats eat the corn—moles eat the gubbers—hawks eat the chickens—the minks killed three of our ducks in one night—cholera kills the hogs—and the other night one of my nabor's mules cum along with the blind staggers and fell up a pair of seven steps right into my front gate and died without kickin'. Then there is briars and nettles and tread safts and smartsweed and poison oak and Spanish needles and cuckle burrs and dog fennel and snakes, that's always in the way on a farm and must be looked after keerfully, especially snakes, which are my eternal horror, and I shall always believe are sum kin to the devil himself. I can't tolerate such long insects. But we farmers hav to take the bad with the good, and there is more good than bad with me up to the present time.

I wonder if Harris ever saw a pack saddle. Well, its as pretty as a rainbow, just like most all of the devil's contrivances, and when you crowd one of 'em on a fodderblade you'd think that forty yaller jackets had stung you all in a bunch and with malice aforethought. And there's the devil's race horse which plies around about this time and, Uncle Isam says, chaws tobakker like a gentleman and if he spit in your eyes you'd go blind in a half a second. And one day he showed me the devil's darning needle which mends up the old fellow's stockins, and the devil's snuff box which explodes when you mash it, and one ounce of the stuff inside will kill a sound mule before he can lay down. Then there's some flowers that he wears in his button-hole called the devil's shoestring and the devil in the bush.

I like farmin'. Its an honest, quiet life, and it does me so much good to work and get all over in a swet of presperation. I enjoy my umble food and my repose, and get up every mornin' renewed and rejuvenated like an eagle in his flight, or words to that effect. I know I shall like it more and more, for we have already passed over the Rubycon, and are beginnin' to reap the rewards of industry. Spring chickens have got ripe, and the hens keep bloomin' on. Over 200 now respond to my old 'oman's call every morning, as she totes around the bread tray a-singin' teheeky, tehecky, tehecky. I tell you, she watches those birds close for she knows the value of 'em. She was raised a Methodist, she was, and many a time has watched through the crack of the door sadly, and seen the preachers helped to the last gizzard in the dish. There was 54 chickens 7 ducks, 5 goslins, 12 turkeys and seven pigs, hatched out last week, and Daisy had a calf and Mollie a colt, besides. This looks like bisness, don't it? This is what I call successful farmin'—multiplying and replenishing according to Scripter. Then we have a plenty of peas and potatoes and other garden yerbs, which helps a poor man out, and by the 4th of July will have wheat bread and buiskit and blackberry pies, and pass a regular declaration of independence.

I like farmin'. I like latitude and longitude. When we were penned up in town my children couldn't have a sling-shot, or a bow and arrow, nor a chicken fight in the back-yard, nor sick a dog on another dog, nor let off a big Injun whoop, without some neighbor making a fuss about it. And then, again, there was a show, or a dance, or a bazar, or a missionary meeting most every night, and it did look like the children were just obleeged to go, or the world would come to an end. It was money, money, money all the time, but now there isn't a store or a milliner shop within five miles of us, and we do our own work, and have learned what it costs to make a bushel of corn and a barrel of flour, and by the time Mrs. Arp has nursed and raised a lot of chickens and turkeys, she thinks so much of 'em she don't want us to kill 'em, and they are a heap better and fatter than any we used to buy. We've got a great big fire-place in the family room, and can boil the coffee, or heat a kettle of water on the hearth if we want to, for we are not on the lookout for company all the time like we used to be. We don't cook half as much as we used to, nor waste a whole parsel every day on the darkey, and we eat what is set before us, and are thankful.

It's a wonder to me that everybody don't go to farmin'. Lawyers and doctors have to set about town and play checkers, and talk politics and wait for somebody to quarrel or fight, or get sick; clerks and book-keepers figure and multiply and count until they get to counting the stars and the flies on the ceiling, and the peas in the dish, and the flowers on the papering; the jeweler sits by his window all the year round, working on little wheels, and the mechanic strikes the same kind of a lick every day. These people do not belong to themselves; they are all penned up like convicts in a chain-gang; they can't take a day nor an hour for recreation, for they are the servants of their employers. There is no profession that gives a man such freedom, such latitude, and such a variety of employment as farmin'.

While I was ruminating this morning, a boy come along and said the dogs had treed something down in the bottom. So me and my boys shouldered the guns and an ax, and took Mrs. Arp and the children along to see the sport. We cut down a hollow gum tree, and caught a 'possum and two squirrels, and killed a rabbit on the run, and had a good time generally, with no loss on our side. We can stop work most any time to give welcome to a passing friend and have a little chat, and our nabors do the same by us; but if you go into one of these factories or workshops, or even a printing-office, the first sign-board that greets you says, "Don't talk to the workmen." Sociable crowd, aint it?

There's no monotony upon the farm. There's something new every day, and the changing work brings into action every muscle in the human frame. We plow and hoe, and harrow and sow, and gather it in at harvest-time. We look after the horses and cows, the pigs and sows, and the rams and the lambs, and the chickens, and the turkeys, and geese. We cut our own wood, and raise our own bread and meat, and don't have to be stingy of it like city folks. A friend, who visited us not long ago, wrote back from the town that his grate don't seem bigger than the crown of his hat since he sat by our great big friendly fire-place.

But they do git the joak on me sometimes, for you see, I'm farmin' accordin' to schedule, and it don't always make things exactly luminous. Fur instance, it said that cotton seed was an excellent fertilizer. Well, I had 'em, and as they was a clean, nice thing to handle, I put 'em under most everything in my gardin. I was a-runnin' inyun sets heavy, and one mornin' went out to peruse 'em and I saw the straight track of a big mole under every row. He had jest histed 'em all up about three inches. He hadn't eat nary one, and thinks I to myself, he's just goin' around a-smellin' of 'em. Next mornin' all my sets was a settin' about six inches up in the air and on top of the thickest stand of cotton you ever did see. Now, if I had known about spilin' of 'em, as my nabors call it, before we used 'em it would have been more luminous. Howsoever, I knifed 'em down and set the inyuns back again, and nobody ain't got a finer crop.

It's a great comfort to me to set in my piazzer these pleasant evenings and look over the farm, and smoke the pipe of peace, and ruminate. Ruminate upon the rise and fall of empires and parties and presidents and preachers. I think when a man has passed the Rubicon of life, and seen his share of trouble, smokin' is allowable, for it kinder reconciles him to live on a while longer, and promotes philosophic reflections. I never knowed a high-tempered man to be fond of it.

I may be mistaken, but it seems to me a little higher grade of happiness to look out upon the green fields of wheat and the leafing trees and the blue mountains in the distance and hear the dove cooing to her mate, and the whippoorwill sing a welcome to the night, and hunt flowers and bubby blossoms with the children, and make whistles for 'em and hear 'em blow, and see 'em get after a jumpin' frog or a garter snake, and hunt hen's nests, and paddle in the branch and get dirty and wet all over, and watch their penitent and subdued expression when they go home, as Mrs. Arp looks at 'em with amazement and exclaims, "Mercy on me; did ever a poor mother have such a set? Will I ever get done making clothes? Put these on right clean this mornin', and not another clean rag in the house! Get me a switch, right straight; go! I will not stand it!" But she will stand it, and they know it—especially if I remark, "Yes, they ought to be whipped." That saves 'em, and by the time the switch comes the tempest is over, and some dry clothes are found, and if there is any cake in the house they get it. Blessed mother! Fortunate children! What would they do without her? Why her very scolding is music in their tender ears. I'm thankful that there are some things that corner in the domestic circle that Wall street cannot buy nor money kings depress.

CHAPTER IX.

THE SOUNDS ON THE FRONT PIAZZA.

It was after midnight. About the time when deep sleep falleth upon man, but not upon woman, for Mrs. Arp's ears are always awake, it seems to me. I felt a gentle dig in my side from an elbow and a whispered voice said; "William, William, don't you hear that?" "What is it?" said I. "Somebody is in the front piazza," said she. "Don't you hear him rocking in the rocking chair?" And sure enough I did. The chair would rock awhile, and then stop, and then rock again. "Is the gun loaded?" said she; "they are robbers, but don't shoot, don't make a noise; can't you peep out of the window? Mercy on us, what do they want to rob us for? Maybe they come to steal one of the children. Slip in the little room and see if Carl is in his bed. Don't stumble over a chair, maybe somebody is under the bed." The rocker took a new start and I had another dig in my side. "It is the wind," said I. "No, it is not," said she. "There is no wind, the window is up, and the curtain don't move. They are robbers, I tell you. Hadn't you better give them some money and tell them to go?" "I havn't got any money," said I. "It's all gone." "Lord have mercy upon us," said she. "William, get your gun and be ready."

I gently slipped out of the bed and tiptoed to the window and cautiously peeped out, and there was the pointer puppy *sitting straight up in my wife's rocking chair* and ever and anon he would lean forward and backwards and put it in motion. I whispered to Mrs. Arp to come and see the four-legged robber, which she did, and in due time all was calm and serene.

Last night there was another sensation in the back piazza, and it was sure enough feet this time, for they made a racket on the floor and moved around lively, and the elbow digs in my side came thick and fast; took me a minute to get fairly awake, and after listening awhile I exclaimed in audible language, "goats, Carl's goats," and I gathered a broom and mauled them down the back steps. "I told you, my dear," said I, "that those goats would give us trouble, but I can stand it if you can."

Carl and Jesse have been begging for goats a good while and I was hostile, very hostile to goats, for I knew how much devilment they would do, but the little chaps slipped up on the weak side of their mother, and she finally hinted that children were children; that old folks had their dotage and children had their goatage and her little brothers used to have goats, and so the pair of goats were bought and Ralph worked two days making a wagon, and contrived some harness out of old bridle-reins and plow lines, and it took all hands to gear 'em up, and at the first crack of the whip they bounced three feet in the air, and kept on bouncing, and jerked Carl a rod, and got loose and run away and turned the wagon up side down, and they kept on leaping and jumping until they got all the harness broken up and got away. It beat a monkey show. We all laughed until we cried, but the little chaps have reorganized on a more substantial basis, and there is another exhibition to come off soon.

Mr. Shakespeare says that a man has seven ages, but to my opinion a boy has about ten of his own. He begins with his first pair of breeches and a stick horse, and climbs up by degrees to toy guns and fire crackers and sling shot and breaking calves and billy goats, and to sure enough guns and a pointer dog, and the looking glass age when he admires himself and greases his hair and feels of his downy beard, and then he joins a brass band and toots a horn, and then he reads novels and falls in love and rides a prancing horse and writes perfumed notes to his girl. When his first love kicks him and begins to run with another fellow he drops into the age of despair, and wants to go to Texas or some other remote region, and sadly sings:

"This world is all a fleeting show."

Boys are mighty smart now-a-days. They know as much at ten years as we used to know at twenty, and it is right hard for us to keep ahead of 'em. Parents used to rule their children but children rule their parents now. There is no whipping at home, and if a boy gets a little at school it raises a row and a presentation to the grand jury. When my teacher whipped me I never mentioned it at home for fear of getting another. I got three whippings in one day when I was a lad:

I had a fight with another boy and he whipped me, and the school teacher whipped me for fighting, and my father whipped me because the teacher did. That was awful, wasent it. But it was right, and it did me good. One of these modern philanthropics was telling my kinsman the other day how to raise his boy. "Never whip him," said he. "Raise him on love and kindness and reason," and then he appealed to me for endorsement. "And when that boy is about twelve years old," said I, "do you go and talk to him and if possible persuade him not to whip his daddy. Tell him that it is wrong and unfilial, and will injure his reputation in the community."

The modern boy is entirely too bigity. I was at church in Rome last Sunday and saw two boys there, aged about ten and twelve years, and after service they lit their cigarettes and went off smoking. An old-fashioned man looked at 'em and remarked: "I would give a quarter to paddle them boys two minutes. I'll bet their fathers is afraid of 'em right now." The old-fashioned man never was afraid of his. He worked 'em hard, but he gave 'em all reasonable indulgence. He kept 'em at home of nights, and he made good men of them. They have prospered in business and acquired wealth, and are raising their children the same way, and they love and honor the old gentleman for giving them habits of industry and economy. He was a merchant and didn't allow his boys to sweep out a string or a scrap of paper as big as your hat. Habits are the thing, good habits, habits of industry and economy; when acquired in youth they stick all through life.

And the girls need some watching too. They are most too fast now-a-days. Too fond of fashion, and they read too much trash. The old fashion retiring modesty of character is at a discount. They don't wait for the boys to come now, they go after 'em; they marry in haste and repent at leisure; they run round in their new-fashioned night gowns and call it a Mother Hubbard party. The newspapers have got up a sensation about the arm clutch; well I don't see any difference between that clutch and any other clutch. The waist clutch in these round dances is just as bad or worse. They are all immodest and there is not a good mother in the land that approves of them. A girl who goes to a promiscuous ball and waltzes around with promiscuous fellows puts herself in a promiscuous fix to be talked about by the dudes and rakes and fast young men who have encircled her waist. A girl should never waltz with a young man whom she woold not be willing to marry. Slander is very common now, slander of young ladies, and there are not many who escape it; the trouble is it is not all slander, some of it is truth. In the olden times when folks got married they stayed married, but now the courts are full of divorces and the land is spotted with grass widows, and in many a household there is a hidden grief over a daughter's shame. It is a good thing for the girls to work at something that is useful. There is plenty of home work to do in most every household. If there is not then they can try drawing and sketching or painting or music, something that will entertain them. There are as many female dudes as males, and they ought to marry, I reckon, and go to raising fools for market.

We have got a cook now and my folks are taking a rest. She is an old-fashioned darkey and flies around with a quick step and lightly. Anybody could tell that "Sicily" had had good training from a white mistress. When she gets through her work she brings up a tub of water and goes to washing up the floors without being told; she washes the dishes clean and is nice about the milk and the churning, and is good to the children. She lets them cook a little and make boys and horses out of the biscuit dough. The like of that suits Mrs. Arp exactly. If I was a darkey I would know exactly how to get Mrs. Arp's money and her old dresses and a heap of little things thrown in. Yesterday morning Sicily's husband knocked at the door very early and said his wife was sick, sick all night, and Mrs. Arp turned over and exclaimed, "Oh my." I told him to go to the next room and tell the girls, and I heard 'em groan and say "goodness gracious," but they got up and gave us a first-class breakfast, and I praised 'em up lots. I promised to let 'em go to town and tumble up the new goods and bring back a big lot of samples. Girls should be encouraged when they do well.

CHAPTER X.

Mr. Arp Feels His Inadequacy.

Sometimes a man feels entirely unadequate to the occasion. A kind of lonesome and helpless feeling comes over him that no philosophy can shake off. I dident have but five sheep. They were fine and fat and followed us about when we walked down to the meadow, and our little shepherd dog thought they were the prettiest things in the world, and they would eat salt out of the children's hands, and we were thinking about the little lambs that would come in the spring. There was a house for them in the meadow and it was full of clean wheat straw where they could take shelter from the rain and the wind.

Alas for human hopes. It looks like everything is born to trouble, especially sheep. Yesterday morning I walked down to the branch with my tender offspring, and before I was prepared for it the torn and bloody form of the old he ram was seen lying in the water before me. While I stood and pondered over this sad calamity, the children soon found the others scattered round in the mire and bullrushes stiff and cold and dead. I thought of Mrs. Arp, my wife. What would she say. I thought of that passage of Scriptures which says "beware of dogs." I thought of Joe Harris and the Constitution and that confounded legislature. I thought of guns and striknine and the avenger of blood. Slowly and sadly we returned to the house, and when the children had unfolded the mournful tale Mrs. Arp, my wife, stopped washing the dishes and sat down by the fire. For awhile she never spoke. She seemed unadequate. There was a solemn stillness pervading the assembled family. The children looked at me and then at their mother, when suddenly says she, choking up, "The poor things; torn to pieces by the dogs right here in a few steps of the house. I heard Juno barking furiously in the piazzo and I heard the cows lowing like something was after their calves, and I thought I would wake you, but I didn't. Poor things, if they had only blated or made a noise. After a solemn pause, she rose forward and exclaimed: "William Arp, if I was a man I would take my gun and never stop till I had killed every dog in the naborhood. A little while back they killed all our geese in that same meadow. These trifling people round here hunt rabbits all over your plantation with their sheep killing dogs, and you won't stop 'em for fear of hurtin their feelings, and now you see what we get by it. I'd go and shoot their dogs in their own yards, and if they made a fuss about it I would——well, I don't know what I wouldn't do."

"If I knew the dogs that did it—" said I, meekly.

"Knew the dogs!" said she. "Why you know that big, brindle that got hung by his block down there in the willows, and you ought to have killed him then, and you know that white dog, and the spotted one that prowls around, and those dogs that them boys are always hunting with—you can kill them anyhow. We will never have anything if you don't protect yourself, and the Lord knows we've got little enough now."

"They will come back to-night," said I, and shore enough they did, and the boys laid in wait for 'em and got some revenge, and we've given the naborhood fair warning that henceforth we will kill every dog that puts his foot on our premises, law or no law, gospel or no gospel. We've declared war. A dog that won't stay at home at night ain't fit to be a dog. The next man who runs for the legislature in this county has got to commit himself against dogs or I'll run against him whether the people vote for me or not, and if he beats me I reckon I can move out of the county, can't I, or quit trying to raise sheep. My nabor, Mr. Dobbins, says they have killed over a hundred for him in the last two years and he has quit. He won't try to raise any more.

But we are reviving a little. The ragged edge of our indignation has worn off. We skinned the poor things and the buzzards have preyed upon their carcasses, and once more our family affairs are moving along in subdued serenity. Last night Mrs. Arp, my wife, told the girls she didn't think their lightbread was quite as light and nice as she used to make it, and she would show them her way, so they could take pattern. She fixed up the yeast and made up the dough and put it down by the fire to rise, and this morning it had riz about a quarter of an inch, which she remarked was very curious, but reckoned it was too cold, and so she put it in the oven to bake and then it got sullen and riz downwards, and by the time it was done it was about as thick as a ginger cake, and weighed nigh unto a pound to the square inch. She never said anything, but hid it away on the top shelf of the cupboard. I saw the girls a blinking around, and when lunch time came I got it down and carried it along like it was a keg of nails and put it before her. "I thought you would like some lightbread," said I.

She laid down her knife and fork, and for a moment was altogether inadequate to the occasion. Suddenly she seized the stubborn loaf, and as I ran out of the door it took me right in the small of my back, and I actually thought somebody had struck me on the spine with a maul. "Now, Mr. Impudence, take that," said she. "If a man asks for bread will you give him a stone," said I. Seeing that hostilities were about to be renewed, I retired prematurely to the piazzo to ruminate on the rise of cotton and wheat, and iron, and everything else but bread. She's got two little grandsons staying with her, and unbeknowing to me she hacked that bread into chunks and armed five little chaps with 'em, and she came forth as captain of the gang and suddenly they took me unawares in a riotus and tumultuous manner. They banged me up awfully before I could get out of the way. My head is sore all over, and take it all in all, I consider myself the injured person. I mention this circumstance as a warnin' to let all things alone when your wife hides 'em, especially bread that wouldent rise. Mrs. Arp, my wife, has most wonderful control of these little chaps—children and grand-children. She can sick 'em onto me with a nod or a wink, but I can't sick 'em onto her; no, sir. I never tried, and I don't reckon I ever will, but I just know I couldn't. I don't have much of a showing with these children. This morning I found one of 'em climbin' up on the sash of the flower pit and while I was hunting for a switch the little rascal ran to his grandma, and that was the end of it. She never said nothing, but sorter paused and looked at me. My only chance is to get 'em away off in the field or the woods and thrash 'em generally for a month's rascality, and then honey them up just before we get home to keep 'em from telling on me. For thirty years Mrs. Arp, my wife, has labored under the delusion that the children are hers, and that I had mighty little to do with 'em from the beginning. I would like to see somebody try to take 'em away with a habeas corpus or any other corpus. Goodness gracious! Talk about a lioness robbed of her whelps or a she bear of her cubs. Well, it couldn't be done, that's all.

CHAPTER XI.

A Feast in a Sycamore Grove.

THE LAMB AND THE PIG—THE WATERMELON AND THE BRUNSWICK STEW—AN ANECDOTE OF JUDGE JUNIUS HILLYER—PEELING PEACHES.

I was peeling nice soft peaches for dinner just to save Mrs. Arp the trouble, and get an approving smile, when suddenly she came up behind me and said, "William, are your hands right clean?" I held them up for her to look at as I remarked, "If they were not at first I reckon they are now." It seems to me that some folks get more particular about such things as they grow older, and it takes more water and soap and whitewash and sweeping and scouring than it used to. Maybe the appetite is not so good, and the spectacles magnify too much. I used to could knock the ashes out of my pipe on the piaza floor and get a little dirt from my shoes on the banisters and leave some dirty water in the pan at the back door, but I am gradually quitting these little things for the sake of being calm and serene in my declining years. Cleanliness is a good thing, I know, and the scripters say it is next to godliness, and if so I know some good women who are mighty nigh sanctified already. But somehow I like a little clean dirt scattered around, just to enjoy the contrast when we do clean up. I don't think a man can enjoy a clean shirt until he gets one dirty. When I showed Mrs. Arp my fingers that the peaches had made so clean it reminded me of the venerable Judge Hillyer, the old patriarch, whom I used to venerate when I was a boy, for he was handsome and eloquent, and used language with such precision and accent. He was always looking into the reason of things—the why and the wherefore, and if he saw anything strange he stopped and perused and inquired until he got to the bottom of it. The first time he ever went to New York, Howell Cobb was his companion, and Howell had a hard time in getting the judge along, for he wanted to see everything and to know everything. "Now, Howell," said he, "just stop right here and tell me what that is, and what is it for?" "Howell, do you suppose that all these people have got pressing business that hurries them along so fast?" "Howell, have you any idea what that store of Stuart's cost?" Cobb was hurrying him along a back street, when the judge stopped and looking over a window screen into a room, saw the heads and shoulders of two men going up and down with a curious motion. His curiosity was excited and says he, "Howell, what are those men doing?" "Oh, I don't know, Junius. Come along," said Howell. "We will never get to the hotel if we keep stopping to examine everything you see." "But, Howell, I want you to look at those men. They are engaged in something very peculiar, and conscientiously, I would like to know what it is."

Howell peeped through an opening in the screen and said, " Why, Junius, they are treading up dough in a trough; they are making baker's bread. Don't you see?"

The judge was amazed. He looked earnestly at them as they tramped the dough with their bare legs.and feet, and with great emphasis, said slowly and distinctly, " Howell, do you suppose their feet are clean?" " I haven't a doubt of it, Hillyer," said Cobb. " I know they are clean by this time." And he hurried him along.

Cobb said afterwards that the judge was very fond of baker's bread, but he noticed that he didn't eat much more of it in New York.

But folks get tired of eating the same kind of vittels every day, and in the same room and keeping off the same flies and kicking the same cat from under the table, and so the other day I took a notion to change the programme. Mrs. Arp had told me many a time that she had never eat any barbecued meat since she was a child, and she thought then that it was the best meat she ever did eat. And so I got an old-fashioned darkey who said, " Yes, boss, I used to barbecu meat for old master away back when Mr. Polk run agin Mr. Clay, and the old master and all of us niggers was for Mr Clay, and we used to give barbecues and have a powerful time just afore de 'lection."

I cleaned up the ground and trimmed the trees in a beautiful little sycamore grove down by the branch, and I had a little pit dug, and we sacrificed a fat lamb and a fat pig, and hung them up over night, and we hauled a load of bark and stovewood, and the old darkey had a big bed of coals by daylight, and had the meat on, and after breakfast we built a table and some plank seats, and put up a swing for the children and swung the hammock, and toted down some chairs and put everything in shape for the company. Of course I invited Mrs. Arp first and foremost, and then the kindred and friends who are our welcome guests. The girls fixed up the vinegar and pepper and butter to baste the meat with while it was cooking, and they made an old-fashioned Brunswick stew, and I roasted a lot of green corn in the shuck under the hot ashes at one end of the pit, and while everything was in a weaving way about twelve o'clock I blowed the horn for the company, and about a score of them came down and were delighted with the prospect and the place. Everybody seemed happy, especially the children, and Mrs. Arp organized herself a toasting committee of one, and in due time pronounced it all very good and ready for business. Gallant gentlemen carved the odorous carcasses and prepared it for distribution. The stew was declared splendid. I noticed that the married women all flavored it with hot onion sauce, and it always seemed strange to me how soon after marriage a woman begins to love onions. The meats came on in due time, and everybody got a sweet and juicy rib. The ribs are the best part of anything, and I reckon that is why a woman is so sweet, for she was made of a rib while man was made of dirt. After this course was over the girls surprised us all with lemon pies and cake and frozen sherbet, and after that we all rested and played cards, and had music and song on the banjo, and the men told some big yarns, which the young ladies believed and the old ones didn't. Can't fool a married woman long with yarns. One of our party told about hunting deer up in the Cohutta mountains, and he rode up a cliff so steep that when he got most to the top he pulled the top burrs from a pine tree a hundred feet high that grew at the base of the mountains. Another one told about killing nineteen wild turkeys at one shot away out in the Indian nation where he said they broke down the trees, and there was fifteen thousand killed on one creek in the month of December. These sort of yarns are catching and one calls for another, and so I was just about to wade in when I noticed that Mrs. Arp was perusing me and modestly I refrained and postponed my adventures to a more convenient season. It is not prudent for an old man to tell the heroic exploits of his youth if his wife lived in the same settlement and knows his raising, and so I never do brag much when she is about.

Well, we had a splendid afternoon, and wound it up with melons from the spring, and then adjourned to the house feeling all the better for this little episode in our daily life.

CHAPTER XII.

TRIALS AND TRIBULATIONS.

"All the world's a stage," as Mr Shakespeare says, and all the men and women merely travelers. It is a mighty big stage, of course—in fact, an omnibus, for it carries us all, and we are traveling along and getting in and getting out all along the line, and ever and anon stopping by the wayside to nurse our sick and bury our dead. There is nothing else that puts on the brakes as we move down the big road on the journey of life. Sickness and death are a veto upon all progress, and upon plans, and schemes, and hopes, and ambition, and fame, and fashion and folly. We suffer awhile and stop awhile, but if we don't die we get in the stage again and move on with the crowd. Sickness knocks up a man and humbles him quicker than anything. Just let the pitiless angel of pain come along suddenly and seize him by some vital part and twist him around a time or two and shake him up, and he will know better what the word torture means when he reads it in a book. I thought I was a strong man and tough, and so the angel has had no terrors for me. I've had the toothache and mashed my big toe with a crow-bar and got around lively with a green-corn dance, but after it was over I forgot the sting of it and only remembered the joke. But there are some things without any joke, and that won't let you forget 'em, and when they come and go they leave you humbled and hacked and meek as a lamb with his legs tied. They take away your pride, and your brag and your starch and stiffening. They strip you of flowers and frills and thread lace and jewelry and leave a poor mortal like a dependent beggar for the charity of health, good health. "If I was only well again," the poor victim sighs; "Oh, if I was only well again."

When a man gets along to my age he forgets that he is on the down grade; that he is like a second-hand wagon patched up and painted and sold at auction to the highest bidder. It will run mighty well on a smooth road and a light load and a careful driver, but it won't do to lock wheels with another, or run into a gully, or over stumps, or up to the hubs in the low grounds. A man is very much like a wagon, anyhow, for his shoulders and hips are the axle-trees and his arms and legs are the wheels and the wagon-body is his body and the coupling pole is his spine and the hounds are his kidneys—his reins, as the Scriptures call 'em—and they brace up everything and hold up the tongue and the coupling pole, and if the hounds are weak and rickety the hind wheels don't track with the fore wheels, and the whole concern moves along with a hitch and a jerk and a double wabble. "He tryeth the reins of the children of men," for that was the test of a man. If the kidneys were sound and well ordered the man was right before the Lord, for in them was supposed to be centered the affections and passions and emotions of a man. Those oldtime philosophers attached a good deal of importance to the kidneys, but I thought it was a superstition of their ignorance, and I never cared much about my kidneys. In fact, I didn't care whether I had any kidneys or not, for I was a thinking what Judge Underwood told me a long time ago about the spleen, which he said was only put there to make men splenetic and cross, and keep 'em from getting overjoyful in this subloonary world. I thought that maybe the kidneys were like the liver of a man over in California, which was crushed out of him in a mine some fifty years ago, when he was about fifty years old, but he was sewed up and got well, and he is a hundred years old and not a hair turned grey, nor a wrinkle come, nor his eyes grown dim, nor his teeth come out, and he keeps well and sound and plumb and active, and goes to balls, and never has an ache or a pain, and its all because his liver is gone. Jesso.

Well, you see I had promised to build a dam across the branch down in the willow thicket and make a bathing pool for the children; and so a few days ago I went at it with a will, and got my timbers across and my boards nailed on slanting up the stream to a rock bottom, and then I put on some old boots and old clothes and went to chinkin' up the leaks with turf and gravel and willow brush and sand bags, and as fast as I stopped one leak another broke out; but I worked fast and worked hard, and the children waited on me and brought me material, and after awhile the water began to rise on me, and got higher till it went over the dam. It was then about noon, and the hot sun was blistering down, and the cold spring water was chilling me up, and I begun to feel age and infirmity; so I took a bath myself, and put on dry clothes and retired to rest from my labors. That evening I listened to the shouts of happy children as they frolicked in the pool, and I rejoiced, for it always makes me happy to see them happy. The next day I dident get up well, and as I was a knockin' around in my garden, a holdin' up my back, shore enough, without any warnin', the unfeelin' angel of pain come along suddenly and snapped me up by the left kidney like he wanted to wrestle, and took all underholt, and he spun me around with such a jerk I almost lost my breath with agony, and he pummeled me and humped me all the way to the house, and threw me on the bed while I hollered. "What in the world is the matter with you, William?" says my wife, Mrs. Arp, says she to me; and the children all gathered round and thought I was snake bit. "I've got a turrible pain round here," says I; "turrible, turrible. Oh, Lordy!" They filled up the stove in a hurry, and brought water; and they gave me camphor, and paregoric, and one thing another; but I got worse, and groaned and grunted amazingly, for I tell you I was a sufferin'.

"I expected it! I expected it!" says Mrs. Arp, as she moved round lively. "I just knew some trouble would come from all that dam business of yesterday." My stomach had suddenly got out of order—I don't know how—for everything they give me come up before it was down; and so they tried salts and quinine and hot water and painkiller, and morphine, and magnum bonum and everything in the house, but nothing would stick, and at last the pain just left as suddenly as it came on, and I went to sleep. But my system was all out of order; the machinery wouldn't work nowhere. The cold sweat poured from me all night, and I dreamed I was away off in a wet prairie, lying down in the cold grass, hiding from a herd of buffaloes, and I woke up with a shaking ague and had to have my night clothes changed and dried off like a race horse. The morning brought another attack still worse than the first, but the good Dr. Kirkpatrick came in time and put me on morphine and spirits of nitre, a hot bath and shortened up the time, and told me my trouble was in the kidneys, and what was going on, and when he left me I was easy and meek and humble, and could look around upon wife and children like nobody was a sinner but me. When I was awake I could look up at the old whitewash that was peeling off from the ceiling and see all sorts of pictures I never saw before. They took shapes innumerable, for there were monkeys, and camels, and bears and buzzards, and turtles, and big Injuns, and little Frenchmen, and old witches, and anacondas and other menagerie animals all out of shape, and funny and fantastic; and while I was asleep I dreamed ridiculous dreams, and the quinine that was in me made me to hear waterfalls and milldams, and once I imagined the dam I had built had grown and swelled until Niagara was but a circumstance compared to it. But alas, there is no rest for the wicked, for although I had escaped for a day and night, and was banking upon bright hopes and returning health, the unfeeling angel came along again, and seeing me recovering from the fight, began on me with a second assault, and beat up my left kidney again till it was all in a jelly and as sore and as sensitive as a carbuncle. While he was beating me I seemed to hear him say, "You didn't know you had kidneys, did you? How many do you think you have now?" "About a dozen," said I; "eight or ten anyhow, and they are as big and as heavy as shot bags." The fact is that my left side was so sore and I was so nervous that it almost gave me a spasm to think of anybody touching me there with a stick. But the torture all of a sudden left me, as suddenly as it came, and the breath, good and free, could get way once more. But now I think I am all safe, and Richard is himself again. Good nursing and the doctor's skill and patience has got the wagon in traveling condition, and now I think I will make friends with my kidneys and a treaty of peace with the angel, and the treaty is that I am to build no more dams during life, if I have to wade in the water to do it.

CHAPTER XIII.

Love Affairs.

Married and gone. It is the same old story. Love and courtship. Then comes the engagement ring and a blessed interval of fond hopes and happy dreams, and then the happy day is fixed—the auspicious day that is never to be forgotten—a day that brings happiness or misery and begins a new life. Then comes the license, the permit of the law which says you may marry, you may enter into bonds. The State approves it and the law allows it, and it will cost you only a dollar and a quarter. Cheap, isn't it? And yet it may be very dear. Then comes the minister, and the happy pair stand up before him and make some solemn vows and listen to a prayer and a benediction, and they are one. In a moment the trusting maid has lost her name and her free will, and is tied fast to a man. Well, he is tied fast, too, so it is all right all round, I reckon, but somehow I always feel more concern about the woman than the man. She is a helpless sort of a creature and takes the most risk, for she risks her all.

We gave him a cordial welcome into the family, and we kissed her lovingly and bade them good-bye, and the children threw a shower of rice over them and an old shoe after them, and they were soon on their way to the land of flowers. She was not our child, but was almost, for Mrs. Arp was the only mother she ever knew, and we loved her.

I sat in my piazza ruminating over the scene, and I wondered that there were as many happy matings as there seem to be. Partners for life ought to be congenial and harmonious in so many things. When men make a partnership in business they can't get along well if they are unlike in disposition or in moral principle, or in business ways and business habits. But they can dissolve and separate at pleasure and try another man.

A man and his wife ought to be alike in almost everything. It is said that folks like their opposite, their counterparts, and so they do in some respects. A man with blue eyes goes mighty nigh distracted over a woman with hazle eyes. I did, and I'm distracted yet whenever I look into them. But in mental qualities and emotional qualities and tastes and habits and principles and convictions and the like, they ought to class together. Indeed, it is better for them to have the same politics and the same religion. And so I have observed that the happiest unions, as a general thing, are those where the high contracting parties have known each other for a long time, and have assimilated from their youth in thought and feeling. When a man goes off to some watering place and waltzes a few times with a charming girl and falls desperately in love and marries her off hand, it is a long shoot and a narrow chance for happiness. Why, we may live in the same town with people and not know as much about them as we ought to. I never made any mistake about my choice of a partner for the dance of a life, but I've thought of it a thousand times that if Mrs. Arp had known I loved codfish and got up by daybreak every morning, she never would have had me. It was nip and tuck to get her anyhow, and that would have been the feather to break the camel's back. Well, I'm mortal glad she didn't know it, though I am free to say that if I had known she slept until the second ringing of the first bell for breakfast and was fond of raw oysters, it would have had a dampening effect upon my ardor for a few minutes, only a few. But I have seen some mighty clever people eat oysters raw and sleep late in the morning. But still a man and his wife can harmonize and compromise a good many of these things, and it is a beautiful illustration of this to see Mrs. Arp cooking codfish for me and fixing it all up so nice with eggs and cream, and it is a touching evidence of my undying devotion to her, to see me wandering about the house lonely and forlorn every morning for an hour or two, and forbidding even the cat to walk heavy while she sleeps. That codfish business comes to me honestly from my father's side, and my mother put up with it like a good, considerate wife, and we children grew up with an idea that is was good. I've heard of a young couple who got married and went off to Augusta on a tour, and the feller stuck his fork into a codfish ball and took a bite. He choked it down like a hero, and when his beloved asked him what was the matter, replied: "Don't say anything about it, Mandy, but as sure as you are born there is something dead in the bread."

Well, we can make compromises about all such things as habits and tastes, but there are some things that won't compromise worth a cent. If a girl has been brought up to have a good deal of freedom, and thinks it no harm to go waltzing around with every gay Lothario who loves to dance, and after she gets a feller of her own, wants to keep at it and have polluted arms around her waist, she had just as well sing farewell to conjugal love and domestic peace, for it is against the order of nature for a loving husband to stand it, and he oughtn't. There is another thing that ought to be considered, and that is age. A few years makes no difference, but an old man had better be careful about marrying a young wife. He wont be happy but about two weeks, and then his misery will begin and it will never end. It may be better for a woman to be an old man's darling than a young man's slave, but she had better be neither. When a young girl marries an old man for his money she has gone back on herself, for money don't bring happiness. Money helps, but money with a dead weight is a curse—an aggravation. I was talking one day to an old man, a Frenchman, who had made a hermit of himself, and was living all alone in the woods, and he said: "Mine frien', I have make one grand meestake. Mine first wife whom I marry ven I vas young vas an angel from heaven, God bless her, but mine last wife she did not come from up dere, she come dis vay—and he pointed downwards. "I vas old and she vas young. I had money and she had none. I marry her in haste and repent at my leisure. I try to live wid her tree years, but we were not compatible. It was against the order of nature and I find myself a fool and a prisoner, and so I geeve her half my monies and run away from her and hide in dis vilderness, and here vill I live and here vill I die, and ven I go oop to St. Peter and tell heem how dat voman trouble me on earth de good man vill open de garden gate and say, come in my brother, for you have had trouble enough."

Country marriages are generally happier than those made in cities among the families of the rich. Children raised to work and to wait on themselves make better husbands and better wives than those raised in luxury. It is mighty hard for a man to please his wife and keep her in a good humor if she has been petted by her parents and never knew a want and had no useful work to do. She soon takes the ennui or the conniptions or the "don't know what I want," and must go back to ma. A young lady who never did anything after she quit school but dress for company and make visits and go to the theatre or the dance, will never make a good wife. This wife business is a very serious business. It is right hard work to play wife. The mother of six, eight or ten children has seen sights. She knows what care is and work is, and one of these do-nothing women can't stand it. If she is a used up institution with one child, two will finish her, and if it wasn't for condensed milk the children would perish to death in a month after they were born, and sorter like the cows in Florida. I heard a Florida man say the other day that a Florida cow dident give enough milk to color the coffee for breakfast, and they had to raise the calves on the bottle. Getting married ought to be a considerate business. Folks oughtn't to get married in a hurry, neither ought they to wait four or five years; six months is long enough for an engagement. I don't mean children. I mean grown folks who have settled down in life and know what they are about. There is no goodlier sight in all nature than to see a good-looking healthy young man, who is making an honest living, standing up at the altar with a pure, sweet, good-tempered, affectionate, industrious girl, and the parents on both sides approving the match. Then the big pot ought to be put in the little pot, and everybody rejoice.

CHAPTER XIV.

Tells of His Wife's Birthday.

It is impossible for a man or a woman either to be calm and serene when surprised by awful and terrible things, unless they are always prepared for 'em, which they ain't. I have been wanting to see some big thing all my life, but I wanted to be in a safe place while it happened, and at a very respectable distance. I would like to have been there when Vesuvius run over and swallowed up Herculaneum and Pompeii, and I want to feel the shake of a big earthquake a mile or two away from the crack. I would enjoy a storm at sea and a genuine shipwreck if I knew we were to strike some rock not far from shore and eventually be saved. I've been reading every now and then about those awful storms and winds that of late years have been perusing the country below us and blowing wagons up in the tree tops and shingles through solid oak trees and carrying houses away and twisting off timber like it was wheat straw, and I thought I would like to see a young cyclone meandering around, just to get the hang of the thing, and shore enough a little one come along here last Sunday and made a call without any premonition, and now I'm satisfied, and don't hanker after any more such visitations. We were sitting on the piazza watching the black clouds as they loomed up in the west, and listening to the rumbling thunder, when suddenly the roar of coming winds was heard, and the storm came in sight over the brow of Mumford's mountain, and came down the valley before us with the big drops of rain in front, and then the hail following after, and the wind like a tornado. We hurried down the window sash and took in the chairs, and before we knew it, it took two of us to shut the front door, and so we retreated to the back piazza, and by the time we got there the roof was rattling like a million buck-shot was being poured on it from a big dump-cart away up yonder, and it covered the ground and banked up in the back yard about three inches deep, and while we were all a wondering what the thing would do next, the wind shifted around and around and come from the east as hard as it did from the west, and pretty soon it was coming from all points of the compass and everywhere else all at once and slammed all the doors and twisted the tree tops around and around, and I was a-fixing to move the family down in the basement, when suddenly my wife, Mrs. Arp, says she to me, "Where is Carl and where is Ralph?" "They are down in the barn," said I calmly. "They are all safe, for the barn is under the hill." "Merciful heavens," said she. "I know something will happen to 'em. You must go after 'em." So I put on the oilcloth and fooled round for an umbrel and couldn't find one, and it wouldn't have been any more than a fly in a hurricane no how, and I heard the limbs a-popping and saw the trees a-bending and the hail was getting bigger and more thicker and more denser and I knowed the little boys were safe, and so I kept foolin' round and round until shore enough I dident go and Mrs. Arp she calmed down a little, for about this time the storm abated a little, and we could see the boys looking out from the barn windows. I aint tellin' no lie when I say that fall of rain and hail dident last more than fifteen minutes, but it raised the branch that crosses the big road by my house five feet in half an hour and spread out all over the meadow and up and down the road for a hundred yards, and a nabor come along from town in a buggy and had to swim it horse and all, and he said the road was as dry as a powder horn at Felton's chapel, and another man came from the other way and said it was all dust at Bishops, and this showed me that the storm-path was only about a mile wide, and it was obliged to have been a cyclone, for we have heard of it going on about the same way and tearing things up fearfully. One nabor had a big tree blown on his barn, and a lad of a boy was in there and it skeered him so he tried to run head foremost home, and the wind picked him up and spun him round like a hummin' top and then laid him down flat and told him to stay there, and he stayed. The oats that had not been harvested look just like a big iron roller had been rolled over 'em and then the whole concern ironed out smooth with a flat iron. We've been mighty busy mowing 'em with the machine, and have managed to save 'em pretty well, though it's right hard to tell which is the best end of the bundles. But they will thrash all the same, and no loss on our side. The rail fences on nabor Cotton's hill went to playin' Jack-straws, and the corn looks like the blades had all been drawn through a shuck riddle. Nearly all my tomatoes have got a bruise on 'em, and the grapes are pretty much in the same fix. Squash leaves and cabbage leaves are riddled with holes, but after all I can't see any very serious damage, and we are trying to be calm and serene. Well, I believe the cyclone did sorter surprise two nice young gentlemen who were perusing the girls at our house, and when they went out in the hail to keep their horse and buggy from running away the storm got so bad, and they got so damp and moist all over, they had to go home prematurely, which we didn't approve, for we could have made a fire and dried 'em in a few minutes, or they could have put on some of my garments which would have been more than a foot or a foot and a half too short at both ends. But they are young and hopeful, and went off down the road singing Hail Columbia, happy land, Hail Boreas and be hanged.

We've had a birthday at our house. There are big birthdays and little ones, common ones and uncommon ones, when the female patriarch of a family, the queen of the household, meets her 60th birthday and has got too much good sense to go back on her age or be ashamed of it, it is an event, it is, sorter like a golden wedding or the declaration of independence or some other big thing. But there is no collapse, no surrender, no let down, not a silver thread among the raven hair, no crow's feet or wrinkled brow, no loss of speech or language, no weakness of memory. Sometimes I wish she would forget something, but she can't, and my short comings, like Banquo's ghost, come up before me ever and anon. So the queen had a birthday dinner and she got a nice new dress and a hall lamp and a beautiful chair and a pair of peafowls wherewith to raise her own fly brushes, and that night we had music and dancing and song, for Solomon says old age is honorable, and I never could see any good sense in a woman or a widower trying to conceal it. I never expect to be either the one or the other, and can't appreciate their peculiar feelings, but I never hear of a married woman concealing her advancing years but what I think she is fixing the triggers for a second husband before the first one dies. But one thing is certain—there's no triggers about our house, and there will be no step-father to my children, for, as Mrs. Arp says, sometimes a burnt child dreads the fire. Jesso.

CHAPTER XV.

Mrs. Arp Goes Off on a Visit.

Man was not made to live alone. I don't mean alone like Robinson Cruso, but alone in a house without a woman—a help-mate, a pard. Its an awful thing to come in and find the maternal chair vacant, even for a season. I know she has gone, but still I imagine that she is somewhere on the premises a circulatin' around and around. I am listenin' for the rustle of her dress or the creak of her nimble shoe—she wears number 2's, with a high instep, and walks like a deer. Ever and anon methinks I hear her accustomed voice saying, William William—major, come here a moment.

What wonderful resolution some women have got! Mrs. Arp has at last departed. She has undertook a journey. For several weeks it has been the family talk. Some said she would get off and some said she wouldent. As for herself, she was serious and non-committal, but we daily observed that the big old trunk that contained the accumulated fragments of better days was being diligently ransacked. Scraps of lace, and lawn, and ribbon, and silk, and velvet, and muslin, and bumbazeen, and cassimere were brought forth and aired, and the flatiron kept busy pressing and smoothing the wrinkles that age had furrowed in them. All sorts of patterns from Demarest, and Ehrick and Butterick, were over-hauled and consulted with a kind of sad reality. A woman may be too poor to buy calico at 5 cents a yard, but she will have patterns. Little jackets, and pants, and shirts, little dresses, and drawers, and petticoats, and aprons had to be made up, and nobody but her knew what they would be made of. I tell you, one of these old-fashioned mothers is a mirical of grace. It aint uncommon for folks nowadays to be their own tailors and dressmakers, but it takes sense and genius to get up a respectable outfit from scraps and old clothes outgrown or abandoned for ratage and leakage. It was wonderful to see her rip 'em, and turn 'em, and cut 'em, and twist 'em—getting a piece here and a scrap there, cutting them down to the pattern—running them through the machine, and before anybody knew it she had the little chaps arrayed as fine as a band-box and never called on anybody for a nickel. That's what I call the quintessence of domestic economy. Nobody can beat her in that line. She knows how to put the best foot foremost. Her children have got to look as decent as other people's, or she will keep 'em at home, certain. She don't go about much, and seems to grow closer and closer to the chimney corner; but when she does move it's a family sensation. Every one helps—every one advises and encourages her in a subdued and respectful way. All want her to go off and rest and have a good time for her own sake, but tell her over and over how much they will miss her, and wear a little shadow of sorrow in the nigh side of the face. I think though she suspected all the time they would turn up Jack while she was away.

Well, she did get off at last—on a three hours' journey and to stay a whole week. It was a tremendious undertaking, for she said the harness might break, or the buggy collapse, or the old mare run away on the road to town, and the cars might run off the track or break through a bridge, or not stop long enough for her to get off with the children, or let her off and take the children on, or some of us would get sick, or the house catch afire, or some tramp come along in the night and rob us and cut all our throats while we were asleep, and we wouldent know a thing about it till next morning.

"Now, William," said she, "be mighty careful of everything, for you know how poor we are anyhow." "Poor as Lazarus," said I "but he's a restin' in Abraham's bosom." "Well, never mind Lazarus," said she, "the paregoric and quinine and turpentine are on the shelf in the cabinet. I have hid the laudanum, for its dangerous, and you havent more than half sense in the night time, and might make a mistake. Don't let Ralph have the gun nor go to the mill pond. There are four geese a setting, and you must look after the goslins, and if you don't shoot that hawk spring chickens will be mighty scarce on this lot. And see here, William, I want you to take the beds off the bedsteads in my room and shut the doors and windows and make a fire of sulphur in some old pan. They say it will just kill everything." "Must I stay inside or outside," said I, in a Cassibianca tone. "May be you had better try it awhile inside," said she, "just to see if you ever could get used to it. Now, William, take good care of everything, for you may never see me again. Somehow I feel like something's going to happen to me. Don't whip Ralph while I'm gone—the poor boy aint well—he looks right pekid—and when you whipped Carl the other day the marks were all over his little legs." She always looks for marks—the little willows are soft as broom straws, but she is bound to find a faint streak or two, and there's a tear for every mark.

"William, the buttons are all right on your shirts. Feed the little chickens till I come back. I think the buntin hen is setting somewhere, and there's six eggs in my drawer that old Browny laid on my bed. If the children get sick you must telegraph me." "And if I get sick myself," said I, inquiringly—"Why there's the medicine in the cabinet," said she, "and you musent forget to water my pot-plants. I told Mr. Freeman to look after you and the boys, and Mrs. Freeman will keep an eye on the girls. Goodbye. Don't you cut the hams. I want them for company, and don't go in the locked pantry." I reckon she must have taken the key off with her, for we can't find it. "Goodbye—take care of Bows." She kissed us all round and choked up a little and dropped a few tears and said she was ready. I looked at the clock and told her we could barely make it—five miles in an hour and five minutes, and the road muddy and the mule slow. She said she had never been left by the train in her life, and she didn't think she would be too late. I pressed the old mule through mud and slop, up hill and down hill. She was afraid of that mule, and when I larruped him she told me not to. Then he would put on the breaks, and she declared she would be left if I dident drive faster. We dident say much but leaned forward and pressed forward in solemn energy as if the world hung upon the crisis. When we got within half a mile of town the whistle blowed away down the road and we had a slick hill to clime. I larroped heavily and clucked every step of the way, and we made the trip just in time to be left. The train moved off right before us. It didn't seem to care a darn. We gazed at it with feelings of sublime despair. Mrs. Arp was looking dreamily away off into space when I ventured to remark, "shall we go back?" She quietly pointed to the St. James and replied, "hotel."

I saw her and little Jessie comfortably quartered in a nice room with a cheerful fire. Mr. Hoss, the landlord, was kind and sympathetic and promised she should not be left by the morning train, and so bidding them a sad goodbye, I returned to my bairns. Take it all in all it was a big thing—a mighty big thing at my house. I'm poking around now hunting for consolation. She knows I'm desolate and is sorter glad of it. I know she is homesick already but she wont own it. She would stay away a whole year, before she would own it. She wants me to beg her to come back soon, and I won't, for she left her other little darling with me, and he will bring her. I've half a mind to drop her a postal card and say: "Carl is not well, but don't be alarmed about him," and then go to meet her on the first train that could bring her, for I know she would be there. It does look like a woman with ten children wouldent be so foolish about one of them, but there's no discount on a mother's anxiety. Her last command was, "keep Carl with you all the time, and tuck the cover under him good at night, bless his little heart." I wonder what would become of children if they didn't have a parent to spur 'em up. In fact, it takes a couple of parents to keep things straight at my house. Yesterday the gray mule broke open the gate and let the cow and calf together. Carl left open another gate and the old sow got in the garden. Another boy has got a felon on his finger, and whines around and says his ma could cure it if she was here. He can't milk now, and so I thought I would try it, but old Bess wouldn't let nary drop down for me. I squeezed and pulled and tugged at her until she got mad and suddenly lifted her foot in my lap and set it down in the bucket, whereupon I forgot my equlibrium, and when I got up I gave old Bess a satisfactory kick in the side and departed those coasts in great humility. It's not my forte to milk a cow. The wind blew over more trees across my fences. The clock run down. Two lamp chimneys bursted. The fire popped out and burnt a hole in the carpet while we were at supper, and everything is going wrong just because Mrs. Arp's gone.

It's mighty still, and solemn, and lonely around here now. Lonely aint the word, nor howlin' wilderness. There aint any word to express the goneness and desolation that we feel. There is her vacant chair in the corner—

> Yes, the rocker still is sitting
> Just where she was ever knitting—
> Knitting for the bairns she bore.
> And now the room seems sad and dreary,
> And my soul is getting weary,
> And my heart is sick and sore—and so forth.

The dog goes whining round—the malteese cats are mewing and the children look lost and droopy. But we'll get over it in a day or two, may be, and then for a high old time.

CHAPTER XVI.

THE VOICE OF SPRING.

Hark, I hear a bluebird sing,
And that's a sign of coming spring.
The bull-frog bellers in the ditches,
He's throwed away his winter britches.
The robin is bobbin around so merry,
I reckon he's drunk on a China berry.
The hawk for infant chickens watcheth,
And 'fore you know it one he cotcheth.
The lizzard is sunning himself on a rail;
The lamb is shaking his newborn tail.
The darkey is plowing his stubborn mule,
And gaily hollers, "gee, you fool."
King Cotton has unfurled his banner,
And scents the air with sweet guanner.
The day grows long—the night's declining.
The Indian summer's sun is shining,
The smoking hills are now on fire,
And every night it's climbing higher.
The water warm, the weather fine,
The time has come for hook and line;
Adown the creek, around the ponds,
Are gentlemen and vagabonds.
And all our little dirty sinners
Are digging bait and catching minners.
The dogwood buds are now a-swelling,
And yaller jonquills sweet are smelling;
The little busy bees are humming,
And everything says spring is coming.

It has been a hard old winter on man and beast. Hard in weather and harder in fire and flood and pestilence, and all sorts of unnatural troubles. The horrors of hotels burning up, and theatres and circusses shrouded in flames, and thousands of poor people made homeless and destitute by the raging waters, and smallpox marking its victims all over the land, is pitiful, most pitiful, but I can't get over the shock

COBE.

of those poor little children who were trampled to death in that school-room in New York City. I can't help but seeing them all laid out in the room together, and their parents hovering over their little disfigured and mangled corpses. The distressing scene haunts me. There is a power of trouble in the world that we know nothing about —trouble that we who live in the country do not have. Here there are no storms, no floods, no fires, no pestilence, no scarcity of wood, or of food, or comfortable clothing. A poor man in the country is safer from all calamity than a rich one in the city. A poor man may lament his poverty and envy the rich, but he has no reason to. A man who makes a comfortable living on a farm has a greater security for life and liberty and happiness and long life than any other class that I know of. Cobe says he is getting along "tolerable well, I thank you." Cobe is always calm and serene. He owns a mouse-colored mule, and has owned him ever since the war. That mule is one of the family and he knows it. The children play under him and over him, and between his legs, and the mule is happy too. Cobe has a chunk of a cow and a sow and pigs, and about enough old rickety furniture to move in one wagon load, and that's all Cobe has got except his wife and half a dozen little children, who live on corn bread and taters. And they are smart children, and healthy and good looking, though Cobe is called the ugliest man in the county, and I think enjoys his reputation. His face is of three colors and splotched about, and his mouth is in a twist one way and his nose in another, and his eyes are of a different color, and he is hump-shouldered and walks pigeon-toed, but he don't care. His wife says he is just the best little man in the world. He works hard, he and the mule, and always says he is getting along "tolable," and finds no more trouble in supporting six children than he did one. He says there never was a 'possum born that dident find a 'simmon tree somewhere. Says he is raising his boys more for endurance than for show—for another war will come along about their time of day and he wants 'em to be able to stand it. Cobe is an honest man, and came from an honest family, and his wife did too, and their children are well-mannered and they are getting a little schooling, and my opinion is, that there is more hope and better hope for the country in that kind of stock than in the average children of the rich. They will make good, humble, law-abiding citizens, and they will work and produce something. When war or trouble comes, it is the yeomanry of the land we have to depend on. The children of the poor are running this Southern country now. They are the foremost men in most everything. They are the best merchants in Atlanta and other cities—the best farmers, the best mechanics and the best railroad men. Some of 'em make splendid bankers, if they do spell hog with a double g. Grammar may deceive, but figures don't lie.

We are all mighty busy now in these parts. I can sit in my piazza and see over a good deal of farming territory, and the mules are moving up lively. They seem to know the spring is late, and the farmers are behind time. But I don't sit long at a time, for the garden is to plant, and the rose bushes have to be trimmed, and the flower beds dressed off, and the compost scattered around, and the vines want new trellaces, and everything got ready for a suit of new clothes. The old year is just now dead, and the new one is born with the spring. March used to be the first month and it ought to be now. I don't see what they ever changed it for. One hundred and twenty years ago our English forefathers took a notion to set old Father Time back a couple of months, without any good reason for it, and I think we ought to move up the clock and put him forward where he was. The spring is the new birth of nature, and is the type of our own resurrection. I don't believe that everything that dies will live again, but I do believe that everything that is good and beautiful will, even to animals, trees and flowers. This is a mighty pretty world we live in— mighty pretty, especially in the spring, and for fear of accidents, I am willing to be a tenant a good while longer.

> "I would not live always,
> I ask not to stay,"

is a very beautiful sentiment, provided a man is sure of a better home when he quits this one. But another poet sung with more caution and content when he said:

> "This world is very lovely—oh, my God,
> I thank thee that I live."

I reckon the majority of mankind are like the fellow who said he dident want to go to heaven if he had to die to get there. Many would like for the ages of Adam and Methusaleh to come back again. It wouldent do, though—it wouldent do at all, for if Jay Gould and

Vanderbilt and company should live a thousand years they would gobble up the whole terrestrial concern and crowd us all off onto a plank in the ocean. On the whole I'm obliged to think that everything is fixed up about right—I reckon it is.

CHAPTER XVII.

The Love of Money.

Money is a right good thing and no sensible man will turn up his nose at it. Money brings comfort and leisure, and Solomon says in leisure there is wisdom. A man who has to be digging away every day for a living don't have much time to read and reflect and ruminate. It don't matter whether he is a merchant or mechanic or farmer or a professional man, if he works hard all day he wants to rest at night.

Money promotes domestic tranquility and that is the biggest and best thing I know of. But money ought to be hard to get, so that its real value may be appreciated—money has to be earned to be prized. If it is inherited or drawn in a lottery or won at games of chance or found in the road or obtained by lucky speculation in stocks or bonds or cotton futures, it goes at a discount. It is undervalued and don't stick to a man long. A fortune gained in a year rarely sticks to anybody. Luck is a right good thing when it follows along with labor and honesty, but luck by itself is a deceiver. "Trust to luck" is the devil's maxim. I knew a hard working man who was so anxious to get ahead that he stinted his family and invested part of his earnings in the Louisiana lottery for five years and never drew but ten dollars. He told me he had lost five hundred dollars that way, and every time he saw the list published of the lucky numbers and read about the lucky men who drew the prizes it fired him up and he tried it again. Sometimes I wish Uncle Jubal and General Beauregard would tote fair and publish a list of them fellows who dident draw anything. But I reckon that would be so long and occupy so many columns in the newspapers they couldent afford it.

It is just human I know to want more money than we have got, especially if we are hard run and living on a strain. I want more myself, and if I was to find a hundred dollars in the road I couldent help hoping that the owner would never miss it, and never call for it.

Just like a boy who finds a pocket knife and feels like it is his, but that sort of money is not as solid and satisfactory as money we work for. I know an old preacher who had ten dollars and his son had ten dollars and the young man went down to Atlanta and took all the money to buy some things, and he came across a wheel of fortune and saw a fellow win ten dollars just as easy, and so he was persuaded to try his luck, and shore enough he won ten dollars, and it hope him up mightily and he tried it again and won some more, and he kept on until he had won fifty dollars and become a fool, for right then his luck changed and he lost it all and his ten dollars and his daddy's ten besides, and had to borrow a dollar and a half to get home on, and like to have perished to death in the bargain. Well, he belonged to the church and they had him up and tried him and he made a clean breast and told how he was overtaken and tempted and how he went on and on until he had made fifty dollars clean. "And right there" said the old man, "is whar John's sin begun. If he had stopped right there it would have been all right but, like a fool he went on and on to destruction." Well, John wasent such a dreadful sinner after all, for he wanted the money to buy something to please the old folks. But money don't come that easy very often. I know a man who has been kept on a strain for five years working out of his losses on cotton futures. Sometimes luck runs along with a man for ten years and more and that makes him vain and he thinks his judgment is infallible and suddenly he collapses like Seney and Eno and Keene. No money is safe except that made by honest men.

The rewards of labor are mighty good and sure. Here I set in my piazza and look over my farm and see the wheat and the oats all in a strut and waving so beautiful in the breeze, and I feel proud and serene, for I sowed that wheat myself and helped to prepare the land, and it is my wheat and my oats and come honestly and wasent made out of somebody else, and it does me good to cut a few choice heads and bunch 'em and take 'em to town and show the folks what I can do. It beats money made by luck all to pieces, and so does walking in my garden and digging the potatoes I planted and working them ever so nice and bringing them in the house to show to my wife and hear her say, "they are very fine." She never says much on that line, she don't, but a little goes a great ways with me. She never indulges in rapture; she never uses adjectives to any excess, such as lovely, exquisite, splendid and the like, but I know what she thinks about anything just as well as if she did. I'm going to get her a mess of raspberries to-day, the first of the season, and I'll surprise her with 'em at dinner time. She likes that. Women like these little thoughtful attentions. They are like oil on the axletree, and makes the machinery run smooth. But then there ought to be a little money to mix up with such things. Money is a good domestic lubricator itself. A man feels more like a gentleman with some change in his pocket, and he ought to always have a dollar or so just to feel of. It stiffens him up and keeps him from feeling like a vagabond. And woman wants some too. When a pedler comes along with tin ware, or a wagon load of jugs, or the Gypsies come along with lace, or the book agent comes along with pictures; and besides it is such a dignified comfort to have a little hid away for the children when they are just obliged to have something to wear and don't want to ask papa for the money, for he is so hard run and talks so poor all the time.

This is the money that goes for all it is worth. Money that comes hard, money that is earned. Even woman does not prize money when she has oodles of it and has every want supplied. Folks must be cramped to be happy. They must have something to stimulate them. Something to provoke economy and industry and I'm thankful we've always had these stimulants at my house.

CHAPTER XVIII.

COBE TALKS A LITTLE.

"Everything is adopted." Says I, "Cobe, you musent say adopted, for you mean adapted." "Well, I reckon so," says he. "Everything is adapted. Everything fits to everything. There is that houn' dog a-runnin' that rabbit and the dog is adopted to the rabbit and the rabbit is adopted to the dog. One was made for the tother to run. If there wasent any rabbits there wouldent be any houn' dogs. Boys is adopted to squirrels. If there wasent any boys there wouldent be any squirrels. If there wasent any chickens there wouldent be any hawks, for hawks is adopted to chickens, and if there wasent any chickens and birds there wouldent be any bugs and worms; and the bugs and worms is adopted to the leaves and vegetables, and there is always enough left of everything for seed and for white folks to live on. Hogs is adopted to acorns, and if there wasent any hogs there wouldent be more than eight or ten acorns on a tree—just enough for seed; and hogs is adopted to folks, and if there wasent any folks there wouldent be any hogs. There wouldent be any use for 'em. I'll tell you, major, everything was fixed up about right, as shore as you're born, and most everything was fixed up for us. Hogs has got sausage meat and tripe and cracklins, and souse and backbone and sparerib and lard and ham and shoulder and jowl to eat with turnip-greens, and it's all mighty good and its all adopted."

"That is all so, Cobe," said I; "everything is adapted whether it is adopted or not."

"Yes," said he, "and I've noticed it for a long time, when the wheat is cut off the land the grass comes up for hay, and if we cut it off another crop comes up and keeps the hot sun off the land and one crop follows another, and if we make a poor crop one year we make a better one the next year, and if we don't we can live on hope and cut down expenses and work the harder to fix up, and some how or other or somehow else we all get along, and when there is a gap we fill it up with something, and we all get along and nobody perishes to death in the name of the Lord, for everything fits and everything is adopted."

"Well," says I, "Cobe, that is all so—not only so, but also, but there are a heap of things come along that don't seem to be adopted, as you call it. Here comes the army worm, and the grasshoppers, and the caterpillars, and all sorts of vermin, and they are not adapted, and what are we going to do with them? What are you going to do with snakes, mad dogs, and storms, and pestilence, and diptheria, and smallpox, and all such afflictions? Are they adopted or are they adapted, or what are they?"

"Well, sir," says Cobe, "I'll tell you. I havn't been troubled with them things yet, but if I was I know there would be some offset. Something to balance the account. I never knowed a man to have a big trouble but what there was something to balance off the trouble. I never knowed a man to go to Texas but what he writ back that there wasn't anything to brag off after he got there. The good things of this life are pretty equally distributed if we only did know it. A rich man haint got much advantage of a poor man if the poor man is any account. Some poor folks is bad stock and don't want to work and goes about grumbling. They is just like a bad stock of horses or cattle or dogs and ought to die out and quit the country. We don't send round the settlement to git a poor dog or a poor cat, or a poor hog or a poor cow. We want a good stock of anything; and there is about the same difference in folks that there is in anything else. There are some rich folks that are clever and some that are mean— some grind you down and some help you up, but them who grind you down don't have much enjoyment. They are too mean to enjoy good health. They are never happy unless they are miserable. I'd rather be poor than to be some rich men that I know. My children have a better time eating simmons and black haws and digging gubbers and hunting possums than their children do in getting to parties and wearing fine clothes and fussing with one another and doing nothing for a living. There is nothing like work—working for a living and being contented with your situation. I love to see rich folks doing well, for they help out the country and build railroads, and factories, and car shops, and open up the iron mines, and I know that if everybody was as poor as I am the country wouldent prosper, and it looks like everything was adopted, and we need rich folks to plan and poor folks to work, and they couldent get along without us any more than we could get along without them. I don't want their fine clothes, nor their fine house, nor their carriage and horses, and they don't want my little old mule, nor my bobtail coat, and so its all right all round, and everything is adopted. It don't take me but a minute and a half to git ready to go to meetin', for all I've got to do is to put on my coat and comb the cuckleburs outen my hair and wash my face and git a couple of chaws of tobacco and take my foot in my hand and go. I can squat down at the door when I git there, and hear all the preachers has to say, and thank the Lord for his goodness, and that is worship enough for a poor man, I reckon, and its all adopted. When I see fine things and fine people I'm always thankful for some favors that are pow'ful cheap considering that money runs the world, for we have got good health and good appetites at my house and can sleep well on a hard bed, and a drink of spring water is the best thing in the world to a hungry man. We haint got no dishpepshy nor heart burn, and nobody haint suing me for my land for I haint got any, and my wife can make as good corn bread as anybody, and our tables is a good kind and the old cow lets down her milk about right and can live and do well without being curried and fed up like a Jersey, and she understands my children and they understand her and so it looks like everything is adopted. I was a thinking the other day how much service this old coat Mrs. Arp give me has done, for if it had been a new one I would have been afeerd of it, but I've wore it now for six months, and its good yet, and the children have wore the old clothes she give them, and they are all adopted, and now, major, if you have got a chaw or two of that good tobacco you always have I want a bite or two, for that is one thing that I like better than poor folks' tobaccer. Its one thing that I think is a leetel better adopted than anything else. At least I like it better."

Cobe got his tobacco and flanked his little mule with his heelless shoes and galloped away in peace. If he is not adapted, I know he feels adopted. Cobe has peculiar ideas and a peculiar language. He always says that thunder killed a man, and when I told him that it was lightning he said, " Well, I know they say it is lightning, but I've always noticed that when it strikes a tree or a man or a mule the thunder and the lightning comes all in a bunch, and you can't tell tother from which." "But, Cobe," says I, "when a gun shoots, the noise don't hurt anything; it is the shot." "Just so," says he, "but there is no shot about this thunder business."

CHAPTER XIX.

THE UPS AND DOWNS OF FARMING.

I never could write like a school-master, and now my fingers are all in a twist and I am as nervous as a woman with the neuralgia. Me and my hopeful boy set out yesterday morning to cut an acre of second-crop clover, for these lazy niggers round here wanted a dollar a day and board, and I wouldn't give it, and so me and him undertook the job for our vittles alone, and he had a good mowing-blade and I rigged up an old scythe that belonged to a wheat-cradle, and it was about six feet long and took a sweep accordin', and the clover was rank and mixed up with morning glories, and for the first ten minutes it looked like we would just walk through it like one of McCormick's reapers; but you see, that kind of work brought into play a new set of nerves and muscles that hadent been used in a long time, for mowin' clover with a long blade is an irregular, side-wipin' business that swings a man in all sorts of horrizontal attitudes, for sometimes he don't put on enough power for the reach of his blade, and then again he puts on a little too much and it comes round with a jerk that twists him up like a corkscrew, and so the first thing I knew I was blowin' worse than a tired steer and my shirt stuck to me and my heart was beating like a muffled drum, and I rather look back at what I had cut than ahead of me what I hadn't. But I was too proud to surrender, for, though I say it myself, there's grit in me, and ever and anon it shows itself, under peculiar circumstances. I heaved ahead of my boy with my long-sweepin' simiter, that give me time to stop and git my wind and wait for my palpitatin' bosom to quit thumpin', and then I would rally my wastin' forces and go it again until I couldent go it any longer. My boy was as willing to quit as I was, for the sun was hot and the air was close, and, I say now after due reflection it was the hardest morning's work I ever did, and I'm not for hire to repeat it at a dollar a day or any other insignificant reward, for it has twisted me out of all decent shape and I go about hump-shouldered and sway-backed and as sore all over as if I had been beat with a thrash-pole. I don't think I would have made such a fool of myself, but you see some of my wife's female relations had come a long ways to see us and all the family paraded over to the clover field like a general and his staff, and as they stood around I put on as much style as possible in swingin' my blade and could hear 'em admiring us how gracefully and easily we handled the instruments, when the truth was we had mighty nigh mowed ourselves to death and saved the king of terrors the job.

What a power of influence these female smiles do have upon us. What undertaking is there that we will not undertake if they will stand by and look on and encourage. Why sir, I have thought in moments of enthusiasm that if my wife, Mrs. Arp, was to unfold her angelic wings and soar away to Chimborazoes top, and call me with a heavenly smile, I'd go too if I could. I wish they were all rich, for these two traits about woman have always struck me. They can live on less when they are obliged to, and make a little go a heap further than the men, but when money is handy they can spend more and take more satisfaction in gettin' rid of it than anybody.

I read the other day in a farming paper that moles dident do any harm, but on the contrary they did good in eating up bugs and worms; well, I caught one on the first day of this month, a nice, slick, fat fellow; and as my folks had been making an April fool of me all day, I just emptied the sugar bowl and shut the sweet little innocent up in there. Mrs. Arp is a dignified woman, especially at the table. She takes her seat the last of all and after grace she arranges the cups in the saucers, and the next thing is to put in the sugar and cream and give it a little stir with a spoon. Mrs. Arp is afraid of rats, and so when she stretched forth her sweet little hand and removed the sugar dish top the varmint rose suddenly to a perpendicular position, and stuck his red snout just above the top edge. She saw him—I know she did from the way she done. Anticipating a catastrophy, I had slipped around to the rear and reached her just in time to receive her in my affectionate arms as she was reclining backward in a riotous and tumultuous manner. Shutting up the animal again, I departed those coasts, and it took me two days to mole-ify her lacerated feelings and make things calm and serene. The next morning I turned him loose in the garden, and before night he had run his under-ground railroad right under a row of peas that was about ten inches high, and cut the peas from the seed, and the tops was lying flat and wilted, like a cabbage plant when the cut worms find it.

Farmin' is a good deal like fishin'. Every time you start out you can just see yourself catchin' 'em; but after tryin' every hole in the creek you go home sorrowfully, with a fisherman's luck. But we are not complainin' by no means, for we've got wheat enuf for biskit every day and light-bread on Sunday, and a few bushels to spare for them angels that's to cum along unawares sum of these days. We finished cuttin' the oat crop this mornin', and what with them and the clover already housed, the cattle are safe for another year. I imagine they look sassy and thankful; but as for me, I am a used up individual. Durin' harvest I have had to be a binder, and if you don't know what that is, ask Harris. The ends of these fingers which are now inscribin' this epistle are in a bad fix. Skarified and stuck up with bull nettles and briars, they are as sore as a school-boy's bile. There was sum variation to my business, such as catchin' young rabbits, and findin' partridge nests, and pickin' dewberries; but the romance wore off the first day, and by the end of the next my wife says I was as humble a man as any woman could desire. Its a mighty purty thing to write about and make up oads and pomes. The golden grain, the manly reapers, the strutten' sheaves, the song of the harvesters, and purty Miss Ruth coquettin' around the fields of old man Boaz, and "how jokin' did they drive their team afield," is all so sweet and nice to a man up a tree with an umbrel, but if them poets had to tie wheat half a day in a June sun, their sentimentality would henceforth seek another subjek. I tried swingin' the cradle awhile, but somehow or somehow else, I couldn't exactly get the lick. It wasent the kind of a cradle I've been used to, and I am too old a dog to learn new tricks now.

The branches are getting low. The corn is curling in the blades. The mills grind a little in the morning and then wait for the pond to fill. The locust is singin' a parchin' tune. Summer flies keeps the cows' tails busy, and all nature gives sign of a comin' drouth. I don't like this, but am tryin' to be resigned. Before I turned farmer such weather dident concern me much if I could find a cool retreat, but now I realize how dependent is mankind upon the farm, and the farmer upon Providence. The truth is, its a precarious business all around, and I sometimes catch myself a wishin' I was rich or had a sorter side-show to my circus.

A sorry farmer on a sorry farm is a sorry spectacle. A good farmer on poor land and a poor farmer on good land are purty well balanced, and can scratch along if the seasons hit; but I reckon a smart and diligent man with good land to back him is about as secure against the shiftin' perils of this life as anybody can be; and then if a man could have besides a few thousand dollars invested in stocks and draw the intrust twice a year he ought to be as happy as subloonary things can make him. Then, you see, he could send off his children to school, and visit his kin, and keep a cook and a top buggy, and lay in some chaney ware and a carpet for the old 'oman, and new bonnets and red ear-rings for the girls, and have a little missionary money left. If the drouth or the army worm or the caterpillar comes along he would have something to fall back on and make him always feel calm and sereen. I think I would like that—wouldent you?—and I reckon there ain't no harm in prayin' for it as Agur did when he said, "give me neither poverty or riches." Most every aspirin' man I know of in the towns and cities is lookin' forward to this blessed state. They work and toil and twist, and dodge in and dodge out, and do a thousand little things they are sorter ashamed of, with a view at the last of settling down on some good farm with creeks and springs and meadows and mills and fine cattle, and windin' up a perplexin' life in peace with mankind and communion with honest nature. No ambitious man becomes lost to such pleasant hopes as these, and the more trouble he has the more he longs for it, for its about the fittenest way I know of to get time to repent and make preparation for shuffling off this mortal coil. But to all such the outside investment is highly necessary. Even Beecher could not get along without it—for there are a thousand little leaks in farmin' that a man without experience can't stop, and without capital can't remedy. Why, only this mornin' one of my boys was driving across a bridge and the mule Joe got skeered at his shadder and shoved Tom over on the hand rail and it broke, and he fell in the creek and dragged Joe with him, and the wagon, too, and broke the tongue all to pieces, and the houns and the haims and the harness and the driver, and both the mules set into kickin' with the front end of the waggon on top of 'em, and the hind end up on the bridge, and you could have heard the racket for two miles without a telefone, and the girls ran and screamed, and Mrs. Arp liked to have fainted every step of the way, for she said she knew Paul was killed as he fell, and kicked to death by the mules and drowned afterwards, and it took two hours to clear the wreck and restore the wounded and passify the women and get everything once more calm and sereen. Now, you see, there's some unforseen damages to pay and nobody to pay 'em, and all we can do is to charge it up to the mule. I do think that we farmers ought to have some protection agin the like of this, and I want to introduce a bill the next session, for they've been protecting manufactures for 75 years and neglectin' agriculture, which is the very subsill of a nation's prosperity. I wonder if our law-makers who can save a State couldn't fix up an arrangement that would give everybody a good price for what they had to sell, and put everything down low that we had to buy, and then abolish taxes and work the roads with the chain-gang, and let the bell-punch run the government. Such a aw would give universal satisfaction and immortalize its author.

CHAPTER XX.

The Family Preparing to Receive City Cousins.

It's a thrillin' time when a country family have invited their city cousins to visit 'em, and are fixin' up to receive 'em in a hospitable manner.

The scouring mop and the floor-cloth and an old jar of lie soap and a pan full of sand are not very elegant things to handle but they are useful and can't be abolished with decency.

Everything around and about our premises is mighty clean and nice now. I wish it would stay so. I don't care so much about it myself, but it harmonizes with Mrs. Arp and the girls and the Scriptures. I'm afraid I'm a little heathenish about such things, for I don't like to live under such constraint—to have to scrape my shoes so much and shut the doors and hang up my hat and empty the wash-bowl. I don't like to see the ashes taken up quite so clean and so often and so much sweeping and scrubbing. I don't think the broom ought to be set in the corner upside down nor the clean towel hid in the wash-stand where me and the little boys can't find it. I think I would like a room somewhere close about where me and the children could do as we please and enjoy a little dirt on the floor and throw the saw and the hammer and a few nails around and kick off our muddy shoes and mould bullets and pop corn and play horse and marbles and tumble up the bed and do as we please and clean up things about once a month. But there's no room to spare and so I have to endeavor to live like a gentleman whether I want to or not. I've got an idea that a little clean dirt is healthy. I'm afraid that little tender children are washed and bathed too much. They get puny and pale, and delicate. Poor little things. It's very disagreeable to 'em. I never saw one that liked it, and that's pretty good evidence it's not accordin' to nature. Once a week is very reasonable, but this every night's business is a sin. They say it keeps the pores open, but maybe they oughtent to be kept open all the time. The surgeons say that a handful of fresh earth bound on a flesh wound or a bruise will cure it up, and I've found out that the best cure for scratches in horses' feet is walking in fresh plowed ground. I never saw a healthy child that didn't love to play in the dirt, and the sand, and make frog houses and mud pies. But still I don't go to extremes. I don't want 'em to get so dirty their skin hasn't got any pores at all and their little ears would sprout turnip seed. Everything must be done in reason and in season. There's some things I am mighty particular about—such as clean dishes and butter and milk and sausage-meat. I saw a woman milking the other day, and she pulled the calf away by the calf's tail and then wiped off the cow's tits with the cow's tail and went to milking. I thought there was too little water and too much tail in that.

But to return to the preparations for the reception. The girls took matters in charge, and for several days the exciting episode went on. It was like clearing the deck of a man of war for a fight. The house has been scoured and scrubbed and sand-papered. Everything in it has been taken down and put up again, and moved to a new place, and I can't find anything now when I want it. The old faded carpets have been taken up and beaten, and patched all over, and curtailed and put down again. They get smaller and smaller, which they say is a good way to wear 'em out without taking cold. The furniture has been freshly varnished with kerosene oil; the window glass washed on both sides, and the knives and forks, water buckets, wash pans, and shovel and tongs brightened up. The hearths have been painted a Spanish brown, the soiled plastering whitewashed, the family portraits dusted, and the pewter teapot and plated castors and spoons and napkin rings polished as fine as a jewelry store.

I surveyed the operations from day to day with affectionate interest, for it does me good to see young people work diligently in a meritorious cause; nevertheless my routine of daily life appears to be somewhat demoralized. On the first day our humble dinner was dispensed with and me and the boys invited to lunch on bread and sorghum at a side table. The next day we were allowed to lunch in the back piazzer, for fear we would mess up the dining room, and the next we were confined to the water-shed to keep us from messing up the piazzer and after that I meekly prepared myself to be shoved out doors on a plank, but we wasn't. Mrs. Arp lectures me every day on manners and she don't confine her lectures to my private ear. The last time we had turkey we had company, and when I asked a lady if she would have some of this fowl, my wife, Mrs. Arp, she looked at me indignantly, and said: "William, that is not fowl—it is turkey." When I asked the lady if she would have some of the stuffing, Mrs. Arp, my wife, observed sarcastically, "Of course she will have some of the 'dressing.'" You see, I thought that dressing was generally worn outside, but it seems that a turkey is not dressed until it is undressed. Well, she overlooked me when the pie was sent around; she overlooks me a great deal, and when I ventured to remind her that I would take some of the dessert, she said she didn't have any Sahara, but maybe a desert of mince pie would do just as well. We took tea at a nabor's once and when the servant handed me a little glass dish of peaches in a waiter, I thought the whole concern was for me and set it down by my plate. But my wife, Mrs. Arp, she watches me pretty close and whispered to me to take some of the preserves if I wanted any, as the servant was waiting for the dish. So after awhile I was handed a saucer of canned peaches, and when I took one out and put it on my plate, my wife, Mrs. Arp, kindly requested me to eat out of the saucer. She has never got reconciled to the way I imbibe my coffee, for you see I was raised to pour it out in the saucer, and when I try to take it from the cup it burns me so I have to give it up. Some folks will endure a heap for style, but I am too old to begin it now. I think I do pretty well considering all things and deserve credit.

Delicate hints have been given that it ain't polite to set down to dinner with one's coat off, or eat hominy with a knife, or smoke in the parlor. The wash bowl has been turned upside down to keep us from using it. With this side up it holds about a pint and a half, and as I was washing my face with the tips of my fingers they surveyed me with a look of unutterable despair. When I raise my workin' boots on the banister rail for an evening rest they wipe it off with a wet rag as soon as I leave. I mustn't step on the purty red hearth to make a fire or put a back log on that weighs fifty pounds. They've put pillows on my bed about half as big as a bale of cotton and fringed all round like a petticoat. They are to stay on in day time and be taken off at night. When I'm tired and feel the need of a midday nap that bed was a comfort, but the best I can do now is to sit up in a chair and nod. The dogs don't understand the new system at all. Old Bows has been coming in the house to the fire or lying in the piazza for fourteen years, and it does seem impossible to break him of it in a sudden though dogmatic manner. Broom-handles and fishing-poles move 'em out at one door, but they slip in at another.

I think the best thing I can do is to vamoose the ranch and take the dogs and cats and children with me. We can sleep on the hay in the loft and eat peas and drink water and swell to keep from starvin'. Maybe Mrs. Arp and the girls will take pity on us then and let us come back to the old regulations. When the cousins come all will be well. I wish they were here now.

CHAPTER XXI

Bad Luck in the Family.

It's bad luck now at our house. One of those peculiar spells when everything goes wrong and nobody to blame for it. Saw the new moon through a brush, I reckon. On Monday two of my pigs, just littered, got drowned in the branch; Tuesday my shoats got into my potato patch; Wednesday a nigger was found struttin' around town with my equestrian walking cane, which was a present, and which I dident know was lost, and yesterday mornin', while Mrs. Arp was away, I thought it was a good time to cut little Jessie's hair off, for it was continually gittin' down over her eyes like any other country gal's, and so I shingled it all over after a fashion of my own, and when her mother came home I dident know at first but what she had took the highsterics, but I soon found out better without much assistance, if any, and all that day I had right smart business away from the house. I gently suggested that it was all owin' to the way she looked at the moon, but that dident screen anything, for you see she was countin' on showin' off the child at the fair, and now she can't. I am hopeful, however, that when the ambrosial locks grow out again our conjugal life will once more be calm and sereen. Husbands! fathers! martyrs to wedded bliss, don't cut your little girl's hair off without permission—don't.

It looks like my bad luck all comes in a bunch. You see, I had dug a flower pit and rigged it up with shelves and put glass windows in the top of it, and Mrs. Arp and the girls had managed one way and another to fill it with geraniums and all sorts of pretty things, and some of them were in bloom and everything growing so nice and smelt so sweet and the women folks were proud of 'em and nursed them and watered them and showed them to everybody; but yesterday they discovered some little varmints, about as big as a gnat, were gathering on the leaves and doing damage, and when they told me about it, I didn't say nothing, but I thought I knew what would kill 'em, for I had tried it in the hen house, and it worked like a charm. So I got some sulphur and put it in an old pan and set it afire and shut down the sash. Well, I have killed all the bugs, that's a fact, and the misery of it is I have killed most everything else. I'm not going to enlarge upon the melancholly consequences, but will just say I wish my folks would put on mourning and be done with it. I can't stand this sort of resigned sadness that's hovering over us much longer. If they would tear around and cut up awhile and quit, I wouldent mind it, but this drooping way they've got of going to the flower-pit like it was a graveyard is just a-killen me. They don't say nothing and I don't say nothing, so I have been reading history for consolation.

Old Bows is dead, my loving and trusty friend, the defender of my children, the protector of my household in the dark and silent watches of the night. For thirteen years he has been both fond and faithful, and now we feel like one of the family is dead. Bows was the best judge of human nature I ever saw. He knew an honest man and a gentleman by instinct. He never frightened a woman or a child—he never went tearing down the front walk after anybody but the very looks of him would mighty nigh skeer a nigger to death. When they had to come to our house they begun to holler "hello" a quarter of a mile off. Bows loved to skeer 'em, he did. He had character and emotions. Having no tail to wag (for he was not cur-tailed) he did the best that he could and wagged where it ought to be. Bows was a dark brindle. He was a dog of ancestors. His father was named Shylock, and his grand-father's name was Sheriff. They were all honorable dogs. He was not quarrelsome or fussy. I never knew him to run up and down a nabors pailings after the dog on the other side. He was above it—but he never dodged a responsibility. He has come in violent personal contact with other dogs a thousand times, more or less, and was never the bottom dog in the fight. And then what an honest voice he had. His bark was not on the C, but it was a deep, short basso profundo. We have buried him on the brow of the hill where he used to sit and watch for tramps and stragglers. Slowly and sadly we laid him down. Talk about your sheep—I wouldn't have given him for a whole flock. Sheep are to eat and wear, but Bows was a friend. It's like comparing appetite with emotion—the animal with the spiritual. But I am done now. Let Harris press on his dog law. I've got nothin' agin sheep—in fact, I like 'em. Ever since Mary had a little lamb I've thought kindly of sheep, and I am perfectly willin' to a law that will exterminate all houns and suck-egg pups and yaller doggs and bench-leg fices. They are a reflection on Bowses memory.

Yesterday morning about the broke of day a big clap of thunder come along and shook a month's rain out of the clouds in half an hour. My old friend Peckerwood says he's lived here 35 years and never seed the like before. It dident rain nor pour, but jest come down in horrizontal sheets, and the little branches turned into creeks, and the creeks into rivers and they swelled out of their channels and all over the bottom land, and tore down fences and bridges and water-gates and carried off rails and planks and watermelons and punkins, and the low ground corn ain't nigh as high as it was, and there's a dozen places in the farm where my nabors' hogs can walk into my fields and help themselves if they want to, and they always want to, you know, for I never saw a gate open or the bars down that there wasent an educated hog in sight somewhere. I reckon a hundred people have told me I had the well-waterdest farm in the county, and now I believe it; but if you know of a man who has got one that ain't quite so well-watered, and is a mile or two high, and not subject to the avalanch, and I keep in my present humor, please send him along and I'll swap.

Everywhere that a fence crossed a slew or a branch it's washed away for a dozen panels, and the big long logs that swung the water gates are gone, and the plank fences on both sides of the big road are gone, and now it takes all the hands and the dogs to keep the nabors' hogs back while we are repairin' damages, and reminds me of the time we used to guard the road to keep the small-pox from comin' to town.

The meandering swine whose fourfathers ran down into the sea, have been perusin' the pasture and now its open to the tater patch, and so we've had to pen up everything in the barn-yard together, and the old sow has been samplin' the young chickens and the Governor (that's our man cow) tried to horn General Gordon, the finest colt perhaps you ever laid your eyes on, and this morning as I was a movin' about with alacrity, Mrs. Arp told me the flour was out and I told her to run us on shorts, and she said the shorts was out, and I hollered back to run us on meal, and she said the meal was out, and then I surrendered, and had some wheat and corn sent to the mill, and in about an hour Ralph come back and said one mill dam had washed away and the other mill had up the rocks a peckin' of 'em, and the creek was still a risin' and he couldn't cross any more, and I sent him to one nabor to borrow and they had locked up and gone a visitin', and another nabor didn't have but a handful in the house, and so here we are jest a perishin' to death in the name of the state, and if you and your folks have got any bowels now is the time for you to extend to me and my folks your far reachin' sympathies—ain't it?

And Mrs. Arp thought it a good day to clean up the kitchen and scour up the pans and cook-vessels, and the girls said shorely nobody would come foolin' around in such wether, and they went to moppin' and sloppin' over the house, and shore enuf about four o'clock this evenin' p. m., in the afternoon a couple of nice young gentlemen swum their horses all the way from town to get to see 'em, and there was no darkey to open the door and my black-eyed Pocahontas had it to do, and she got behind it and hid and ax'd 'em in, and about sundown I come home and told 'em I was agoin' to put up their nags and they must stay all night, which was the boldest venture on the least capital I ever made in my life, but they respectfully declined, which was fortunate for them, for although bright eyes and rosy cheeks and bang'd up hair may have some effect on a young man's heart, they are mighty little comfort to his stomach—aint they?

And it aint done freshin' yet, for the frogs are croakin' and the air is full of swet and the salt sticks together and the camphor bottle is cloudy, and I don't think Mrs. Arp is as smilin' as usual, and all of these signs hardly ever fail at once you know.

Such is life and I can't help it. The bad and the good, the wet and the dry, is all mixed up together. I have spread forth my trouble and feel better. There's lots of folks in my fix, and I want 'em to know I sympathize. I'm sorry for 'em, and if they are sorry for me it's all right. As Cobe says, it's all right. We have got a power of good things to be thankful for. A little boy was drowned in my nabor's mill-pond yesterday, but he wasn't mine. The doctor passes my house most every day, but he don't stop. There was a barn full of corn and mules burnt up in the settlement last week, but it wasent mine. The poor house is just up the road a piece, but we don't board there. I'm not a candidate for any office. I've got plenty to eat right now, and when we get tired of our homely fare we can just step over to nabor Freeman's and fare better. There's nothing like having a good nabor in eating distance—for we don't have to dress up nor put on any particular style about it, but just send up word we are coming up to supper and it's all right. Folks can't do that way in town.

CHAPTER XXII.

The Struggle for Money.

I don't hear of many folks getting rich. I don't know of but a few who are making more than a good fair living, and there's ten to one who are powerfully scrouged to do that. The majority of mankind are always on a strain. Most of them work hard enough but somehow or somehow other, they can't get ahead, and a good many are in old Plunket's fix who said he was even with the world for he owed about as much as he dident owe. Some folks are just like hogs. They won't stay in one place or keep at one business long enough to make anything, but are always a rooting and ranging around for new places. I've noticed children picking blackberries— some will stay at a bush until they have gathered 'em all and others will spend nearly all the time in hunting for a better place. You can tell 'em by their buckets when they get home. My good old father used to say he never knew a man to stick closely to a business for ten years but what he made money—toat is, excepting preaching and politics. The one don't want to make it and the other can't keep it, as a general rule, for money made easy goes easy. When a lawyer gets five dollars for writing a deed he spends it before night, but if he had to make ten bushels of corn to get it he would carry it in his pocket just as long as he could. It's altogether another sort of a V. But it's all right, provided we are happy, and I don't think there is very much difference in this respect between the poor and the rich. I used to be sorter curious of rich people, and wondered at Providence for letting them have so much more than they needed, but I ain't now; I've got more sense, for I perceive they are no happier than I am, and then, besides, when they begin to get old their grip weakens, and they build up colleges and churches, and orphans' homes, and establish libraries and other institutions. If they don't do that, their children get it, and as a general rule they scatter it all before they die, for it comes easy and it will go the same way. So it's all right in the long run and if it aint I can't help it, and I'm not going to grieve over what I can't remedy. Honest industry and a contented disposition is the best insurance company for happiness in this world and will make a man independent of fine houses and fine clothes and the luxuries of life on the one side and court houses and jails and pinching poverty on the other. It seems to me that somebody has said something like this before, but I'll say it again anyhow. There's one thing I consider settled—my children will have no chance to waste and squander my money, for there won't be any left to speak of and it will be such a long division the fractions will be too small to fuss about. Time about is fair play, and if we take care of them in infancy and youth and spend the last dollar we get on 'em, they must look after us when we get old and helpless—and they will, I know. We've tried to make their young lives happy. I've mighty nigh wore myself out playing horse and marbles and carrying 'em on my back, and rolling 'em in a wheelbarrow, and doing a thousand things to please 'em, and that's more than a rich man will do, who is all absorbed in stocks and bonds and speculation, and goes home at night with money on the brain. He's no father—he ain't; he's a machine. The average family man is hard run. There's nobody perishing or freezing in this sunny land, and very few folks boarding at the poor house, but still there is a general struggle going on in the town and the country. Most everybody is in debt more or less, and what one crop don't pay has to lap over on the next. The merchants say that money is awful tight right now, and I reckon it is. I'm sorry for the merchants, for as a general thing money is their sole dependence. If he hasent got money he is a busted institution, and that is where the advantage of being a farmer comes in. He can be out of money and still squeeze along, for he has corn and wheat and sheep and hogs and chickens, and don't have to wear store clothes to any great extent, and his children can wear their old ones a long time and go bare headed and bare footed when there's no company around. Town folks have to dress better and dress oftener, whether they can pay for 'em or not. But it is a hard time all round to make a living, and I don't know exactly what is the matter. The average family is not extravagant. They understand the situation at home and try to conform, but it looks like they are just obleeged to fudge a little and go in debt, and then the misery begins. When the good man gets his mail from the post-office, he is most afraid to open it for fear of a dun. These darned little just debts as Saul McCarney used to call 'em, hang around him like a shadow. The four D's are mighty close kin—debt, duns, death and the devil—and one is nearly as welcome as the other. A man who was born rich and managed to keep so or a man who was born poor and has gotten rich, don't know much about the horror of debt and hasent got much sympathy for the debtor class and is very apt to lay it all to their imprudence or bad management, but the fact is most of our rich men got a start before the war or built up on the ruins of it before society with its extravagance got hold of 'em. They couldent do it now. I know lots of rich men who, if they were to lose their fortunes, couldent start now and make another. They think they could, but they couldent; mankind are too smart and too sharp now for an old-fashioned man to stand any chance. He would get licked up in his first experiment. Money makes money and money can keep money after it is made, but there is a slim chance now for a young man to make money and save it and keep in gun-shot of society. He can bottle himself up and remain a bachelor and turn his back on society and accumulate a fortune, but the trouble is that most of 'em want to marry and ought to marry, and if he bottles himself up and spends nothing and dresses common he is not the sort of man the girls are waiting for. And so if he spends freely and rides around, he is apt to get married, and then comes house rent and servant's hire and clothes according, and he squeezes along and is always on the strain. There are mighty few getting rich now-a-days, but when a man does get a start, he can get richer than they used to. A half a million now is about what fifty thousand dollars used to be. But the average man is not going to get rich, and I reckon it is the common lot, and therefore it is all right. Nobody ought to distress himself about it, or hanker after money, but somehow I can't help wishing that our common people were a little better off.

Let us encourage the boys—the rising young men and middle aged men. Let us pat 'em on the back and point to the flag and say, "Excelsior." It will help 'em climb the mountain. Jesso—but I said awhile back that this generation will not produce men as grand as our fathers, and it won't. There are no young men who give promise of equaling Clay or Webster or Calhoun or Crawford or Forsyth or Troup or Howell Cobb or Toombs, in the days of his splendor, or Stephens or Joseph Henry Lumpkin or Warner or Walter T. Colquitt, and a score of others I could name. I am talking about grand men—men who stood away above their fellows and adorned society like mountains adorn and dignify a landscape. Nobody is to blame about it that I know of, for it comes according to nature's laws and the decrees of Providence, and I reckon its all right. Those grand men of the olden time have served their day and accomplished their work. They moulded manners and statesmanship and great principles and patriotism and the masses looked up to them and learned wisdom. All this was in the days of Southern aristocracy, and these grand men had abundant leisure and dident have to be on the wild hunt for money. It was the aristocracy of dominion, for dominion dignified a man then, and it does now just as it did in the days of the centurion, who said: "I say unto this man, go, and he goeth, and to another come, and he cometh." Dominion over men makes a man feel a responsibility that nothing else does, and this responsibility enlarges his moral nature and ennobles him as a gentleman and a philosopher. It is this feeling that dignifies judges and railroad presidents, and captains of ships, and generals in armies. They can all command men and be obeyed.

But the time came in the Providence of God for a change. The masses of the people were under a cloud. They were overshadowed, and the wreck of the slave aristocracy, together with the results of the war, made an opening for them and their children. Humbler men have come to the front and now run the machine. The masses are looming up. Overseers have got rich. Poor boys, who had a hard time, are now our merchant princes. The old lines of social standing are broken down, and one man is good as another, if he succeeds. Success is everything now, especially success in making money. Statesmanship has gone down. Great learning is at a discount, money rules the roost, and everybody knows it, and everybody is pushing for it. Money makes presidents, and governors and members of congress. We talk about a candidate's "bar'l" now just as we used to talk about his eloquence or his service to his country. Everywhere there is a wild rush for money, and it don't matter how a man gets it so he gets it.

Now, how can this sort of an age produce great men? How can the young men escape the infection? Where is any purity or honor in' politics or in the court house? When a man has to resort to deceit or hypocrisy or questionable means to support his family he loses his self-respect, and when his self-respect is gone, his ability to be a great man is gone. He can't do it. No man is truly great who is not honest and and sincere and a lover of his fellow-men. A lawyer who lies or resorts to tricks—a merchant who conceals the truth may get rich, but they will never be great. I tell you the grand old men are gone, or going, and their places will not be filled by this generation nor the next. The next generation will be worse than this, for these people who have sprung up and got rich are going to get richer, and they will spoil their children with money and a fashionable education. They are doing it now, and by and by these children will get to be proud and vain and no account, and won't work, and finally go down the hill their father climbed. Stuck up vagabonds will marry the girls, and the boys will loaf around town and play billiards and drive a fast horse. A man who was raised poor and by a hard struggle gets rich, is the biggest fool in the world about his children. He came from one extreme and puts his children on the other.

Nevertheless I am hopeful, and if I do sometimes take the shady side, I mean no harm by it. I am always reconciled to what I cannot help. The wild rush for a big pile of surplus money alarms me, for the older I grow the surer I am that the surplus will not bring happiness or be a blessing to the children. There is no security except in honest industry, and boys won't work whose fathers are rich. Old Agur was right. "Lord give me neither poverty nor riches, lest if I be sick I take thy name in vain or lest I be poor and steal." But there is some comfort in this great change from the old to the new. The common people have a better chance than they used to have. All classes are assimulating and becoming more alike—more on an equality. One man is about as good as another now, if not better. The Joe Brown type is in the ascendant, and the humblest man has an equal chance for the highest honors. So let it rip along, for a wise Providence is above us.   *   *   *   *   *

Cobe says he "aint makin' a blessed thing—no corn, no 'taters, no cotton, no nuthin'—and Willy is down with the new-mony, and the chickens all died with the cholera;" and then he gave a three-cornered grin and squeezed his tobacco between his teeth as he remarked, "but, major, it ain't nigh as bad as it mout be; it ain't nigh as bad as war." Then he stuck his heels in the little mule's flanks and away he went galloping up the road. There used to be a bureau called the bureau of refugees and abandoned lands, and Cobe says if them yankees will revive it now he is about ready to jine the concern. Says he will do most anything except beg or steal, or go to the poor house. So when I feel melancholly I think about Cobe and cheer up. The truth is, we all borrow too much trouble. It is better to look back once in awhile and recall the vast amount of fears and forebodings that were wasted and maybe that will give us brighter hopes of the future.

* * * * * * *

There's a new lot of boys a circulatin' around us now. *Grandchildren* have come to visit us and see the spring show open in our country home. Penned up for months in a little city, they have lived in a sort of prison home and feel now like school boys when recess comes —want to go out and rock somebody. They hardly took time to kiss and say howdy and shuck off their store clothes before they were off —dabblin' in the branch, rockin' the ducks in the little pond, fightin the ganders as they stand guard over their sitting mates, digging bait, fishing for minners, rollin' an old hogshead down the hill, breakin' the bull calf and every half hour sendin' to grandma for some more gingerbread. Here they go and there they go, while their poor mother jumps up every five minutes to see if they havent got killed or drowned or turned over the hen-house. She had like to took a fit this mornin' as she looked out of the window and seen 'em coming down the big road with a calf a pullin' a little wagon with gum-log wheels. One a pullin' haw, another pullin' gee, and four of 'em a ridin' and all a hollerin' tell they made such a racket the calf took a panic and run away with the whole concern and never stopped tell he got in the branch and landed their gable ends in the water.

Blessings on the children and the children's children. How I do love to have 'em around and see 'em frolic and ever and anon hear one squall with a cut finger or a stumped toe, or the bark knocked off his hide somewhere. What a pity they have got to grow up and see trouble and be sent to the legislature or congress, and there get a little behind in morals and money. But sufficient unto the day is the evil thereof.

P. S.—Now is the time to plant potatoes. Be shore to plant 'em in the dark of the moon and then plant some more just two weeks later, and they'll be "allee samee." I tried it last year.

* * * * * *

Breaking the Bull Calf.

My little boy geared up an imitation bug last night, made of black cloth with horse-hair legs—an awful looking varmint—and slyly swung it before me on a stick, and I had like to have a fit, trying to knock the ugly thing out of my face. The little rascal just laid down and hollered, and the family ain't done laughing about it till yet. Mrs. Arp sometimes tells me I let them take too many liberties with the dignity of their paternal ancestor, but it's all right, I reckon. And I noticed the other night when the girls jerked her up from the sofa and whirled her round the room to the music of the dance, she submitted to it with a humility and a grace that was impressive. I like that. I like an affectionate familiarity between parents and children, though I want it understood that I'm the boss of the family, that is, when Mrs. Arp is away from home. I give 'em butter on their biscuit as a regular thing, but when I put sugar on the butter I expect 'em to be more than ordinarily grateful.

CHAPTER XXIII.

ON A STRAIN.

In a numerous family of eight or ten children and some poor kin, it is right hard to maintain them, and keep up with the nabors in style and appearances. That is, it is right hard to do it from the profit of a little farm, and so if a man can't make a little money outside, he has to live on a strain. Folks are just obliged to keep up with the nabors, strain or no strain. The children must have as good clothes and the parlor as good furniture, and there must be as much good eating when company comes, and as good china ware to eat out of, and so on and so forth. But it is all a pardonable pride, for mothers are proud of their children, and their greatest pleasure is to see them look as well as other people's. Mothers have to stay at home all the time, and home ought to be made as attractive as possible. The men and the boys can go about and see folks and talk and joke and have a good time, and they don't care so much for show or ornament, but woman is penned up at home and has to look at the same old thing from morning till night and night till morning. I don't mean to say that she is a prisoner or unhappy by her fireside, for she is not, but her mind is active and her emotions are wide-awake, and it is her nature to love the beautiful, both in art and nature. Men too frequently forget this, and neglect many little things that would give the good wife and daughters pleasure. A man would let a worn-out curtain hang and hang until it was all faded out by the sun or speckled by the flies, and he had just as leave see it tacked up as hung from a cornice. If a window glass gets broken he is content to paste a piece of paper over the hole, and sometimes he won't do that, and the poor wife has to stick a pillow or some old rags in it to keep out the wind. I've seen the like of that at poor folks' houses, and I always blamed the man for it, for it is his business, and he could fix it up if he would. Woman gets discouraged after awhile about fixing up, and then she becomes careless and sloven, and maybe goes to eating snuff on the sly—on the sly at first, but after awhile as a regular thing.

She makes that compromise with her indifferent husband, and after that they just live along after a fashion, and call it life.

In such cases there is a sad difference between the pretty, nice, sweet girl he married a few years ago and the wife he has got now, and he is more to blame for it than she is. Why dident he fix up some home-made pleasures for her? He could make some cornice for the curtains, and a hanging shelf for the books, and he could buy a cheap chromo or two for the walls, and put a scraper on the door-step, and whitewash the fence, and plant out some rosebushes, and get a woodbine and a jessamine from the swamp and grow them by the front piazza, and then border the garden walks, and do a lot of little things, and keep doing them for her sake; and it would pay him well, for it would bring smiles and loving words, and above all, it would bring content and happiness. Woman loves ornament, for it is her nature, and why shouldent she? Our Heavenly Father painted nature in beautiful colors. He adorned the birds with plumage, and the fields with flowers, and the heavens with stars. All these costs us nothing to look at and admire. The best thing and the most beautiful things in nature are the cheapest. Riches can't buy them, nor hoard them, nor hide them from the poor. Air and sunlight, and water, and shade trees, and fruit, and flowers, and the sweet songs of happy birds, and the love of children, and good health, and refreshing sleep and the happy union of loving hearts—all these cost nothing, and are worth more to make us happy than anything else. Well, of course we must have something to eat and something to wear, but it is only the rich who don't have a good appetite and who have nothing to wear. All the poor folks in this region have enough to eat and enough clothes to make them comfortable, but I do know of some rich ones who are always troubled because they have nothing to wear. Some of them can't go to church for want of a new dress or a new bonnet or a shawl, or a set of jewelry as fine as their nabors.

The most important food in the world is bread, and it is the cheapest, and then comes milk and molasses, and meat, which are all within the reach of a workingman's purse. It is a wise provision of a kind Providence that the labor of one man, whether upon the farm or in the workshop, will feed and clothe eight persons and keep them comfortable—that is, eight dependent persons, as a wife and six children, and himself. When there are more than six children in a family, the older ones are big enough to help—that is, unless the good wife has doubled on him and has a whole passel of twins, which she ought not to do if she can help it. But poor folks for children and poor folks for twins, and when I remonstrated with Cobe about it, he smiled and said: "It's all right, it's all right, and me and the old 'oman ain't sorry nary bit, for the Lord never sent a 'possum in the world but what He planted a 'simmon tree close by."

In this country most any laboring man can earn his dollar a day, and that will buy bread and molasses for a family of eight, and have fifty cents left for clothing and other things. It is mighty little, I know, and I wish it was more, but nobody need to starve or steal. The trouble is, that it don't leave anything for schooling, or for sickness, or doctor's bills, or any of the little luxuries of life. That misfortune is the man's own fault, when you sift it down, for he ought to have laid up something before he got married, and something more before the children come along so numerous; but we are all thoughtless creatures in our youth, and like Cobe, are relying upon luck and the 'simmon tree. I can look back now and see my own mistakes, and sometimes feel like singing that old song:

> I wish I was young again,
> I'd lead a different life,
> I'd save my money and put it away
> To comfort my loving wife.

Money is a right good thing for old age, and every patriarch ought to have some. It dignifies him and his wife to have a surplus that they can draw upon when the children and grandchildren come to see them. It is so nice to be able to help those along that need help and to give little presents around, and then when Christmas comes, and there is a family gathering, it takes money to give all things a pleasant direction. I've heard it said that an old man without money is without friends, and had as well be dead, but that is a slander upon our humanity. I know a number of aged people who are loved and honored, not only by their children and children's children, but by the community; and, although they are poor, their every want is provided for. If a man raises his children right, they are not going to turn their aged parents off or neglect them. We have no fear of want at our house. There is no poor house waiting for us. We have done all we could for our children and they love us, and they are not waiting for us to die either, so as to divide out the remnant of their patrimony. Our fondest ambition now is to always have a home, a gathering place, a sacred ancestral spot where, as long as we live, they will love to come, like pilgrims to Jerusalem, and for awhile be happy and make us happy. That is the highest and best earthly joy for old folks, and if they are too poor to entertain their posterity as they would like to, why, then the posterity must bring their rations with them and help the old folks out. That is the way to do it. I know a venerable man now in his ninetieth year, who lives not far from me, at his old homestead, where he has lived for half a century, and his children are all married and gone but one, and she wouldn't leave him. I remember when he was a distinguished member of congress and when he was a statesman of reputation, and when he was a monarch in his rule over hundreds of slaves and dependents, and was loved and honored by them, and when his draft was good for thousands of dollars. But the war left him penniless, and all he saved was his homestead and a few acres of land on the banks of the river. He is very poor and goes about with tottering gait and trembling fingers, but he is grand and noble still, and never complains. Rich in memory and in love for his race, it is still a feast to visit him and listen to his counsels. His children and grandchildren gather there once or twice a year and make him happy, and they always go laden with the comforts and luxuries of life—enough and more than enough for him. This is the bright side of our love and our humanity, and it is pleasant to think of it.

Children, "Honor thy parents, that thy days may be long in the land."

CHAPTER XXIV.

New Year's Time.

I was discoursing Mrs. Arp, my wife, about that last night. You see, it was New Year, and I called on her. I dident have any swallow-tail coat and white kids, but I called. I had procured a bunch of misseltoe full of pearly berries, and I got the girls to make it into a wreath with some heliotrope blossoms, and sweet violets, and geraniums, and strawberry blooms which they had in the pit, and as she sat by the parlor fire I came in and addressed her: "Fair lady, I come with the New Year's greeting. May it bring you joy and peace, and love and rest, and happy days. Thirty long years of devotion and arduous duty in the infantry service of your country entitles you to be crowned the queen of love and beauty. Allow me to encircle your brow with this wreath." She enjoyed that first-rate, and when the girls took off the chaplet to show it to her, she remarked with a touch of sadness, "It is very beautiful, but your promising parent has been promising me a tiara of diamonds for thirty years, and now he pays me off in mistletoe and flowers." "Solomon," said I, "in all his glory, had no such gems as these. You know, my dear, I have always desired to be able to purchase a diamond ring and breast-pin and a diamond tiara for you, not that you need any ornaments to make you beautiful and attractive, for all the gems of Golconda could add nothing to your natural loveliness." "Ralph," said she, "your father has got a fit; you had better throw some water on him."

"But then," continued I, "the love of ornament is natural to women; Isaac knew her weakness when he sent Rebecca the ear-rings and bracelets. The ear-rings weighing half a shekel apiece, which, according to the tables, made the pair worth exactly sixty-two and a half cents. It rejoices me, my dear, that I shall soon be able to present you with a full set of genuine diamonds of the first water."

"When did you get so suddenly rich?" says she. "Have you drawn a prize in a lottery?" "Not at all, by no means," said I.

"But a London chemist has just discovered how to make diamonds of charcoal. They have known for 20 years how to make charcoal out of diamonds, but now they reverse the process and pure diamonds will soon be manufactured on a large scale, and it is predicted, will be sold at about 8 dollars a bushel. When they get down to that price, my dear, I am going to buy you a whole quart and you can string 'em all over you and cook in 'em and wash in 'em and make up the beds in 'em. I'm going to stick a kohinor in the end of the broom handle. What do you think of that, my dear, won't it be elegant?"

"No it won't," said she. "I don't want any of your charcoal diamonds. Eight dollars a bushel is 25 cents for the quart you propose to spend on me. I wouldn't be so extravagant if I were you. No I thank you. Isaac spent more than that on Rebecca, and didn't hurt himself. Buy me a carriage and horses and I'll do without the diamonds. They were intended for homely folks, and I am so beautiful and lovely I don't need them. Suppose you try me with a pearl necklace. I reckon your London man is not making pearls out of charcoal, is he?"

"Why, that's an old trick," said I. "Parisian jewelers have them at fifty cents a string and you can't tell them from the genuine. What does it matter if they are cheap so they are beautiful? What are all the gems of the ocean to be compared to these fragrant and lovely flowers that cost us nothing? Beautiful flowers that "weep without woe and blush without a crime." I never liked golden ornaments, nohow, as Tom Hood says, it's "bright and yellow, hard and cold," you can't tell it from brass without close inspection, and it wouldent be worn as jewelry if it was cheap. I wish everything was cheap—cheap as the air and the water. Then we wouldent be tied down to one little spot all the time, but we would travel—we would go to Florida and California and London and Paris and all over the Alps, and see the pyramids and the city of Jerusalem, and when we got tired we would come back home again and rest. Wouldent that be splendid?"

"Oh, yes," said Mrs. Arp. "All that is very romantic, but it sounds very much like 'college talk,' as old Mr. Dobbins would say. Whenever he hears anybody gassing around or talking extraordinary he says, "Oh, that don't amount to anything. Its college talk." He says he never knew a college-bred man that didn't build air-castles, and imagine a heap more than ever come in sight. We are right here on this farm and we will never see California nor the pyramids, and I'll never see the diamonds nor the pearls, and I don't care to, but I never like cheap things for they are not much account—so will fall back on the flowers, and when you have a little money to spare I want to send on for a few choice ones and a collection of seed. Do you understand?"

"I do, madam," said I, "you are a sensible woman. You shall have the money if I have to sell my Sunday boots. 'Bring flowers, bring flowers to the fair young bride.'"

I believe it's a good rule for everybody to attend to their own business. The other night I was reading aloud to the family about a feller who was standing at the forks of the road with an umbrella over him, when a flock of sheep came along and got tangled up, and so he thought he would help the driver by shooing 'em a little and waving his umbrel. An old ram dident like that and suddenly made for him and went through his umbrel like it was a paper hoop, and having knocked him down in the mud, he had to lay there until about a hundred sheep jumped over him one at a time. When he arose and took in his dilapidated condition, he remarked: "The next time I see a drove of sheep a-coming I reckon I'll attend to my own business."

Next day Mrs. Arp, my wife, was fixing to grind up sausage meat and I ventured to remark that if she would salt the pieces before she put them through the machine, it would save her a heap of trouble. Her sleeves were rolled up and as she looked at me she assumed a chivalric attitude and remarked: "There will be an old ram after you the first thing you know." Of course I retired in good order, and now I can't make a remark about domestic affairs without having that old ram thrown up to me. You see a woman has more liberty of speech than a man, for its mighty nigh the only liberty she has and I don't begrudge her the use of it. But then their five senses are more sensitive and acute than ours. In fact I think my wife, Mrs. Arp, has seven or eight, for she can come to a conclusion about things so quick it makes my head swim, and I know she must have some perceptions unknown to the books. She can hear more unaccountable noises in the night, and see more dirt on the floor, and smell more disagreeable odors than anybody in the world. I won't say she can point partridges, but a few years ago our nabor come over one day and said he had lost his dog, and my wife, Mrs. Arp, laid down her knitting, and says she: "That dog is in our well. The water has tasted and smelt like a dog all day." We all laughed at her and continued to use the water for two or three days, but she dident. Finally we give it up that something was wrong, and I sent a darky down a hundred feet to the bottom, and shore enough there was the dog.

Well, the rats took possession of our house not long ago and we could hear 'em at all times of night ripping around overhead and playing tag and leap-frog, till it was past endurance. So I got some rat poison that was warranted to drive 'em away to water, and shore enough they disappeared and we were happy. The next morning my wife, Mrs. Arp, was snuffling around about the mantel-piece, and says she, "William, these rats are dead, but they never went after water —they are all in these walls." Well, we dident pay much attention until next day, when some of the family thought there was a very slight taint in the atmosphere. We waited another day, and then had to take down the mantel-piece and found six dead ones behind it as big as young squirrels, and we have mighty nigh tore the house all to pieces hunting for the rest of 'em. Fact is, we had to quit the room, and it's just gittin' so now we can live in it. There's no fooling such a nose with fraudulent combinations. If a man ventures to take a little something for his stomach's sake and his often infirmities, she can tell what kind of medicine it was by the time he gets to the front gate, which to say the least of it is very inconvenient.

CHAPTER XXV.

Old Things Are Passing Away and All Things Have Become New.

That is the way it used to be in Scripture times, and it is the same way now. I wonder what were their old things? In those primitive days there were not very many things of any kind—not much invention or contrivance—no steamboats, or steam cars, or telegraphs, or telephones, or sewing machines, or telescopes, or spectacles, or cooking stoves, or reaping machines, or threshing machines, or patent plows, or cotton factories, or wool carders, or printed books, or the like. But still I suppose they did improve some, and shook off the old ways of living, and cooking, and dressing. I was looking at a venerable patch-work quilt the other day that a good old lady made some forty years ago, and it was very nice and pretty; and right beside it, on another bed, was a printed one that was pretty, too. One costs days and weeks of labor, and the fingers got tired, and so did the eyes, and I reckon the back; and if the labor and time could be fairly computed, it was worth twenty-five dollars, and now one can be made for a dollar that is just as good and just as pretty. What a world of trouble our forefathers and foremothers had! And yet they were just as happy and got along about as easy as we do. They dident want much and they dident have much. They had simple ways and simple habits. They prized what they made a good deal more than we do what we buy. When the good housewife put the last stitch in a woolen coverlet, or even a pair of woolen socks, she felt happy. Her work was a success and it was a pride.

The other day I received a present of a pair of socks, knit with golden silk, and the good old lady wrote me a note with her trembling fingers that this was the 865th pair that she had knit upon the same needles; that she began more than half a century ago and had knit for young and old, for silver weddings and golden weddings, and for weddings that were new-born—when the lily and the rose put their first blush upon the maiden's cheek; that she had knit scores of pairs for the soldiers in the last terrible war, both in the field and in the hospital, and that she had never lost any time from her other household duties, but knit only after her other labors were done.

Well, it is a wonderful amount of work to think about. I know some venerable women, who are close akin and very dear to me, who have been working in the same way, too. They havent knit as much, but they have sewed and patched and darned for large households and never complained. It is a world of work for a mother to keep her children clothed, especially in these days when it takes more clothes than it used to. How many little jackets, and waists, and breeches, and shirts, and drawers, and petticoats, and dresses, and aprons, and socks, and stockings! When the great pile of clothes comes in from the washerwoman, and Mrs. Arp sits down beside it to assort out and put away in the different drawers, I look on with amazement, and wonder when she made them all. Why, it takes about sixty different garments for our youngest child, who is only ten years old, and she hasent got anything fine—not very fine. There are about ten little dresses, mostly calico, and a like number of undergarments and stockings and aprons, but it takes work, work—lots of work—and the sewing machine rattles away most all the time. What a blessing that wonderful invention is to woman, for society is exacting and progressive, and the families of moderate means could hardly keep in sight of the rich if all the stitches had to be made by hand. As it is, we keep up pretty well—that is, we keep in a respectable distance—and our folks can fix up well enough to go to church and send the children to school.

The old ways were pretty hard ways, and the next generation is not going to work like the last. I am glad that it won't have to, for it is a waste of time and toil to make a patch-work quilt now, or to knit the stockings, or to beat the biscuit dough, or to bake them in a spider with coals underneath and coals on top of the heavy old-fashioned lid. Our mothers used to do all that "when niggers was," but the cooking stove came along just in the right time, and now it is much easier to cook "when niggers wasent."

Everything was hard to do in the old times. It was hard to thresh out the wheat with a couple of hickory flails. I have swung them many a day until my arms were tired, and I could find only a few bushels under the straw after a half day's work. But it made me strong and made the wheat bread taste mighty good. I remember the first cotton gin that was put up in our county, and the long round bags we used to pack with a crow-bar, and how we used to wagon it to Augusta and camp out at night and hear the old trusty wagoners recite their wonderful adventures. It was a glorious time to us boys, and when we got back home again and brought sugar, and salt, and coffee, and molasses and shoes all round for white and for black with the wooden measures in them, and the names written upon them all, the family was as happy and merry as if Christmas had come before its time. I remember when a pocket-knife was a wonderful treasure, and a pair of boots the height of all ambition. But now a pocket-knife is nothing to a boy. He can lose it in a month and get another, and if he isent born in boots, he gets them soon after.

> "I remember, I remember
> The house where I was born,
> The little windows where the sun
> Came peeping in at morn."

Well, there was no glass in that window—only a shutter—and there was no ceiling overhead. But we boys kept warm under the cover of a winter night, and when the rain pattered on the shingle roof above us it was the sweetest and most soothing lullaby in the world. Folks would complain now if their children had to put up with such a shelter, and I reckon they ought to, for this generation haven't been raised that way and they couldent stand it. But we found out during the war what we could stand, and it dident take us very long to get used to it. A shingle roof and a plank window would have been a luxury then. But even war is not as hard as it used to be. Here is a road in front of my house that Gen. Jackson's soldiers cut out, and is called Jackson's road yet. He cut it out for a hundred miles during the war of 1812. In those days, when the soldiers wanted to march across a country, they had to carry the roads with them. They had to make them as they went along; but now the railroads pick up an army and hurry it along—everything is lightning now.

Truly, the old things are done away. Farewell to home-made chairs, and home-made jeans, and the old back log, and the crane that swung in the kitchen fire-place, and to home-made baskets, and shuck collars, and shuck foot-mats, and dominicker chickens and old-fashioned cows, and castor oil, and paregoric, and opodeldoc, and salts, and sassafras tea. Farewell to marigolds and pinks and holly-hocks, for there are finer flowers now. Farewell to simplicity of manners, and water without ice, and temperate habits, and contented dispositions. Farewell to abundance of time to come and to go and to stay, for everybody is in a hurry now—a dreadful hurry—for there is a pressure upon us all, a pressure to keep up with the crowd, and the times, and with society. Push ahead, keep moving, is the watchword now, and we must push or we will get run over, and be crushed and forgotten.

So let us all work and keep up if we can. We must fall into line and keep step to the new music that is in the air. "Old Hundred" is gone, and "Sweet Home," and "Kathleen Mavourneen," and "Billy in the Low-grounds," and now it is something else that passeth comprehension. But there is no use in complaining about what we cannot help, for some things are better, even if others are worse. We can still do our duty and put on the brakes for our children. We can tell them to go slow and go sure. Be honest. Money is a good thing, but money gained by fraud or by luck will do no good. Money earned by honest, diligent labor is the only kind that will stick to a man and do good. Money is a social apology for lack of brains or lack of education or graceful manners, but it is no apology for lack of honesty or good principles. Make money, save money, but not at the sacrifice of self respect or the respect of others. Some things pay in the short run and for a little while, but honesty and truth and diligence pay in the long run, and that is the run we have to die by. Folks differ about religion and politics, but all mankind agree on this. It is old-fashioned talk, I know, but some old-fashioned things are good yet. I have even got respect for my rheumatism, for it has stuck by me like a friend for a long time, and is nearly the only disease that has not changed its name and its pain since I was a boy.

CHAPTER XXVI.

The Country.

I have now been farming six years, and, take it all in all, I like it better than anything else that I have tried. They say that a rolling stone gathers no moss, and a man who is Jack-at-all-trades is good at none; but I don't regret what I have learned about merchandise and carpentering and law, for my experience in these different pursuits has broadened my views and enlarged my charity and give me a better knowledge of human nature than I would have learned by running a bee-line all my life. A man is happier if he acquires a variety of knowledge, but it is fortunate for mankind that some folks get absorbed in one thing and pursue it diligently, and develop and im‑ prove and invent, until they bring it to protection. A wise Providence has created just such men in all ages, and the world is indebted to them more than to any other class for its progress in art and science. Still, I am satisfied that the Germans have overdone this thing. A German father will pick out a trade or a profession for his boy before he is in his teens, and will drive him into it whether he likes it or not, and keep him at it about fourteen hours in a day until he is twenty-one. The best music teacher and one of the finest musicians I ever saw, told me he never liked it, and the unwilling pursuit of it withered all his youth. He had a taste for mathematics, and wanted to be an engineer and build railroads and bridges; but the door was shut in his face. We had a Belgian civil engineer at Rome who stood at the top of his profession, but he didn't know anything outside of it. He didn't know a mule's parentage until I told him. When he saw cotton in the field for the first time, he said he thought it grew on the cotton-wood tree, and he asked me what kind of a plant silk grew on. Outside of his calling he had but little more sense than an idiot. He reminds me of a feller that Jules Verne wrote about. A compiler of Logarithms had offered ten thousand dollars reward to anybody who could find a mistake in any of his figures, and so this feller, "Polander," set about on logs and stumps from day to day doing all the sums over in his head, and one day the tide rose on him and the alligators came around him and were just about to grab him, when he suddenly flourished his umbrella and exclaimed, "I've found it! I've found it! and the ten thousand dollars are mine!" I like to see a man earnest in his profession or business, but a man oughtn't to become so absorbed as to let the alligators eat him up. These over-earnest men sometimes accomplish great things, but they are not much account to their families. A woman had just as well marry a machine, for she has no husband, and her children have no father, and he is a nabor to nobody. There is no good sense in burning midnight oil. It is contrary to nature. A young man can sit and study and rack his brain until he loses his appetite, and then he loses his health and prematurely dies. The stomach has got to be nursed, and exercise is the best doctor. If the stomach is out of order, the whole man gets sick. The stomach is the most important part of the human machine. Some folks talk about the heart being the seat of the affections and the emotion, but the heart can be diseased and the man not know it. It has no effect upon the brain or upon man's cheerfulness or hilarity; but if the stomach is out of order the whole machine is demoralized until it is fixed up again. Old Solomon understood it when he wrote about bowels of mercies and bowels of compassion. From their good, healthy condition comes the best reward of labor—out-door labor, on the farm or in the workshop. Good health, good appetite, good sleep—why a city man can't enjoy his dinner without whetting up his appetite with a drink, and that is a poor thing to grease the wagon with. It cakes and cuts and wears out the axles. City folks eat their meals more from habit than hunger, but country folks love to hear the horn blow. Seven-tenths of the people live in the country, but seven-tenths of the whisky and wine and beer is drank in the towns, and most of 'em drink it because they are not hungry and want to be. A right hungry man doesn't want whisky. He wants something to eat—something solid; and so, after all the fuss about the temperance problem, work, toil, sweat is the best remedy, for a laboring man can't cheat his stomach with juices. Ben Franklin was a smart man, and he said that man was a bundle of habits, and he said also, that idleness was the parent of all vice. So it is best for a man to raise his boys in the country, where he will get a habit of work, and where there are not many temptations. A man can't throw off his habits like he does his coat. If contracted in youth they will stick in manhood and old age, whether they be good or bad. I've got an old mare that will quit a good pasture and let down the bars to go into a poor one, and it's just because she got into a habit of letting the bars down. Habits are stronger than principles. They are not cast-iron, for you can break that, but they are more like green withes and new ropes—the more you wet 'em the tighter they draw, especially if you wet 'em with whisky.

A farmer's life is a pretty hard one in some respects, and not one in a hundred makes any clear money at it—money to lay up and put away for hard times or old age; but the law of compensation comes in and balances off all its troubles. There is an independence about it that belongs to no other profession. The farmer belongs to nobody. His time is his own. If he can't get rich, he can live comfortably and raise his children to industry, and that is the best legacy in the world. It is very natural for a man to imagine that other people are better off than he is, and to wish that he had chosen some other business. Very few are content with their lot. Old man Horace, who lived 2,000 years ago, alluded to this when he said, "How comes it that most everybody is dissatisfied with his calling and thinks he would be better off and happier if he were pursuing some other?" But Horace, like all other poets, gave the preference to a country life. He says, "The city is the best place for a rich man to live in, and the country is the best place for a poor man to die in; and, inasmuch as riches are uncertain and death is sure, it becomes a man to move to the country as soon as he can get there." It is amusing to me to see how all the famous poets, who never plowed a furrow in their lives, go off into raptures and ecstacies over rural life:

> "God made the country, man made the town."
> "How jocund did they drive their team afield."
> "Delightful toil! There must be husbandry in heaven."

And they write gushingly of fields and flowers and harvest moon and mountains and brooks and grand old woods and setting suns and happy birds and tinkling bells and the cotter's Saturday night.

All that is mighty pretty, and there is comfort in it; but there is mighty little fun in pulling fodder right now, or in carrying a load of it through the long, hot rows and stepping, like a blind horse, over morning glory vines and bending corn stalks. There ain't very much hilarity about getting stung with a packsaddle or fodder-blade or waking up a yallerjacket's nest. Farmers are not tickled to death over picking cotton all day as hard as they can pick, and thinking they will get 200 pounds and it weighed out about 150. There is not very much fun in getting up in the morning and finding half a dozen of your nabor's hogs or cows in your field, and having to run after 'em all through the wet grass and then can't make 'em go out at the same break they came in. There is many a little trouble that these spectacled poets know nothing about, and never will until they try it. There is not much fun in any kind of toil, but it is the common lot, and we are all happier when at work than when sitting down or loafing around in idleness. A man who was raised a pampered youth, and knew no wants and had no falls or hair-breadth escapes, no stumped toes or mashed fingers, no horse to run away with him, no colts to break, no bull calf to drive, hasn't been much of a boy, and will never be much of a man. He has no marvelous things to tell his little boys if he ever has any, which he oughtn't to have, considering his fitness to raise 'em.

When boys have learned to farm and built up their constitutions and settled their habits, why then is time enough for 'em to try the city and soar to more ambitious things; but the country is the place to raise 'em. I've a poor opinion of a boy raised in town to strut around and then be sent to college to raise cain.

CHAPTER XXVII.

But Once a Year.

Another busy year has gone—gone like the water that has passed over the dam—gone never to return. It has carried many friends along with it and left sad memories in our household, but on the whole it has been a good year to us all, and Providence has been kind. Now is the time to look back and review the past—to take an account of stock like the merchants do—a time to be thankful for what we have received, and to compare our condition, not with those who are better off, but with those who are worse off.

It is a good time to feel happy, for there is something about Christmas that seems like a recess from a long year of work, and toil, and tribulation. Man needs just such a rest for body, and mind, and spirit. These periods of relaxation prolong life, both of man and beast. If it were not for the Sabbath we would wear out before we got old, and I remember reading a long time ago, about some emigrants going overland to California. Some of them rested their teams every Sunday, and some did not, and the first got there several days ahead, and were in the best condition at the end of the long journey. But one day in seven is not enough—we want a whole week at the end of the year, and according to scripture it is a good thing to have a whole year in seven—a year of jubilee when even the land we till shall have rest and a time to recover itself and renew its wasted energies. Blessings on the holy fathers who established the Christmas holidays, and on the good men who for eighteen centuries have preserved it for us and our children. It is a blessed heritage and belongs to all alike—the rich and the poor, the bond and the free, the king and his subject. But these good old ways are changing and becoming circumscribed. Mankind is growing too stingy of time. Christmas used to last from the 25th of December to the 6th of January, and for twelve days there was neither work nor toil, nor official business, nor suits for debt, dunning, nor preparations for war, but all was peace and pleasure and kindly feelings. The peasant was on a level with the prince, and the girls and boys wore chaplets of ivy and laurel and holly and evergreen, and it was no sin for them to take a sly kiss while the rosemary wreaths encircled their brows, for a kiss under the rose was an emblem of innocence and had the sanction of heaven, and love whispered while wearing the mistletoe crown was too pure to be lost or betrayed.

I love the old superstition that clusters around this season of my joy and gladness. Long did I lament the day when my childish eyes were opened and I learned there was no Saint Nicholas nor Santa Claus, no reindeer on the roof, no coming down the chimney to fill the stockings that hung by the mantel. Even now I would fain believe, with Skakespeare, that for these twelve days witches, and hobgoblins and devilish spirits had to fly away from the haunts of men and hide themselves in the dark pits and caves of the earth while the good spirits who love us and watch over us, nestled their invisible forms among the evergreens that hung upon the walls. It was pleasant to think that on the last day of the twelve the cattle knelt down at midnight and humbly prayed that souls might be given them when they died, so that they, too, might live in heaven and worship God. I hope the poor things will have a good time in the next world, for they see a rough one in this, and I reckon they will, considering what a splendid pair of horses came down after the prophet Elijah. Heaven wouldn't be any the less heaven to me to find my good dog Bows up there, all renewed in his youth, and to receive the glad welcome that wags in his diminished tail.

How naturally we become reconciled to the approach of death. How tired we get fighting through the hard battle of life. I remember when it was the grief and horror of my young life that sometime or other I would have to surrender and give it up, but I don't care now. Let it come. I would not live it over again if I could. I do not lament like Job that I ever was born, but still I have no desire to hold on and worry and struggle for several hundred years longer, as did the old patriarchs before the flood. If I was a good man, and everything moved along serenely I wouldn't care, but there's a power of trouble, and we make the most of it ourselves. Like David and Solomon, we keep sinning and repenting, and the memory of it haunts a man and cuts into him like a knife, and all sorts of friends come along and clutch the handle and give it a gentle twist. Not one in a thousand will pull it out and put a little salve on the wound.

I always thought it a pretty idea to weigh a man—to put his life in a pair of balances, the good on one side and the bad on the other, and let him rise to heaven or fall below it, as the scales might turn. I know it's not an orthodox doctrine exactly, for they say that one bad deed will outweigh a thousand good ones. Nevertheless, Belshazzar was weighed, and the Scriptures abound in such figures of speech. It will take miracles of grace to save us all anyhow, and it becomes everybody to help one another, for the devil is doing his best. David committed murder, and Solomon worshipped idols, Cain killed his brother, and Jabob cheated Esau out of his birthright, and Noah got drunk and Peter denied his Master, but they all repented and got forgiveness, and if there's any difference between folks now and folks then I don't know it, unless it is that they had the strongest support and the least temptation to fall.

But then, a man ought not to take too much comfort from such comparisons, for they savor of vanity, and vanity don't save anybody nor keep him from doing wrong. A man who moves along the pathway of life happily and serenely in the midst of cares and temptations, is a long ways better off than one who don't. A man who brings no sorrow to his friends and nabors lives to a better purpose than one who does, and it must be a blessed bed to die on when a man gets old and has no stinging memories in his pillow case. There is no goodlier sight in nature than a good man going down to the grave in graceful composure. I recall one who, not long ago, reached his fourscore years and died. He was a model of that sweet decay that has no odor of dissolution. He was never a burden nor a cross, and to the last received his children and his children's children with a rejoicing smile. Would that I, too, like him, might go down behind the everlasting hills—not in a cloud nor yet in a blaze of glory, but rather like the sun when his rays are softened and subdued by the Indian summer sky.

Our family frolic is over. The show of it and the pleasant hilarity of the occasion, with all the delightful surprises and rejoicings, passed away most happily, but the sweet perfume of love and kindness that Christmas brought remains with us still. It is more blessed to give than to receive, and the purest pleasure we can feel is in making others happy. In the good old times Prince Rupert used to go round in disguise and find out who was needy and grateful and kind, and when Christmas came he distributed his gifts according to their deservings. It seems to me that if I was Mr. Vanderbilt I would like that, but maybe not.

> Then a rich and merry Christmas to the rich,
> And a bright and happy Christmas to the poor;
> So their hearts are joyful it doesn't matter which
> Has the fine velvet carpet on the floor.
>
> For riches bring a trouble when they come,
> And money leaves a pain when it goes,
> But everybody now must have a little sum
> To brighten up the year at its close.

* * * * *

Pleasing the children is about all that the majority of mankind is living for though they don't realize it and if they did they would hardly acknowledge it. It is emphatically the great business of this sublunary life. We look on with amazement at the busy crowd in the town and cities that are ever going to and fro, and the most of them are working and struggling to please and maintain children. It is the excuse for all the mad rush of business that hurries mankind through the world. It is the apology for nearly all the stealing and cheating and lying in the land. One time a man sold me a Poland China sow for $15 and she eat up $5 worth of chickens the day I got her, and when I asked him why he didn't tell me she was a chicken eater, he smiled and said he thought I would find it out soon enough. He spent that money on his children and so I had to forgive him. Sometimes when I ruminate upon the meanness of we grown-up folks, I wish that the children would never get grown, for they don't get very mean or foolish until they do.

Now the biggest part of all this Christmas business is to please the children. Of course there is service in the churches, and the good pious people celebrate the day in prayer and devotion, but most of it is for the children. The stores are thronged with parents hunting something for them. The Christmas trees are for them, and all the dolls and wagons and tea-sets and pocket-knives and harps and firecrackers and a thousand other things too numerous to mention. Why there will be five thousand dollars spent in this county this week for

Christmas gifts. There will be half a million in the State. There will be twenty millions in the United States, and it is nearly all for children. So, my young friends, you must understand how very important you are in this world's affairs, but you needent get uppity nor bigoty about it, for that spoils all the old folks' pleasure.

Now, let us all imagine we are around the cheerful Christmas fire and talk about Christmas and tell what it means. Of course you know that it is the anniversary of the birth of Christ, and all Christian people celebrate it. It is very common everywhere to celebrate birthdays. Americans make a big fuss over Washington's birthday because he was called the father of his country. My folks make a little fuss over my birthday and my good wife's birthday. They don't toot horns nor pop fire-crackers, but they have an extra good dinner and fix up a pleasant surprise of some sort. We used to surprise the children with a little present like a pocket-knife, or a pair of scissors, or sleeve buttons or something, but so many children came along that there was a birthday in sight almost all the time, and as we got rich in children we got poor in money and had to skip over sometimes. The 4th of July was the birthday of a nation and so the nation always celebrates that day.

Christians began to observe Christmas about 1,500 years ago at Jerusalem and Rome. They had service in the churches and made it a day of rejoicing. In course of time the young people rather lost sight of the sacredness of the day and the devotion that was due to the occasion, and made it a day of frolic and feasting. They sang hilarious songs, because they said the shepherds sang songs at Bethlehem. They made presents to each other because they said the wise men from the east brought presents to the young child and its mother. They kept up their festivities all night because the Saviour was born at midnight. The Roman Catholic church has observed these annual celebrations for centuries, and the Church of England took them up, and so did the Protestants in Germany and other countries. Christians everywhere adopted them, and Christmas day became a universal holiday except among the Puritans of New England, who forbade it under penalties. They never frolicked or made merry over anything. In a great painting of the nativity by Raphael, there is seen a shepherd at the door playing on a bagpipe. The Tyrolese who live on the mountain slopes of Italy always come down to the valleys on

Christmas eve, and they come carroling sweet songs and playing on musical instruments, and spend the night in innocent festivities. A century or so ago there were many curious superstitions about Christmas. It was believed that an ox and an ass that were near by when the Saviour was born bent their knees in supplication, and so they said the animals all went to prayer every Christmas night. Of course, they might have known better if they had watched all night to see, but when folks love a superstition they humor it. If a child believes in ghosts they are sure to see them, whether they are there or not. Those old-time people believed that when the rooster crowed for midnight on Christmas night all the wizzards and witches and hobgoblins and evil spirits fled away from the habitations of men and hid in caves and hollow trees and deserted houses, and stayed there for twelve days.

Nations have superstitions just like individuals have them. The Persians had their genii and fairies; the Hindoos their rakshar; the Greeks and Romans had all sorts of wonderful gods and godesses, such as Jupiter and Juno and Hercules and Vulcan and Neptune, and they built temples for them to dwell in. The more learned and enlightened a people are the more sublime are their superstitions. The uncivilized Indians are mystified and "see God in the clouds, and hear Him in the wind." The native Africans come down to crocodiles and serpents and owls for their Gods. Some of the negro tribes take a higher grade of animals and set their faith in brer fox and brer rabbit, as Uncle Remus has told you. When I was a boy we could tell the difference in the negro character by the stories they told us in their cabins at night; and good negroes always told us funny, cheerful stories about the tar baby, and the bear and the bee-tree, and about foxes and wolves; but the bad negroes told us about witches and ghosts and Jack-o'-lanterns, and raw-head-and-bloody-bones. I used to listen to them until I didn't dare to look around, and I got up closer and closer to the fire, and when my brother called me I had to be carried to the house in a negroe's arms. But what about the evergreens the holly and laurel and ivy and mistletoe and the Christmas tree? That is a curious history, too, and it all came from the poetry and romance that belongs to our nature. Evergreens have for ages been used as symbols of immortality. The victors returning from the wars were crowned with them; chaplets of green leaves and vines were made for the successful ones at the Olympic games. The poets of Scripture tell us of green bay trees and the cedars of Lebanon. Churches and temples have been decorated with them for centuries. Evergreens have always had a poetic prominence in the vegetable kingdom. We all love them, for they cheer us in midwinter when there are no other signs of vegetation to gladden our longing eyes.

Now, children, these superstitions are all fancy, as you know, and are not even founded on fact, and yet it is human nature to love them. We are all fond of anything that is marvelous, especially if it turns out well for the good. We love to read the Arabian Nights and we rejoice with Alibaba who outwitted the forty thieves, and with Aladdin who found the wonderful lamp. Just so we rejoice with Cinderella for marrying the prince, and we take comfort in it, although we know it never happened. It is human nature to want good to triumph over bad, and on this heavenly trait in our humanity is our government and our social system founded.

You know all about St. Nicolas and Santa Claus, and where that pleasant superstition came from, but the traditions of the Germans about the good Knight Rupert are just as good, and, I think, are more stimulating to the children. In every little village Knight Rupert comes out just after twelve o'clock, and nobody knows where he comes from. He has a beautiful sleigh and four fine horses, all dressed up in silver spangles and silver bells, and he dashes around from house to house and calls out the mother and whispers something to her and she whispers something to him, and he bows his head and wags his long gray beard and dashes away to the next house. You see he is going around to find out from the mother which ones of her children have been good and which ones have been bad, so as to know what presents to bring and how many. If the good mother says sorrowfully, "Well, Knight Rupert, my Tom has not been a good boy; he is not kind to his sisters, and he is selfish and has fights with other boys, and he won't study at school, but I hope he will get to be better, so please bring Tom some little thing, won't you." She is obliged to tell the truth on all her children, and it goes very hard with her sometimes. So after Knight Rupert has been all around he drives away about dark and nobody knows where he went to. That night he brings the presents while the children are all asleep, and sure enough Tom don't get anything. Now, that is what they pretend to believe, but of course

Knight Rupert is some good jolly fellow about town, and he is all bundled up and disguised and cuts up just such a figure as old Santa Claus does in the pictures.

The year is almost gone, and all of us ought to stop a minute and think about how much good we have done since the last Christmas. How many times we have tried to make our kindred happy—not only our kindred, but our nabors and companions. As I came out of the Markham house, in Atlanta, one cold morning, two little dirty newsboys came running to me from opposite directions to sell me a paper. They are not allowed to go inside the hotels to sell papers, and so they stand outside in the cold and watch for the men to come out. One of these boys was a stout lad of ten years, and the other was a little puny, pale-face, barefooted chap, and although he was the farthest off, he got to me first. I said to the biggest boy, "Why didn't you run? You could have got here first." He smiled and said, "I dident want to." "Why not?" said I. "Is that boy your brother?" "No, sir," said he, "but he's little, and he's been sick." Now, that was kindness that will do for Christmas or any other day. I gave them a dime apiece, and they were happy for a little while. Children, if you can't do a big thing you can do a little thing like that. I wouldent let the little ragged newsboys get ahead of me.

We keep Grier's almanac at our house. We get a good many almanacs from the merchants as advertisements, but Grier's is the old standard and is the one that is always hung by the mantle. If you have that kind at your house and will look at the bottom of the last page to see what kind of weather we are to have this Christmas week you will find it put down this way: "Be thankful for all the blessings you have enjoyed this year and try to do better the next." That is a curious kind of weather, but it is mighty good weather.

CHAPTER XXVIII.

GRANDFATHER'S DAY—THE LITTLE URCHIN OF THE THIRD GENERATION.

This is a most blessed land—where everything grows that man is obleeged to have, and a power of good things throw'd in just to minister to his pleasure. The summer sun is now ripening the fruits of the earth, and when I see children and grandchildren and nefews and neeses rejoicin' in their wanderin's over the fields and orchards, it carries me back to the blessed days of childhood. The old-field plums and the wild strawberries and cherries, mulberries and blackberries were worth more then than gold, and it made no difference who was priest or president, or how rich was Astor or Girard or any of the nabors, or whether Sal Jackson's bonet was purtier than Melyann Thompson's or not. What a glorious luxury it was to go barefooted and wade in the branch and go saining and climb trees and hunt bird's nests and carry the corn to the mill and leave it, just to get to run a horse-race home again. I know now that those days were the happiest, and so I won't rob my posterity of the same sort, if I can help it. I want 'em to love the old homestead, and I want children's children to gather about it and cherish its memory. What a burlesque on childhood's joy it must be to visit grandma and grandpa in a crowded city, penned up in brick walls with a few sickly flowers in front and a garden in the rear about as big as a wagon sheet. But that's the way the thing is drifting. Them calculatin' yankees have long ago done away with the 'old back log' and the blazing hearth-stone and substituted a furnace in the basement and a few iron pipes running around the walls and a hole in the floor to let the heat in. All that may be economy, but in my opinion a man can't raise good stock in no such way. They'll be picayunish and nice and sharp featured and gimlety, but they won't do to bet on like them children that's been bro't up 'round a fire-place on a hundred acre farm and had plenty of fresh air and latitude.

Pleasin' the children is about all the majority of mankind are livin' for, though they don't know it; and if they did they wouldn't acknowledge it. It is emphatically the great business of life. We look on with wonder and amazement at the busy crowds in a great city that are ever goin' to and fro like a fiddler's elbow, and eight out of ten of 'em are workin' and strugglin' to please and maintain the children. It's the excuse for all the mad rush of business that hurries mankind through the world. It's the apology for nearly all the cheatin' and stealin' and lyin' in the land, and in a heap of such cases I have thought the good angels would drop tears enuf on the big book to blot 'em out forever. The trouble is, that most people are always livin' on a strain, tryin' to do a little too much for their children, and scufflin' against wind and tide to git just a little ahead of their nabors. Some of 'em won't let a ten year old boy go to meetin' or to Sunday-school if he can't fix up as fine as other boys. They won't let him go barefooted nor wear a patch behind nor before, nor ride bareback, nor go dirty, and so the domestic pressure for finery becomes tremendous. Jesso with bonnets, and parasols, and kid gloves, and silk dresses, and chanyware, and carpets, and winder curtins—and a thousand things that cost money and runs up the outgo a heap bigger than the incum. Generally speakin' this home pressure ain't a noisy one, but, on the contrary, is very silent and sad—so sad that a body would think there was somebody dead in the house, and so after awhile sumhow or sumhow else the finery comes, and thus for awhile all is sereen. But the collapse is shore to cum sooner or later, and the children ain't to blame for it. Sumtimes when I ruminate upon the meanness of mankind I wish the children never got grown, for they don't get mean or foolish until they do. Just think what a sweet time of it old mother Eve and Mrs. Commodore Noah, and aunt Methusaler had with thirty or forty of 'em wearin' bibs and aperns until they were fifty years old, toggin' along after their daddies until they were a hundred. I don't think old father Woodruff could have stood that. When a man who ain't no yearlin' gits married, and ten or a dozen of 'em cum right straight along in a row, and by the time he gets on the piazza, tired and grunty, they begin to climb all over him and under him and betwixt him, and on the back of his chair and the top of his head, it's a little more than his venerable nature can stand. On such occasions, it ain't to be wondered at that he gently shakes himself aloose and exclaims, "Lord have mercy upon me." But, then, the like of this must be endured. 'Tis a part of the bargain, implied if not expressed, as the lawyers say, and no man ought to dodge it. Humor 'em, play hoss and frolic with 'em, wash 'em, undress 'em, tell 'em stories about Jack and the bean stalk, and what you done when you was a little boy; scratch their backs and put 'em to bed, and if they can't sleep, get up with 'em away in the night, and nod around in your nightgown until they can. Let them trot after you a heap in week days and all day of a Sunday, and don't try to shirk off the trouble and the responsiblity on the good woman who bore 'em. Solomon says: "Children are the chief end of man, and the glory of his declining years," and raisin' of 'em is the biggest business I know of in this life, and the most responsible in the life to come.

When a man begins to get along in years he gradually changes from being a king in his family to a patriarch. He is more tender and kind to his offspring, and instead of ruling them, the first thing he knows they are ruling him. My youngest children and my grandchildren just run over me now, and it takes more than half my time to keep up with 'em, and find out where they are and what they are doing. It rains most every day, and the weeds and grass are always wet, and the children and the dogs track mud all over the house. We can't keep 'em in and we can't keep 'em out. The boys have got traps set in the swamp, and are obliged to go to 'em every fifteen minutes, and if they catch a bird it's as big a thing as killin' an elefant. They built a brick furnace in the back yard, and have been cookin' on it for two days, bakin' hoc-cakes, and fryin' eggs, and boilin' coffee, and their afflicted mother has mighty near surrendered; for she can't keep a skillet, nor a spoon, nor a knife, nor a plate in the kitchen, and so she tried to kick the furnace over, and now goes about limpin' with a sore toe. Some of the older ones have found a chalk quarry in a ditch, and taken a notion to drawin' and sculpture, and made pictures of dogs and chickens and snakes all around the house on the outside; and while the good mother was cookin' the two youngest ones chalked over the inside as good as they could. The mantel-piece, and jams, and doors, and beadsteads, and sewin' machine, and window-glass were all ring-streaked and striked, and as I couldent do justice to the subject myself, I waited for reinforcements. When the maternal ancestor appeared, I was a peepin' through the crack of the door. She paused upon the threshold like an an actor playing high tragedy in a theater. "Merciful fathers!" then a long and solem paus. "Was there ever such a set upon the face of the earth? What shall I do? Ain't it enough to run anybody distracted? Here I have worked and worked to make this old house look decent, and now look at it! I've a good mind to wring your little necks for you. Did ever a mother have such a time as I have—can't leave me one minit that they ain't into mischief, and it's been the same thing over and over and over with all of 'em for the last twenty-nine years. I'd rather been an old maid a thousand times over. I wish there wasn't a child in the world —yes, I do!" (Looks at 'em mournfully for a minute.) "Come here, Jessie, you little pale-faced darling. Mamma ain't mad with you; no, you're just the sweetest thing in the world; and poor little Carl's broken finger makes my heart ache every time I look at it. He did have the sweetest little hand before that boy mashed it all to pieces with his maul; and there's that great scar on his head, where the brick fell on him, and another over his eye, where he fell on the hatchet. I wonder if I ever will raise you poor little things; you look like little orphans; take your chalk and mark some more, if you want to." When I came in she was a helpin' 'em make a bob-tail dog on the closet door. "I've found your old tom cat," said I; "Carl had him fastened up in that nail keg that's got a hen's nest in it." "Why, Carl, what upon earth did you put the cat in there for?" "Why, mamma, he's a settin, and I wanted him to lay some little kittens. Me and Jessie wants some kittens."

These little chaps ride the horses and colts over the meadow and pasture, and make the sheep jump the big branch, and they go in a washing two or three times a day, and they climb the grape arbor and the apple trees and stuff their craws full of fruit and trash, and they can tell whether a watermelon is ripe or green, *for they plug it to see.* and every one of 'em has got a sling shot and my pigeons are always on the wing, and the other day I found one of the finest young pullets laying dead with a hole in her side, and all the satisfaction I can get is I dident mean to do it, or I won't do it any more, or I dident do it at all. Jesso. It's most astonishing how the little rascals can shoot with their slings, and now I don't believe it was a miracle at all that made David plump old Goliah in the forehead, for these boys can plump a jaybird now at 40 yards, and we have had to take all their weapons away to protect the birds and poultry. Sometimes I get mad and rip up and round like I was going to do something desperate, but Mrs. Arp comes a-slipping along and begins to tell how they dident mean any harm, and they are just like all other boys, and wants to know if I dident do them sort of things when I was a boy. Well, that's a fact—I did—and I got a lickin' for it, too. You see, I was one of the oldest boys, and they always catch it, but the youngest one never gets a lickin', for by the time he comes along the old man has mellowed down and wants a pet. The older children have married and gone, and the old folks feel sorter like they have been throwed off for somebody no kin to 'em, and so they twine around those that are left all the closer, but by-and-by they grow up, too, and leave them, and it's pitiful to see the good old couple bereft of their children and living alone in their glory. Then is the time that grandchildren find a welcome in the old family homestead, for as Solomon saith, the glory of an old man is his children's children. Then is the time that the little chaps of the second and third generation love to escape from their well ruled home, and for awhile find refuge and freedom and frolic at grandpa's. A child without a grandpa and a grandma can never have its share of happiness. I'm sorry for 'em. Blessings on the good old people, the venerable grand-parents of the land, the people with good old honest ways and simple habits and limited desires, who indulge in no folly, who hanker after no big thing, but live along serene and covet nothing but the happiness of their children and their children's children. I said to a good old mother not long ago: "Well, I hear that Anna is to be married." "Yes, sir," said she, smiling sorrowfully, "I don't know what I will do. The last daughter I've got is going to leave me. I've nursed her and petted her all her life, and I kinder thought she was mine and would always be mine, but she's run off' after a feller she's no kin to in the world, and who never did do a thing for her but give her a ring and a book or two and a little French candy now and then, and it does look so strange and unreasonable. I couldent understand it at all if—if I hadent done the same thing myself a long time ago," and she kept knitting away with a smile and a tear upon her motherly face.

But I am not going to slander these little chaps that keep us so busy looking after them, for there is no meanness in their mischief, and if they take liberties it is because we let 'em. Mrs. Arp says they are just too sweet to live, and is always narrating some of their smart sayings. Well, they are mighty smart, for they know exactly how to get everything and do everything they want, for they know how to manage her, and they know that she manages me, and that settles it. A man is the head of the house about some things, and about some other things he is only next to head, if he ain't foot. A man can punish his children, but it's always advisable to make an explanation in due time and let his wife know what he did it for, because you see they are her children shore enough, and she knows and feels it. The pain and trouble, the nursing and night watching have all been hers. The washing and dressing, and mending, and patching—tieing up fingers and toes, and sympathizing with 'em in all their great big little troubles all falls to her while the father is tending to his farm, or his store, or his office, or friends, or may be to his billiard table. When a woman says "this is my child," it carries more weight and more meaning than when a man says it, and I've not got much respect for a law that will give a man the preference of ownership just because he is a man. I remember when I was a boy, a sad, pretty woman taught school in our town, and she had a sweet little girl about eight years old, and one day a man came there for the child and brought a lawyer with him, and the mother was almost distracted, and all of us boys—big and little—got rocks and sticks and thrash poles and hid the little girl up in the cupalo, and when the sheriff came we attacked him like killing snakes or fighting yaller jackets, and we run him off, and when he came back with more help, we run 'em all off, and the man never got his child, and I can say now that the soldiers who whipped the yankees at Bull Run were not half so proud of their victory as we were, though I found out afterwards that the sheriff was willing to be whipped, for he was on the side of the mother and didn't want to find the child no how. But the world is getting kinder than it used to be—kinder to women and to the poor and the dependent, and kinder to brutes. Away up in New England they used to drown women for being witches, but they don't now. Well, they do bewitch a man powerfully sometimes, that's a fact, but if any drowning is done he drowns himself because he can't get the woman he wants and live under her witching all the time. But a man is still the head of the house and always will be, I reckon, for it's according to Scripture. He has got a natural right to run the machine and keep up the supplies, and if he always has money when the good wife wants it and doesn't wait for her to ask for it but makes her take it as a favor to him, then he is a successful husband and peace reigns supreme. Jesso. When there is money in the till a man can sit in his piazza with his feet on the banisters and smoke the pipe of peace. A woman loves money for its uses. She never hoards it or hides it away like a man—and when I used to be a merchant I thought there was no goodlier combination in all nature than a new stock of dry goods and a pretty woman in the store with a well filled purse in her pocket. Jesso.

CHAPTER XXIX.

MAKING SAUSAGE.

Hog killing is over at last. We had about made up our minds to kill one at a time as we needed them and not cure any for bacon, but the weather got right and the moon was on the increase, and so we slayed them. I don't care anything about the moon myself, but there are some old family superstitions that the meat will shrink in the pot if the moon is on the wane when you kill it. The new moon is quite level this time, which is a sure sign that it will rain a good deal this month, or that it won't. We have pretty well disposed of this greasy business. The little boys had a good time frying liver on the hot rocks and roasting tails in the ashes and blowing up balloons, and now if we had a few darkies to cook up the heads and clean the feet and fix up the skins for sausages and make a nice lot of souse, we could live like princes, but it's troublesome work and costs more than it comes to if we have to do it ourselves.

I am very fond of sausage—home made sausage such as Mrs. Arp knows how to make, and so she delicately informed me that the meat was all chopped and ready for the machine, and said something about my everyday clothes and one of her old aprons. She further remarked that when it was all ground up she would come down and show me how much salt and pepper and sage to put in and how to mix it all up together. Well, I didn't mind the machine business at all, but I remembered seeing her work mighty hard over that mixing of the salt and pepper and sage, and frying a little mess on the stove and tasting it, and then putttng in more salt and work it over again, and cooking another mess and tasting it again, and then putting in more pepper and more sage, and after the job was all over, heard her declare there wasn't enough of anything in it, and so I conjured up a bran new idea, and sprinkled about a hatful of salt and a quart of black pepper and a pint of cayenne and all the sage that was on the premises all over the meat before I ground it. Then I put it through the machine, and cooked and tasted it myself. Well, it was a little hot—that's a fact—and a little salty, and a right smart sagey, but it was good, and a little of it satisfied a body quicker than a good deal of the ordinary kind, and the new plan saved a power of mixing. I took a nice little cake of it up to Mrs. Arp to try, which she did with some surprise and misgiving. By the time she had sneezed four times and coughed the plate out of her lap, she quietly asked me if it was all like that. "All," said I, solemnly. "Do you like it?" said she. "Pretty well, I think," said I; "I wanted to save you trouble, and maybe I have got it a leetle too strong." She never replied, but the next day she made up the little cloth bags and stuffed 'em and hung all overhead in the kitchen, and remarked as she left, "Now, children, that's your pa's sausage. It's a pity he hadn't stayed away another day."

Mrs. Arp has been mighty busy, as usual—always a working, for the house will get dirty, and the children's clothes will wear out, and it's clean up and sew, and patch, and darn, and sew on buttons; and it's the same old thing day after day and week after week; and the little chaps have to be watched all day and washed every night; and their shoe-strings get in a hard knot, and it's a worry to get it undone. They wander over the hill and play in the branch, or frolic in the barn loft, or slip off to Cobe's; and I can hear a sweet motherly voice about forty times a day, as she steps to the door and calls: "Carl—you Carl! Jessie, Jessie e-e! Where upon earth have those children gone to? I will just have to tie the little wretches, or put a block and chain to them." One day she caught me laughing at her anxiety, and I knew she didn't like it, for she said: "Never mind, William, some of these days those children will come home drowned in the creek, or carried off by the gypsies, and you won't laugh then." When she succeeds in getting them home she places her arms akimbo, and with a look of unutterable despair gazes at them and exclaims: "Merciful fathers! did ever a poor mother have such children?—feet right wet, shoes all muddy; and there—another hole in the knee of his pants—and Jessie has torn her apron nearly off of her. Bring me a switch. I will not stand it, for it's sew and patch and worry forever. I could hardly put those shoes on you this morning, for they have been wet and dried, and wet and dried until they are as hard as boards, and your pa won't get you any new ones; and your stockings are worn out and all wet besides; and the diptheria is all over the country, and it's a wonder you don't take it and die. Come into the fire, you poor little orphans, and warm your feet. You may pop some corn, and here's some apples for you. Don't you want some dinner, my darlings?"

The poet hath said that "a baby in the house is a well spring of pleasure." There is a bran new one here now, the first in eight years, and it has raised a powerful commotion. It's not our baby, exactly, but it's in the line of descent, and Mrs. Arp takes on over it all the same as she used to when she was regularly in the business. I thought maybe she had forgotten how to nurse 'em and talk to 'em, but she is singing the same old familiar songs that have sweetened the dreams of half a score, and she blesses the little eyes and the sweet little mouth and uses the same infantile language that nobody but babies understand. For she says, "tum here to it's dandmudder," and "bess its 'ittle heart," and talks about its sweet little footsy-tootsies and holds it up to the window to see the wagons go by and the wheels going rouny-pouny, and now my liberty is curtailed, for as I go stamping around with my heavy farm shoes she shakes her ominous finger at me just like she used to and says, "Don't you see the baby is asleep?" And so I have to tip-toe around, and ever and anon she wants a little fire, or some hot water, or some catnip, for the baby is a-crying and shorely has got the colic. The doors have to be shut now for fear of a draft of air on the baby, and a little hole in the window pane about as big as a dime had to be patched, and I have to hunt up a passel of kinlings every night and put 'em where they will be handy, and they have sent me off to another room where the baby can't hear me snore, and all things considered, the baby is running the machine, and the well spring of pleasure is the center of space. A grandmother is a wonderful help and a great comfort at such a time as this, for what does a young mother, with her first child, know about colic and thrash, and hives and hiccups, and it takes a good deal of faith to dose 'em with sut tea and catnip, and lime water, and paregoric, and soothing syrup, and somtimes with all these the child gets worse, and if it gets better I've always had a curiosity to know which remedy it was that did the work. Children born of healthy parents can stand a power of medicine and get over it, for after the cry comes the sleep, and sleep is a wonderful restorer. Rock 'em awhile in the cradle, then take 'em up and jolt 'em a little on the knee and then turn 'em over and jolt 'em on the other side, and then give 'em some sugar in a rag and after awhile they will go to sleep and let the poor mother rest. There is no patent on this business, no way of raising 'em all the same way, but it is trouble, trouble from the start, and nobody but a mother knows how much trouble it is. A man ought to be mighty good just for his mother's sake, if nothing else, for there is no toil or trial like nursing and caring for a little child, and there is no grief so great as a mother's if all her care and anxiety is wasted on an ungrateful child.

It looks like we will be obleeged to import a doctor in the settlement. Fact is we are obleeged to have a doctor—not that one is needed at all, but just to quiet the female hystericks when any little thing happens. Since we've lived here I've had to send five miles on the run for a doctor two times just to keep down the family hystericks. Both times the patient recovered before the doctor arrived, but then it was such a comfort to have him around and hear him say it is all right, and see him measure out a little yaller powder. It was only day before yesterday that Ralph put our little Carl on the old mare and was leading her along at the rate of half a mile an hour, when the little chap took a notion to fall off and as soon as the wind of it got to headquarters, there was a wild female rush to the scene of great disaster. "Oh mercy, oh the dear child. He's killed. I know he's killed, poor little darling. Oh my child, my child. Ralph, I'll whip you for this if I live. Oh my precious. Just look at that place on his little head. Children, where is your pa? Send for the doctor. Oh mercy—what did we ever move out here for, five miles from a doctor?" I was mighty busy planting peas and so forth in my garden, but I snuffed the commotion in the air, and in a few moments found 'em all bringing the boy to the house, and Mrs. Arp and the girls talked so fast and took on so I couldent find out what had happened to him. Finally I got the bottom facts from Ralph, the reckless—the butt end of all complaints—the promise of a thousand whippings with nary one performed. I looked in vain for wounds and bruises and dislocations. "The boy is not seriously hurt," said I—"he is badly scared and you are making him worse by all this commotion—what he wants is rest and sleep."

"Oh, never," said my wife, "it won't do to let him sleep—when the brain is hurt sleep is the very worst thing—it brings on coma and coma is next thing to death—we must not let him sleep." I was pretty well aroused by this time and said, "he shall sleep," and turned everybody out but Mrs. Arp and she acquiesced in my determination and the boy slept. He slept all night and Mrs. Arp sat beside the bed and watched. He was all right in the morning and ready for another ride.

CHAPTER XXX.

The Old Trunk.

The old trunk was open. Away down in its mysterious recesses Mrs. Arp was searching for something, and as I sat in the other corner with my little table and pen I watched her as she laid the ancient relics on a chair and unfolded first one and then another and looked at them so earnestly, and then folded them up again. "What are you hunting for, my dear?" said I. "Oh, nothing much," said she; "I was just looking over these little dresses to see if there was anything that would do for the little grandchildren. Here is a pretty dress. This dress cost me many a careful stitch. All these plaits were made by my hand, my own hand. There is very little such work done now, for we had no sewing machines then, and it took a long, long time. This embroidery was beautiful then, and it is pretty yet. Do you remember when the first daguerrean came to our town to take pictures? Well, Hattie wore this dress when her picture was taken, and I thought she was the sweetest little thing in the world, and so did you, and she was. Since then we have had ambrotypes and photographs and porcelain pictures, and I don't know what all; but that little daguerreotype gave me more pleasure than anything since, and it is pretty now. Let me see—that was twenty-five years ago, and now I think this same dress will look right pretty on Hattie's child. And here is one that our first boy was christened in, and there is no machine work about it either. That was more than thirty years ago, and now there are four grandchildren at his house, and three more at another one's house, and I don't know what will become of the poor little things, but I reckon the Lord will provide for them. And here is a little garment that Jennie made. Poor Jennie, she had a troubled life, but she is in heaven now, and I'll save this for Pet. She will prize it because her mother made it. And here is a piece of my wedding dress—do you remember it? I know you said then that I looked like an angel in it, but my wings have dropped off long ago, and now I'm only a poor old woman, a faded flower, an overworked mother, ten living children and three more up yonder, and I will be there, too, I hope, before long, for I'm getting tired, very tired, and it seems to me I would like to be nursed, nursed by my mother, and petted like she used to pet me in the long, long ago. And here is a pair of little baby shoes, and the little darling who wore them is in the grave, but he is better off now, and I wouldent call him back if I could. Sometimes I want to feel sad, and I rummage over these old things. There is not much here now, for every little while I have to get out something to mend with or patch or make over again. I wish you would go and see what Carl and Jessie are doing; down at the branch I reckon, and feet all wet, and they have both got dreadful colds. I can't keep them away from that branch."

"Dident you play in the branch, my dear, when you were a child?" said I. "Yes," said she mournfully, "but nothing couldent hurt me then; we were not raised so delicate in those days. You know I used to ride to the plantation, twelve miles, and back again in a day and bring a bag of fruit on the horn of the saddle, but the girls couldent do it now. They can go to a party in a buggy and dance half the night, but that is all excitement, and they are not fit for anything the next day. We dident have any dances—hardly ever—we went to the country wedding sometimes. You remember we went to James Dunlap's wedding, when he married Rebecca Sammons. That was a big frolic—an old-fashioned frolic. Everybody was there from all the naborhood, and there were more turkeys and roast pig and cake than I ever saw, and we played everything we could think of. Rebecca was pretty then, but poor woman—she has had a thousand children, too, just like myself, and I reckon she is faded too, and tired." "But Jim Dunlap hasn't faded," said I. "I see him when I go to Atlanta, and he is big and fat and merry—looks a little like old David Davis."

"Oh, yes, of course he does," said Mrs. Arp. "The men don't know anything about care an anxiety and sleepless nights. It is a wonder to me they die at all." "But I have helped you all I could, my dear," said I, "and you see it's telling on me. Look at these silver hairs and these wrinkles and crows-feet, and my back hurts ever and anon, and this rainy, bad weather gives me rheumatism, but you haven't a gray hair and hardly a seam on your alabaster forehead. Why, you will outlive me, too, and maybe there will be a rich widower stepping around here in my shoes and you will have a fine carriage and a pair of beautiful bay horses, and—"

"William, I told you to go after Carl and Jessie."

"If Vanderbilt's wife should die and he could accidentally see you," said I, "after I'm gone, there's no telling—"

"Well, go along now and find the children, and when you come back I'll listen to your foolishness; I'm not going to let you die if I can help it, for I don't know what would become of us all. Yes, you have helped me, I know, and been a great comfort and did the best you could—most of the time; yes, most of the time—and I might have done worse, and you must nurse me now and pet me, for I am getting childish." "And you must pet me, too," said I. "Oh, of course I will," said she; "am I not always petting you? Now, go along after the children before we both get to crying and have a scene; and I wish you would see if the buff cochin hens have hatched, in the hen house." "She has been setting about fourteen weeks," said I, "but she is getting old, and these old mothers are slow, mighty slow."

I went after the children, and sure enough they were fishing in the spring branch, and their shoes were wet and muddy, and they were bare-headed, and I marched them up tenderly, and Mrs. Arp set them down by the fire and dried their shoes, and got them some more stockings, and then opened their little morning school. How patiently these old-fashioned mothers work and worry over the little things of domestic life. Day after day, and night after night, they labor and watch and watch and wait, while the fathers are contriving some big thing to keep up the family supplies. Parents are very much like chickens. The old hen will set and set and starve, and when the brood comes will go scratching for worms and bugs as hard as she can and be always clucking and looking out for hawks, but the old rooster will strut around and notice the little chickens with a paternal pride, and when he scratches up a bug makes a big fuss over it and calls them with a flourish, and eats it himself just before they get there.

That was a mighty good talk in your last Sunday's paper about sleep, and letting folks sleep until nature waked 'em. He was a smart doctor who said all that, and he said it well, but I couldent help thinking what would become of the babies if the mothers dident wake until they had got sleep enough. There are no regular hours for them. Job speaketh of the dark watches of the night when deep sleep falleth upon a man, but it don't fall upon a weary mother with a fretful child when it is cutting its front teeth and wants to nurse the livelong night. When she is sleeping she is awake, and when she is waking she is half asleep, and the morning brings no rest or refreshment, and I was thinking, too, of what would become of the farm if the boys were not waked up early in the morning. Not many boys will awake up themselves, and they must be called, and in course of time have habits of waking forced upon 'em. A family that sleep late will always be behind with farm work. I do not believe in getting up before day and eating breakfast by candle light, but I do believe in early rising. I don't know how long my children would sleep if I did not call 'em, for I never tried it; but I don't call Mrs. Arp, of course I don't, though she says I had just as well, for I stamp around and slam the doors and whistle and sing until there is no more sleep for her. She wants me to build her a little house away off in the garden, where she can sleep enough to make up for lost time, and be always calm and serene, and I think I will.

CHAPTER XXXI.

THE GEORGIA COLONEL.

Speaking of Georgia colonels, I was thinking the other day how there came to be so many of 'em. We used to have general musters all over the State twice a year. The militia were ordered out to be reviewed by the commander-in-chief, which was the governor. The constitution required him to review 'em, and as he couldn't travel all around in person, he had to do it by proxy, and so he had his proxy in every county, and he was called the governor's aid-de-camp with the rank of colonel. This gave the governor over a hundred aid-de-camps, and they all took it as a compliment and wore cockade hats with red plumes, and epaulets, and long brass swords, and big brass spurs, and pistols in their holsters, and rode up and down the lines at a gallop, reviewing the meelish. The meelish were in a double crooked straight line in a great big field, and were armed with shot-guns and rifles, and muskets, and sticks, and corn-stalks, and thrash-poles, and umbrellas, and they were standing up and setting down, or on the squat, or playing mumble peg, and they hollered for water half their time, and whiskey the other; and when the colonel and his personal staff got through reviewing he halted about the middle of the line and said, "Shoulder arms—right face—march," and then the kettle drums rattled and the fife squeaked, and some guns went off half cocked, and the meelish shouted awhile and were disbanded by the captains of their several companies. These colonels held their rank and title as long as the governor held his office, and they were expected to holler hurrah for the governor on all proper occasions, and they did it. If the governor ran again and was defeated, the next governor appointed a new set from among the faithful, and the old set had to retire from the field, but they held on to the title. For a great many years the old whigs and democrats had it up and down, in and out, and so new colonels were made by the score until the State was chock full again. They had a general muster and a grand review once up at Lafayette, and Bob Barry lived up there and was the b-hoy of the town. Bob never wore shoes or a hat or hardly anything else in those days, and he had petted and tamed a great big long razorbacked hog, and could ride him with a rope bridle, and so as the colonel and his staff came galloping down the lines with their cockades and plumes and glittering swords, Bob suddenly came out from behind a house mounted on his razor-back hog, and a paper cap with a turkey feather in it on his head, and a pair of old tongs swinging from his suspenders, and some spurs on his bare·footed heels, and he fell in just behind the cavalcade, and got the hog on a run, and scared their horses, and the whole concern ran away and the hog after 'em, and such a yell and such an uproar was never heard in those parts or anywhere else. The hog never stopped running until he got home, when he dismounted and took to the woods for fear of consequences. Bob is running a Sunday-school now, and I'm glad of it, for it will take a good deal of missionary work in him to make up for some things the Lafayette people tell about.

But these militia musters got to be such farces that the legislature abolished 'em about thirty-five years ago, though they couldent abolish the colonels. When the war broke loose most of 'em went into the army and got reduced. Many a peace colonel got to be a war major or a captain, or even a high private, and in that way their ranks were thinned. Our governors, however, still make a few new ones as often as they are elected, and so the peace colonel is still destined to live and illustrate the good old State. The Georgia majors are not so numerous. They came from these same militia musters, for every county had her battalions and every battalion had its major. But now his destiny is fixed. There are no more majors to come, and the old stock is passing away. I'm glad you have a paper in your town that is perpetuating the good old name, for the time was in the good old days when he was a power in the land—when he, too, wore epaulets and a sword and marched his cohorts up the hill and marched 'em down again.

After the muster was over then came the horse swapping, and the horse races, and the pugilistic exercises in the town in front of the groceries. No pistols, nor knives, nor sticks were allowed, but the boys stripped to the waist and went at it with nature's weapons. It was short work and quick work and nobody hurt very much, though sometimes Billy Patterson got an awful lick. These fighting boys had no cause to quarrel, but Rancy Sniffle wanted it settled as to who was the best man in his beat. That was all.

CHAPTER XXXII.

On the Old Times, Alexander Stephens, Etc.

Two cents—only two cents. When I look at a postage stamp it carries me away back. Back to the time when my father was postmaster and I was clerk, and had to make up the mails in a country town. The difference between now and then shows that the world's progress in this department is hardly excelled in any other branch of improvement. We couldn't bear to be set back again in the old ways that our fathers thought were pretty good. There were no stamps and no envelopes and no mucilage. The paper was folded up like a thumbpaper, and one side slipped in the other and sealed with a wrapper. The little schoolboys, you know, had to use thumb-papers in their spelling books to keep them clean where their dirty thumbs kept the pages open. Girls didn't have to use them, for they were nicer and kept their hands clean, and didn't wear out the leaves by the friction of their fingers. Boys are rough things any how, and I don't see what a nice, sweet, pretty girl wants with one of 'em. Girls, they say, are made of sugar and spice and all that's nice, but boys are made of snaps and snails and puppy dogs' tails. Josephus says, that when the queen of Sheba was testing Solomon's wisdom, she had fifty boys and fifty girls all dressed alike in girls' clothes and seated around a big room, and asked the king to pick out the boys from the girls, and he called for a basin of water and had it carried around to each one and told them to wash their hands. The girls all rolled up their sleeves a little bit, the boys just sloshed their hands in any way and got water all over their aprons, and so the king spotted every mother's son of them.

The postage used to be regulated by the distance that Uncle Sam carried the letters. It was $12\frac{1}{2}$ cents anywhere in the state, and $18\frac{3}{4}$ cents to Charleston, and 25 cents to New York. It was never prepaid. A man could afflict another with a pistareen letter that wasent worth five cents. A pistareen, you know, was $18\frac{3}{4}$ cents—that is a sevenpence and a thrip. We had no dimes or half dimes. The dollars was cut up into eighths instead of tenths. When a countryman called for letters and got one, he would look at it some time and turn it over and meditate before he paid for it, and very often they would say, "where did this letter come from?" Well, I would say, for instance, "it came from Dahlonega—don't you see Dahlonega written up on the corner?" Then he would say, "well, I reckon it's from Dick, my brother Dick. He is up there diggin' gold. Don't you reckon it's from Dick?" "I reckon it is," said I. "Why don't you open it and see?" "No, I'll wait until I get home. They'll all want to see it." When he got home that letter would be an event in the family, and perhaps it would take them half an hour to wade through it and make out its contents. Nine out of ten of those country letters began, "I take my pen in hand to let you know that I am well, and hope these few lines will find you enjoying the same blessing." My father kept store and his country customers used to ask him to write their letters for them, and he always sent them to me, and most of them told me to begin their letters that way. There was not more than one in five that could write, but they were good, clever, honest people and paid their debts, but they hardly ever paid up in full at the end of the year, and so they gave their notes for the balance and made their mark. My father used to say that he had known cases where a man swore off his written signature, but he never knew a man to deny his mark. Our big northern mail used to come in a stage from Madison twice a week, and I used to think the sound of the stage-horn as the stage came over the hill, was one of the sublimest things in the world, and I thought that if ever I got to be a man I would be a stage-driver if I could. Well, I came pretty near it, for my father had hired a man to ride the mail to Roswell and back twice a week, and the man got sick and so my father put me on a dromedary of a horse and the mail in some saddle-bags behind me, and I had to make the forty-eight miles in a day and kept it up all the winter. I liked to have frozen several times, and had to be lifted off the horse when I got home, and it nearly broke my mother's heart, but I was getting a dollar a trip and it was my money, and so I wouldn't back out. The old women on the route used to crowd me with their little commissions and get me to bring them pepper, or copperas, or bluing, or pins and needles, or get me to take along some socks and sell them, and so I made friends and acquaintances all the way. The first trip I made, an old woman hailed me and said, "Are you a mail boy?" "Why, yes, mam," said I. "You dident think I was a female boy, did you?" I thought that was smart, but it wasent very civil and it made her so mad she never told me what she wanted, and as she turned her back on me I heard her say, "I'll bet he's a little stuck up town boy."

My father was postmaster for nearly thirty years. It didn't pay more than about $200 a year, but it made his store more of a public place. He didn't know that anybody else hankered after it or was trying to get it, but all of a sudden he got his orders to turn over the office to another man, an old line Whig and a competitor in business. It mortified him very much and made us all mad, for there was no fault found with his management, and he never took much interest in politics but voted for the man he liked the best whether he was a Whig or a Democrat. When he found that Alex. Stephens had it done he wasent a Stephens man any more, and I grew up with an idea that Mr. Stephens was a political fraud. I dident understand the science of politics as well as I do now. I told Mr. Stephens about it one night at Milledgeville when we were all in a good humor and were talking about the old times of Whigs and Democrats, and he smiled and said, "yes, we had to do those things, and sometimes they were very disagreeable." I will never forget that night's talk. It was during the session of the first legislature after the war. Jim Waddell took me to Mr. Stephens' room to hear him talk, and there was Mr. Jenkins and Tom Hardeman and Benning Moore and Beverly Thornton and Peter Strozier and Dr. Ridley and some others, and everybody was in a good humor, and Mr. Stephens was reclining on his bed and told anecdote after anecdote about the old Whigs and how he met the Democrats on the stump and what they said and what he said, and he most always got the advantage and carried the crowd with him. I was very much fascinated with his conversation, but couldent help being reminded of a circumstance that transpired some years before in the town of Calhoun. The Whigs of Gordon county had sent for Mr. Stephens to come up and make a speech and rally the boys for the next election, for Gordon was pretty equally balanced between Whigs and Democrats, and the Whigs wanted a big revival. So Aleck accepted, and when the day came the crowd was tremendous.

The Democrats had tried to get Howell Cobb and Herschel Johnson to come up and reply to Aleck, but they couldent come, and so little Aleck had it all his own way. In the meantime the Democratic boys had hunted up A. M. Russell and got his promise to reply to Mr. Stephens. Russell was an original genius. He was gifted in language, gifted in imagination, gifted in cheek, gifted in lying, and was utterly regardless of consequences.

Mr. Stephens made a splendid speech. He arraigned the Democracy and held them up to ridicule, and when he got through the Whigs were more than satisfied, and Mr. Stephens was satisfied, too—he came down from the stand and was receiving the congratulations of his friends, when suddenly Russell mounted the rostrum and, rapping on the plank in front of him, screamed out in one unearthly yell: "Fellow citizens!" Everybody knew him, and everybody wanted to hear him, and hushed into silence. After a sentence or two Mr. Stephens was attracted to him, and with curious and astonished interest inquired, "Who is that man?" After Russell had paid an eloquent tribute to the glorious old Democratic party, and given it credit for every good thing that had been done since the fall of Adam, he then turned to Mr. Stephens, and, with a sneering scorn, said: "And what have you and your party been doing and trying to do? What made you vote away the public lands so that yankees and furriners could get 'em and our people couldent? What made you vote for high tariff on sugar and coffee and raise the price so that our poor people couldent buy it?" Mr. Stephens rose excited and irritated, and stretching his long arm to the audience, screamed out: "I never did it, my fellow-citizens—I deny the fact and call upon the gentlemen for his proof." With the utmost self-possession, Russell said, "You do—you call for the proof. Sir, if I was to go two miles from home to make a speech I would carry my proof with me. I wouldent be vain enough to go without it; but, sir, I am at home—these people know me—they raised me and when I assert a thing they believe it. You are the man to bring the proof." The crowd shouted and laughed as tumultuously as they had done for Mr. Stephens, and he sat down disgusted. Russell continued: "And what was your motive when you were a member of the legislature in voting for a law that prohibited a man from voting unless he was worth $500? Answer me that while you are here face to face with these humble citizens of

Gordon county. At this Mr. Stephens rose again furious with indignation and screamed: "It is false, sir, it is false; I deny the fact."

"You do," said Russell, scornfully, "I supposed you would—you deny the fact. That is just what you have been doing for twenty years—going about over the country denying facts." And the crowd went wild with merriment, for even the Whigs couldn't help joining in the fun. Mr. Stephens turned to his companions and said with a tone of despair, "Let us go to the hotel," and they went.

I thought of all this while Mr. Stephens was telling me of his triumphs over veteran foes, and so when he came to a pause I timidly said: "Mr. Stephens, did you ever encounter a man by the name of Russell up at Calhoun?"

With a merry glistening of his wonderful eyes he straightened up and said: "I did, I did, yes, I did. I will never forget that man. He got me completely. If I had known him I would not have said a word in reply, but I dident know him. He cured me of one expression. I frequently used to emphasize my denial of lies and slander, and that was to say, 'I deny the fact.' I had never thought of its grammatical absurdity, but that man Russell taught me and I quit it. I think he had the most wonderful flow of language and lies of any man I ever met." Mr. Stephens then made a pretty fair recital of his recounter and his "utter defeat," as he expressed it, all of which we enjoyed. Where are they now? Old Father Time has cut them all down but three, Hardeman and Thornton and myself are here, but all the rest of that bright, intelligent crowd are gone. It looks like most everybody is dead. If they are not they will be before long, and another set will be in their places and have their jokes and flash their wit and merriment all the same.

CHAPTER XXXIII.

Sticking to the Old.

As the world grows older mankind becomes more liberal in opinion and less wedded to prejudice and superstition. We rub against one another so closely nowadays, and talk so much and read so much that our conceit is weakening, and we think more and think deeper than we used to, and are more ready to absorb knowledge. A man don't dare nowadays to say anything is impossible, for many impossibilities have already been performed, and we now live in a state of anxious expectation as to what big thing will come next. Still, there are some folks who stubbornly refuse to fall into line, and they stand by the old landmarks. Not long ago I passeed by a blacksmith shop away off in the country, and there was a horse doctor cutting the hooks out of a horse's eyes to keep him from going blind, and he got very indignant when I told him that the horse books were all against it, and said it ought to be prohibited by law. I heard an old hardshell arguing against this idea that the world turned over every day, and he declared it was against common sense and Scripture, and he wouldent let his children go to school to learn any such nonsense, for he knowed that the water would all spill out if you turned it upside down, and the Scripters said that Joshua commanded the sun to stand still, and it stood still; and he asked me how I was going to get over the like of that. I saw that the crowd was against me, and so I replied: "Jesso. Jesso, my friend. And right then the wonderful change took place. The sun used to go around the earth, of course, but Joshua stopped it and he never set it to going again, and it is there yet."

This weakened the old man a little and unsettled the crowd, and I got away from there prematurely for fear the old man would send for his Bible. Answer a fool according to his folly is a good way sometimes. Dr. Harden told me about his father raising a rumpus a long time ago in old Watkinsville by asserting that all horses had botts in 'em, and it was accordin' to nature and the botts were not a disease, and a horse never died on account of 'em. Old man Moore kept the tavern there and he swore that Harden was a luniack, and so one day when they were playing checkers in the tavern a storm came up and a terrible crash was heard, and pretty soon a darkey came running in the house and told his master the lightning had struck his iron grey horse and killed him. Old man Moore thought as much of that horse as he did of his wife, and the crowd all hurried out to the lot to see him. Moore was greatly distressed and used bad language about the catastrophe, and after he subsided a little, Harden says he, "Now Moore, if you say so, I'll cut open that horse and show you the botts, and I reckon that will settle it." So Moore agreed to it, and when he was opened, and the botts began to cut their way out and worm around, Harden looked at Moore with triumphant satisfaction and paused for a reply. Moore had his hands crossed behind his back, and was gazing intently at the ugly varmints, when suddenly he exclaimed, "Harden, I was powerful mad with that lightning for killing old Selim, but I ain't now, for if the lightning hadent struck him I'll be damned if them infernal botts wouldent have killed him in thirty minutes." Moore had a big fighting stump-tail dog by the name of Ratler, and one day a little Italian came along with an organ and a monkey, and as the crowd gatherd around he asked the man if his monkey could fight. "Oh, yes, he fight," said the Italian. "Will he fight a dog?" said Moore. "Oh, yes; he fight a dog—he whip dog quick," said the Italian. Moore pulled out a five dollar bill and said, "I'll bet you this that I've got a dog he can't whip." The little fellow covered it with another five and the money was handed over to a stakeholder and they went through to the back yard, followed by half the folks in the little town. There lay the dog on the grass asleep, and at the word the Italian tossed the monkey on him. In less than a jiffy the little brute had his teeth and his claws fastened like a vise in the stump of that dog's tail and was screeching like a hyena. The dog gave but one astonished look behind as he bounced to his feet and made tracks for another country. The monkey held on until Ratler sprung over a ten-rail fence at the back of the garden when he suddenly quit his hold and sat on the top rail, and watched the dog's flight with a chatter of perfect satisfaction and danced along the rail with delight. The crowd was convulsed. They laughed and roared and hollered tumultuously, all but old man Moore whose, voice could be heard above all others as he stood upon the fence and shouted "Here Ratler, here, here; here Ratler, here; here Ratler, here." But Ratler wouldent hear. Ratler rattled on and on, across field after field, until he got to the woods and was gone from human sight. The Italian shouldered his monkey affectionately, and walking up to Moore, said: "Your dog not well to-day, maybe your dog gone off to hunt rabbeet. Your dog no like my monkey—he not acquint. Maybe ven I come again next year he come and fight some more. Ven you look for heem to come back?" Moore gave up the wager, but he asserted solemnly that Ratler would have whipped the fight if he hadent have run. "The surprise, gentlemen, the surprise was what done it," said he, "for that dog has whipped wild cats and a bear and a she wolf and every dog in ten miles of Watkinsville." And all that evening and away in the night and early the next morning an inviting mournful voice could be heard at the back of the garden calling, "Ratler here;" Ratler, here; and three days after a man brought Ratler home, but he had lost his integrity and never could be induced to fight anything more.

Some men never give up a thing, and some give up too much. Judge Bleckley says that he is in the cautious, credulous state about everything, and just lives along serenely and waits for events. He says that if a man can hear the voice of a friend from New York to Boston by the aid of a telephone, why shouldn't all the other senses be aided in like manner by some invention; and he hints that he wouldent be surprised at an invention that would enable a man to kiss his wife across the Atlantic ocean. I don't think that follows to reason, for hearing and seeing are both for distance, and so is smelling, but feeling is a very different thing. Feeling means contact, and the closer the contact the more intense the feeling. It never was intended to feel afar off, and so I don't believe that any good would come of a man kissing his wife through a machine a thousand miles long. It would be very dangerous, for it might encourage folks to be kissing other people's wives, and the machine would be kept busy all the time, for there are some men who couldent be choked off, and by and by the whole world would be kissing one another, and business would be neglected and mankind would come to want.

But I do believe that everything will come that ought to come. Nature has a mighty big storehouse, and she always unlocks it at the right time. She is very economical of her treasures, and keeps 'em from us until she sees that we are obliged to have 'em. Cotton didcnt come, nor cotton machinery, until the world was bad off for clothing. The sewing machine come along just as the poor women were about worn out, and Tom Hood had written his sad, sweet "Song of the Shirt." Coal was found when wood got scarce in the old world. Railroads and steamships were invented as population increased, and now we couldent possibly do without 'em. Old Peter Cooper said that a million of people would perish in New York city in one month if the cars were to stop running that long. Then came the telegraph, and now the telephone, and I don't think any other very big thing will happen soon, for mankind is very comfortable, and don't need it, so let us all rest awhile and let Dame Nature rest. She has been very kind to her creatures, and we all ought to be thankful.

CHAPTER XXXIV.

A Prose Poem on Spring.

On this pellucid day when the sky is so beautifully blue and the sun so warm and cheerful, when the jaybirds are chanting their safe return from purgatory and the crows are cawing over the sprouting corn, when the sheep bells tinkle merrily in the meadow and children and chickens are cackling around, it seems like everything in nature was happy and everybody ought to be. The darkies are singing to the mules in the cotton field and are happier with a little than the white folks are with a good deal. The darkey never borrows trouble. I wish our race would take a few lessons in contentment from 'em— not enough to make us shiftless and with no ambition to better our condition, but enough to stop this restlessness, this wild rush for money, this wear and tear upon brain and heart that is getting to be the curse of the land. I wish everybody was happy and had nothing against nobody. I wish every farmer had fine horses and fat cattle and plenty of pocket change, and dident have to work only when he felt like it. I wish I had a winter home in Florida with orange groves and pine apples and bananas, and a summer home up among the mountains, and a railroad and palace cars between the two, and a free pass over the line and plenty of money at both ends of it. I wish I was a king with a mint of gold and silver at my command, so I could go about in disguise and mingle with the poor and friendless and lift them up out of distress and make 'em happy. I wish I was a genii like we read of in the Arabian Nights, and could, at a breath, build palaces and make diamonds and pearls and marry all the poor girls to rich husbands, and all the struggling boys to princesses and kick up a cloud of golden dust wherever I went. No I don't, either, for I know now that the like of that wouldent bring happiness in this sublunary world. The best condition for a man is to have neither poverty nor riches. Old Agur prayed a good prayer and he knew how it was—

For riches bring us trouble when they come,
And there's want in the homes of the poor,
But it's good for a man to have a little sum
To keep away the wolf from the door.

Some folks are never happy unless they are miserable. Their livers are green and yellow like melancholy, and they want everything they can get, and would rather see mankind going to hell than to heaven if they could stay behind and play wreckers on eternity's shore. I have seen men whose very presence would dry up all hilarity as quick as a slack tub cools hot iron. Men who never smile willingly, and when they force one the cadaverous visage is lit up for a moment with a brimstone light, and then relapses into its natural scowl. Such people are a nuisance upon society, and ought to be abolished or put into a lower asylum like luniacks. I've no more toleration for 'em than for a mad dog, and if there's any apology it's in favor of the dog.

How inspiring is the earliest breath of spring, when nature like a blushing maid is putting on her pantalets and preparing to bang her silken hair. How quickly it brings to life the slumbering emotions which, though chilled by the frosts and the winds of winter, were not dead, but only lay dormant like a bear in his den. What harmonious feelings spring up in one's bosom and gush forth to all mankind. This balmy weather fills all the chambers of the soul with music that is not heard and with poetry that is not expressed. The very air is redolent with love and peace. Turnip greens are running up to seed, the plum trees are in bloom, the busy bee is sucking their fragrant blossoms, and by and by will be stinging the children as usual. The sweet south wind is breathing upon the violet banks. Alder tags hang in graceful clusters upon their drooping stems. Jonquills are in a yellow strut, and the odorous shallots are about right for the frying pan. The little silver-sides and minnows have opened their spring regattas. The classical robin has ceased to get drunk on the China berry, and the ferocious chicken hawk catches about one a day from our earliest broods. Everything is lively now—

Over the meadows the new-born lambs are skipping,
Over the fields the little boys are ripping.

The country is the best place for children. What a glorious luxury it is for them to go barefooted and wade in the branch and go seining, and climb trees and hunt birds' nests, and carry the corn to mill, and run pony races. It is well enough for a man to live in a town or a city when he is young and active, but when he gets married and the little chaps come along according to nature, he ought to get on a farm to raise 'em. An old man with numerous grandchildren has got no business in a city. What a burlesque on childhood's joy it must be to visit grandpa and grandma in a city penned up in brick walls, wtih a few sickly flowers in the window, and a garden in the rear about as big as a wagon sheet. Might as well try to raise good, healthy, vigorous colts in a stable yard. There is too much machinery about raising children now-a-days anyhow. The race is running out, and nothing but country life can save it. The old back-log is gone, and the big, open, friendly fire-place, and the cheerful blazing family hearth; and now it is a hole in the floor, or iron pipes running around the walls. I reckon that is economy, but in my opinion a man can't improve the stock that way, nor keep it as good as it was. The children will be picayunish and over-nice and sharp-featured, and potty before and gimletty behind. They won't do to bet on like those chaps brought up around a fire-place on a hundred-acre farm.

Raising children is the principal business of human life, and is about all that the majority of mankind are working for, though they don't know it. It is the excuse for all the mad rush of business that hurries su along. It is the apology for nearly all the cheating and stealing and lying in the land. Working for the children is behind it all, and the trouble is that most everybody is trying to do too much for 'em and scuffling against wind and tide to keep up with their nabors or get a little ahead. Too many fine clothes, too many kid gloves and parasols and new bonnets—too many carpets and curtains and pictures, and a thousand other things that run up the outgo bigger than the income, and keep the poor fellows always on a strain. I love to humor 'em and play horse with 'em, and tell 'em stories about Jack and the bean stalk, and what I did when I was a little boy; and I put 'em to bed and rub their backs and let 'em trot around with me a good deal on week days and all day Sunday, but I'm not going to waste my slender substance on 'em, for it's nature's law that they must work for a living and they shall. I'm going to raise 'em in the country, for as Thomas Jefferson said, "the influence of great cities is pestilential to health and morals and the liberties of the people."

CHAPTER XXXV.

Uncle Bart.

Old Uncle Bart, as we call him, wasn't a common drunkard nor an uncommon one either, but every time he came to town he would get drunk. He came mighty seldom, for when he did the memory of it lasted him about three months. He told me after such a spree he felt as mean and lonely as a stray dog. He said he couldn't eat nor sleep, and away in the night wanted water so bad he "felt like he could bite a branch in two and swallow the upper end."

One morning he came in early to see Dolph Ross, who was going to Texas. He came across him before he came across the grocery, and says he: "Hallo, Dolph—gwine to Texas?"

"Yes, Uncle Bart, I am."

"Well, my brother Ben lives over there, and he's *got big rich*, and no family, and I thought if you'd see him and tell him how sorry we was gettin' along he mout do something for us. You see my wheat crop is likely to fail, for the back-water from the spring freshet got over it, and it's all turned yaller, and my corn looks sickly, and my best cow got snake-bit last week and died, and the old lady is powerful puny, and Sal she got to hankerin' arter a likely chap in the naborhood and married him, and he ain't got nothin', and I'm gettin' old and can't stand nigh as much as I used to, and I want you to see Brother Ben, and maybe he'll do somethin'—you see?"

"Yes, I see, Uncle Bart, but where does your brother Ben live?"

"Live? Why, he lives in Texas, I told ye! If you don't meet him in the road you can send him some word by somebody and he'll find you. He's over there, shore."

In about an hour he met Dolph again, and slapping his foot down limberly, he seized Dolph's hand with a loving grip, and says he, "Hello, Dolph—gwine to Texas?"

"Yes, Uncle Bart."

"Will you tell Brother Ben that we are all doin' tol'able; the crop looks 'bout as good as common, and the old 'oman's sweet and sassy as ever, and Sal, she's married and done splendid. Good by, Dolph, God bless you, I love you."

In about two more drinks, from that time, Uncle Bart come weavin' along, and, says he, "Hello, Dolph, gwine to Texas?—*tell Brother Bren* I've got—I've got the brest crop in the—State—to let me know how he's golonging along—if he wants anything—he shall—s'havit—he shan't—he shan't—she shan't suffer—as long as—as I've got nothin'—I can send him—twen or twelve-teen dollars—any time—fwarwell Dolph."

About the close of the day Dolph found him on the lowermost step of the grocery, his head on his knees and his hat on the ground. Thinking it a poor place to spend the night, he aroused him to a glimmering view of the situation.

"Hello—Roff Doss," says he, "gwine to—Texas?—tell Brother Ben—*hell's afloat and the river's a-risin'.*" (Hic.)

CHAPTER XXXVI.

CHRISTMAS ON THE FARM.

A happy New Year to you and your readers. I don't mean just the first day, but all the year round. I wish from my heart everybody was comfortable and contented and everybody lived in peace. I was ruminating over that kind of a millenium which would come if there were no bad folks—no lazy folks, no envy nor spite nor revenge—no bad passions but everybody took things easy and tried to make all around them happy. I wasent thinking about a religious millennium for I have known peoplo to make mighty good, honorable citizens who dident have any religion to spare and some who had a power of it on Sunday but was a juggling with the devil all the rest of the week. I was thinking about that class of folks who gave us no trouble and was always willing to tote fair. The law wasent made for them. I was thinking about the half a million of dollars it costs to run the State government a year and the half a million more it costs to run the counties and courts. If everybody was clever and kind we could save most all of it and in a few years everybody would have enough to be comfortable and to educate their children. The laws are made for bad people only and bad people costs us about all the surplus that's made. I know folks all around me who never violate a law or impose on their nabors or have a law suit, and it seems to me they ought not to be taxed like people who are always a fussing around the courthouse and taking up the time of juries and witnesses. There ought to be some way to reward good citizens who give us no trouble or expense, and to make folks who love strife and contention pay the expense of it.

But I started out wishing for a happy New Year to everybody, and my opinion is that we can all make it happy if we try. Lets try. Lets turn over a new leaf. Lets have a Christmas all the year long. Lets keep the family hearth always bright and pleasant. Fussing and fretting don't pay. Solomon says its like water dropping on a rock—it will wear away a stone. The home of an unhappy discordant family is no home at all. It aint even a decent purgatory. The children won't stay there any longer than possible. They will emigrate and I don't blame 'em.

We've had a power of fun at my house the last few days. Mrs. Arp said she was going to town. She had a little passel of money hid away—nobody knew how much or where she got it, but sometimes when my loose change is laying around or left in my pockets, I've noticed that it disappears very mysteriously. It took about two hours to arrange herself for the expedition and she left us on a mission of peace on earth and good will to her children.

"Now William, you know the Christmas tree is to be put up in the hall. You have very good taste about such things and I know I can trust you without any directions. Put in that large square box in the smoke house and fasten it well to the bottom and put the top on the box for a table, and the girls will cover it nicely with some curtain calico. But I will not direct you for I know you can fix it all right. There are most too many limbs on the tree. There is a lot of pop corn already threaded and you can arrange them in festoons all over the tree, and the oranges that Dick sent us from Florida are locked up in the pantry. Thread them with a large needle and tie them all about on the limbs. The little wax candles and the tins to fasten them are in the drawer of my bureau. I've had them for several years and we will light up the tree to-night. The milk is ready to churn you know. Set the jar in the large tin bucket before you churn. It will save messing the floor. There are two turkeys in the coop—take the fattest one—you can tell by holding them up in your hands. Ralph will help about the turkey. If you think one turkey will not be enough you had better kill a couple of chickens to go with it. I do hope all the children will be here, but I am afraid they won't. It does look like we might get together once a year anyhow. Now do attend to the turkey just as nice as you can, and leave the butter for me to work over when I come back. The front yard ought to be swept and the back yard is in an awful mess. But I will just leave everything to you. Keep the hall doors locked for the children mustent see the tree until Santa Claus comes. That mistletoe must be put over the parlor pictures. Hunt up a few more eggs if you can find them. Don't disturb the mince pies in the closet—never mind about that either, for I've got the key in my pocket."

It always did seem to me that ours was the noisiest, liveliest and most restless set that ever stumped a toe or fell into the branch. They went through the measles, and the whoopin' cough, and chicken pox, and I don't know how many more things, without stoppin' to see what was the matter. A long time ago it was my opinion that I could regulate 'em and raise 'em up accordin' to science, but I dident find that amount of co-operation which was necessary to make a fair experiment. On the contrary, I found myself regulated, besides being from time to time reminded by their maternal ancestor that the children were hern, and to this day she always speaks of 'em as "my children. Well, that's a fact; her title is mighty good to 'em I know, and on reflection I don't remember to have ever heard any dispute about who was the mother of a child.

Well, we can sing the same old song—how the little folks had lived on tip-toe for many days waiting for Santa Claus, and how that umble parlor was dressed in cedar and mistletoe, and the big back log put on, and the blazing fire built up, and the little stockings hung by the mantel, and everything got ready for the kind old gentleman. How that blue-eyed daughter played deputy to him, and was the keeper of everybody's secret; and shutting herself up in the parlor, arranged everything to her notion. How that when supper was over one of the boys slipped up the ladder to the top of the house with his cornet and tooted a few merry notes as the signal that Santa Claus had arrived. Then came the infantile squeal, and the youthful yell, and the Arpian shriek, and all rushed in wild commotion to the festive hall. Then came the joyful surprises, all mixed up with smiles and sunbeams, and exclamations and interjections. Tumultuous gladness gleamed and glistened all around, and the big bucket of family joy ran over. But everybody knows how it is hisself, and don't hanker after a history of other people's frolics.

Well, the old year has buried its dead, and brought forth its living to take their places. And the time is at hand when everybody is going to open a new set of books, and turn over a new leaf and pass a few resolutions to be kept about three weeks. That's all right. Keep 'em as long as you can, but don't repent of this year's sins too much at once. Don't get too much religion at a revival, for by and by the snow will be gone, and the spring will open and the birds begin to sing and the flowers to bloom and man's conceit and independence come back to him and make him forget the winter and his promises, and strut around like he was running the whole macheen. But it's all right, judge, all right, as Cobe says. If a man is good accordin' to his capacity he can't be any gooder.

CHAPTER XXXVII.

DEMOCRATIC PRINCIPLES.

How sweet are the sounds from home. How soothing the consolations of a discerning wife. I was feeling bad and she knew it. My cogitations over the election news were by no means jubilant. Silent and sad, with the newspaper open on my knee, I had been looking dreamily at the flickering flames for about ten minutes while Mrs. Arp sat near me sewing a patch on a pair of little breeches, when suddenly she inquired:

"What did you expect Mr. Cleveland to do for you?"

"Nothing," said I, "nothing at all; but then you see, my dear, its highly important that a Democrat should be at the head of the nation."

She never looked up nor for a moment stopped the graceful jerk of her needle and thread as she again inquired:

"And what would a Democratic President do for you?"

"Well, nothing—nothing at all," said I, "but then you see I feel interested in the success of our party and the promulgation of the great general principles of the Democracy. They are the hope of the country—the—the"

"Please tell me something about those great principles," said she; "what are they?"

"Why, my dear, the great principles of our party are—they—are—they—why they are as old as the government. They underlie the foundation of Democratic institutions—they"—

"But what are they?" said she.

"Well, in the first place," said I, "when Thomas Jefferson was President he eliminated and set forth those principles in a series of state papers that have established in the mind of American patriots a reverence for democratic government that"—

"But what are the principles?" said she.

"Well as I was going on to say, the democratic institutions of our country have contributed more to the peservation of life, liberty and happiness than all other causes combined; indeed the benefits that is adherent partake of are—they are"—

"Justification, adoption, and sanctification," said she.

"No, not exactly; not to that pious extent," said I. "An enumeration of all those great principles would require more time than—than—"

"Well, never mind, William, never mind," said she affectionately, "I don't want to take up your valuable time, but I've been suspecting, for a long time, that those principles were to get in office and draw big salaries, and live high without work, and I reckon one party can do that about as well as another; don't you?"

"Well, yes, my dear; there is, I confess, some foundation for your suspicions; but then, you see, we are trying to nationalize the American people through a national party, and become once more in fraternal union, and—"

"Well, you can't do that, William," said she. "They never did like us and we never did like them. We needn't have any more war, but we can be stately and distant like we have to be with nabors that are not congenial. If I was you I'd let national politics, as you call it, alone, for it's a jack o'lantern business and will never profit you. Look after your farm and your home affairs. You had better go out now and water the flowers in the pit, and see where Carl and Jessie are. The meal is nearly out, and you had better shell a turn of corn this evening, and while you are down there see if the old blue hen has hatched. Her time is about up. Stir around awhile and don't be looking so far away."

Blessed woman! I did stir 'round, and it made me feel better. I shall take no more interest in national politics until—well, until the next election. Consolation is a good thing. I'm going to be reconciled anyway and not give up the ship. Reckon I can stay at home and make corn and cotton, and frolic with the children, and ruminate on the uncertainties of life and bask in the sunshine of the family queen.

"I am afraid you are hankering after an office," said she, "and that would take you away from home and leave me and the children alone. Office is a poor thing; when a man gets one, everybody is envious of him, and he has to give away about half his salary to keep his popularity. We've got a good home, and we are getting along in years, and I think we had better stay here, and be as happy as we can. Don't you, John Anderson, my Joe?" and she placed her little soft hand so gently and lovingly on my frosty brow, my reverend head, that I havent thought about office since. I'm going to camp right here. Dr. Talmage has been preaching a sermon lately on married folks, and he says it's the way the women do that drives their husbands off at night to the club houses, and the stores, and the loafing places about town; says they don't sweeten up on 'em like they did before they was married—don't come to the door to meet 'em—don't play the piano, but sorter give up, and are always complaining about something, or scolding the children or the servants. Well, maybe that's so to some extent, but my observation is that most of them fellers went to the club-houses and loafed around before they were married. I've knowed men to quit home and go up town every night because they said they was in the way while the children were being washed and put to bed. My wife, Mrs. Arp, taught me a long time ago that a man could perform those little offices about as well as a woman, and if they are his children he ought to be willing to do it. There the poor woman sits and sews and nurses the little chaps all the day long, tieing up the cut fingers and stumped toes, and doctoring the little tooth-ache, and leg-ache, and stomach-ache, and fixen 'em something to eat, and helping 'em in a thousand little ways—while the lord of the house is chatting with his customers or sitting in his office with his feet upon a table or against the mantel-piece, and another feller just like him is doing the same thing, and they talk, and swap lies, and laugh, and carry on, and it's "ha, ha, ha," and "he, he, he," and "ho, ho, ho;" and about dark he stretches and yawns and says, "Well, I must go home; it's about my supper time," and brother Talmage wants his poor wife to be a watching at the window, and when she sees him coming she must run out and meet him 'twixt the house and the gate, and kiss him on his old smoky lips and say, "Oh, my dear, my darling, I'm so glad you have come." Well, that's all right, I reckon, if a woman ain't got nothing else to think about but fitting herself for heaven, but to my opinion a man ought to go home a little sooner than he does, and take a little more interest in things when he gets there.

Women are a heap better than men if they have half a chance. They were created better. They begin the world better in their infancy Little girls don't go round throwing rocks at birds and shooting sling-shots at the chickens and running the calves all over the lot and setting the dogs on the barn cats and breaking up pigeons' nests and all that. Never saw a boy that didn't want to shoot a gun and kill something. It's a wonder to me that these kind, tender hearted girls will have anything to do with 'em, but it seems like they will, and I reckon it's all right, but if I was a young marryin' woman I would be mighty particular about mating with a feller round town who belonged to half a dozen societies of one sort or another and was out every night. If I wanted a man all to myself I would look out for some farmer boy who would take me to the country where there ain't no clubs or Masonic lodge or Odd Fellows or Knights of Honor or Pythias or Scylla or Charybdis, or fire companies, or brass bands, or mardi gras, or pate defoi gras. I'd force him to love me whether he wanted to or not, for there wouldn't be anything to distract his attention. But then, if a girl wants to fly round and be everybody's gal, and have all sorts of a time, why then she'd better marry in town. It's all a question of having one good man to love you, or a dozen silly ones to admire. But as I ain't a woman, I suppose it's none of my business.

CHAPTER XXXVIII.

POLITICS.

POLITICS IS A HARD ROAD TO TRAVEL.

Politics are pretty hot, but no hotter than they were forty-five years ago between the Whigs and Democrats. I remember when Dr. Miller, the Demosthenes of the mountains, used to follow Judge Lumpkin on the grand rounds and whip him in everything but gettin' votes; when the democratic school boy couldent nigh kiss a whig girl, nor buck up to her with honorable intentions, party spirit run high in them days, shore. There were party lawyers and doctors, and party clients and patients. If a Democrat got sick, he was afeared a Whig doctor would pizon him, and vice voce. There were party stores and blacksmith shops and gristmills. The line was drawn tite between 'em in almost everything, and they hated one another.

I remember the great Harrison jubilee, when the Whigs of our town fixed up for a big torch-light procession and hifalutin' speechifyin', and sent down to Decatur and borrowed a cannon, and hauled it up with four yoke of oxen, and was to fire it all day to make the Democrats feel just as bad as possible, and that night it poured down rain in great sluices, and ten of the Democrat boys stole the cannon out of a back yard and dragged it off about two miles and hid it in a swamp, and the rain put out all the tracks before day. I've seen a heap of mad critters in my life and hearn tell of some, but nothin' was ever more madder than them Whig boys the next mornin'. They ripped and raved, and snorted, and cavorted, and tore 'round like wildcats and hunted everywhere, and sent off after some track dogs, but that cannon wasent found. It dident come to light until the next Democratic victory, when one dark night it went off right in the middle of the town and like to have skeered everybody to death, but nobody know'd how it got there or who fired it. Well, I tell you, them Whigs did hate powerfully to haul that gun back to Decatur, shore. Ask Luster if they dident, and some of these days, after he is elected, ask him in a confidential way who stole it. But don't you tell Dr. Jim Alexander, nor his brother Tom, for I don't know exactly how long it takes 'em to get over that sort of a thing.

It dident matter much in them days whether a man was a Methodist or a Baptist, honest or tricky; whether he was smart or sorter thickheaded, but it did matter a good deal whether he was a Whig or a Democrat. When Polk was nominated everybody was waitin' for the news, and as soon as the postmaster jerked the wrapper off the newspaper and read it out to the crowd, Nic Omberg threw up his hat and said he was the very best man they could have nominated, and then leaned over and asked the postmaster what he said his name was. Omberg was a fair sample of all of 'em. He was a good man and a devoted Democrat, and it would have been all the same to him if they had nominated Sam Patch. I don't suppose there was one in a thousand could have told the difference between Whig principles and Democratic principles. The fact is, there wasent very much—none to speak of, except the spoils of office. They were like folks are about their religion. Mighty few can tell the difference between one church and another church. Most of 'em are just what their fathers were, and that's reason enough without botherin' their brains with any other.

* * * * * * * *

If our party ever gets in office again we are going to run the political machine on merit and fitness and to suit the people everywhere. We are not going to turn a good man out just because he is a Republican. If the community he lives in are satisfied with him we will let him stay. We will make a few more offices and raise all the salaries a little, I reckon, for our people are mighty poor and powerful hungry, and have waited long. We are going to give protection to the manufacturers and free trade to the consumers. We are going to buy the farmers' corn at a dollar a bushel, and sell it to the poor for twenty-five cents. We are going to issue ten thousand millions of greenbacks so that everybody can have a hat full, and then we will build railroads to every town and open all the creeks and mackadamize all the roads, and give all soldiers and widows and orphans pensions, and have a general jubilee all over the country. I am going to set Cobe up in a phaton behind a spanking team just to see him ride and bob up serenely as it springs up and down over the bumps in the road.

I'll bet you couldn't drag Cobe into a phaton with a steam engine. He has got a little old truck wagon and won't even put a plank across the body for fear of getting sea sick, but he just sets down in the bed and goes singing along:

> Old Eve she did an apple pull,
> And then she filled her apron full;
> Old Adam he came bobbing around
> And spied the peelings on the ground.
>
> Old Noah he did build an ark,
> Of white oak splits and hickory bark;
> The animals they come in two by two,
> The elephant and the kangaroo.
>
> And then they come in three by three,
> 'Possom and coon and bumble bee;
> Old Noah kicked his old tom cat
> For not diskiverin ara rat.

And ever and anon he punches his claybank mule and says, "*Peg along, Tatum.*"

But a nice little office under the State is a good thing, and generally lasts a long time, for our people are kind and considerate and don't turn folks out for nothing. I wouldent mind having an office that was a sort of a "sine qua non," as old Major Dade called it—an office with good, fair pay and not much to do but boss. I always did like to boss. Bossing comes natural to the Anglo-Saxon. They like it. A few years ago the Rome railroad let out a contract for a thousand cords of wood to two fellers and they sub-let it in jobs to eight other fellers, and they sub-let it again to some niggers, and there was ten darkeys doing the work and ten white men bossing the job, and all of 'em made some money out of it and were happy—so that was all right all round, but I much rather play boss than darkey. Hadent you?

CHAPTER XXXIX.

Harvest Time.

The harvest has begun. The harvest sun is shining by day and the moon by night. Our Burt oats, that we sowed in March, have come in ahead of the wheat and are falling before the cradle blade. It is a charming scene. The good, old-fashioned way is not a bad way after all. I've got a reaper and shall use it in the low grounds on the wheat, but the everlasting rains this spring made too many little ruts and furrows on the upland, and the cradles are better. The machine jolts and bumps around so that Ralph could hardly keep his seat. But the oats are good. I have never seen a better upland crop. Carl and Jessie follow along in the wake of the cradlers and tie up their little bundles, and when they get tired of that they pile them into dozens, set them up into shocks and are proud of their work. What a pity it is that we can't all make play of our work. How fond the children are of trying to do grown folks' work. Carl wants a little cradle to reap with and thinks he could do it splendid, but it most kills him to take a bucket of water to the field. That sore on his foot where he snagged it on a nail hurts awful bad then, and he limps all the way to the spring and back, but he can trot to the dewberry patch or the mulberry tree as lively and gay as a colt in the meadow. Grown folks are that way, too. I've known some mighty nice girls get tired, most broke down cleaning up the house, cooking, sewing and the like, but they could wake up to the music that night and dance till the rooster crowed for morning. We can all do what we want to do, and we go at it with alacrity. It is easier to go to a picnic than it is to church. But labor and toil has a sweet reward. We will never reap if we do not sow. The harvest that is now at hand is one of the great lessons of life, for our life is like a field and our years like the acres, and our months and weeks and days and minutes are the roods and rods and yards and feet which sub-divide the whole. Some portions are well sown and tended and some are not, but a good man will make an average crop. We may fail here and there, and have our little sins and weaknesses, but at the last a man must be measured by his average crop. Character is not made or lost in a day or a week, but it takes a life and we can never write a true epitaph until this life is closed and we write it on the tomb.

But a few days ago the fields were beautifully green, and the grain bent its proud heads gracefully before the gentle breeze and seemed conscious of its life and health and consequence. It reminded me of man in his prime, moving to and fro upon the earth acquiring wealth or fame or pleasure, and all unmindful of the reaper. But soon he ripens and must fall and make way for another crop. If the proud has born fruit golden fruit, it is well, and his mission in life is accomplished; but if clogged and tangled and corrupted with cheat and cockle and smut and rust and brambles, the crop is a failure and ought to have been cut down while it was green.

I had worked hard all the morning helping Mrs. Arp take up her carpets for the summer. The hay and dust that was under had to be swept up ever so gently—yes, gently— that was the word she used—"gently, now, William; you are raising the dust and it will be all over the house. Don't be in such a hurry—gently." I got it all up after a fashion and put out of the window in the wheelbarrow, and put the carpets on the fence ready for beating, and then I took her long handled broom and swept the walls, and the ceiling, and the cornices, and behind the pictures, and then our chunk of a darkey brought water and washed up the floors, and the girls worked on the bedsteads with kerosene and turpentine and corrosive sublimate and rat poison and damnation powder, and I don't know what all, and this morning when my wife was making up her bed and lifted up the corner of the mattress she discovered one of the biggest, fattest ones you ever saw, and her heart sank down within her and she reclined on a chair in despair. I was sorry for her, I was, for the pesky varmints are her eternal horror, and if I was rich I would build her a brand new house and fill it with brand new furniture, all made of china wood or camphor wood. I care nothing about these silent perambulators myself, and it has been hinted to me on more than one occasion that it is because I am tough and old and alligatorish, which I reckon is so, though I do know some women who are no spring chickens themselves. But I do suffer from the varmints anyhow, and have my sleep broken, for sometimes I have to get up in the night and help search for them, and when found I assume a theatrical attitude and exclaim in the beautiful language of Mr. Shakspeare: "How now, ye secret, dark and midnight hags! What is it ye do?"

Well, I took Mrs. Arp down in the low land wheat this evening, where it is thick and green and tall, and I explained to her all about wheat being first in the boot and then in the milk and then in the dough, and as we walked along in a water furrow I said it reminded me of the old song of "Coming Through the Rye," that I would change it a little, and say:

> If a body meet a body coming through the wheat,
> And a body kiss a body, wouldent it be sweet.

And she smiled and said the rye of the poet was not a field but a rocky branch named Rye, and the lassie was wading through it when her lover met her on the rocks and kissed her. So that knocked all the poetry out of the situation, and I said no more on the subject. I've seen the day when that wheat field would have been as good a place for the business as a branch, and if anything, better. While we sauntered along old Bob White was whistling to his loving mate, and we talked over the days of our childhood, when we used to follow the reapers in the field and get the partridge eggs from the nests, and have a big frolic over them when they were boiled, and how we caught the young rabbits in their nest, and how everything was so fresh and bright and rosy, and now how serious and earnest everything had become. Such is life and we cannot help it, and I don't want to help it. No matter how old or how poor, there is some happiness for us all if we will find it. The trouble with most of us is we search for it too far away—away off yonder somewhere when it is right near us. Yes, within our reach, if we will only see it. "Carpe diem," says the poet—"enjoy the day." Enjoy to-day and every day as it comes and don't let old father time cheat us out of a moment.

CHAPTER XL.

THE OLD AND THE NEW.

The aristocracy of the South was, before the war, mainly an aristocracy of dominion. The control of servants or employees is naturally elevating and ennobling, much more so than the mere possession of other property. The Scriptures always mention the number of servants when speaking of a patriarch's censequence in the land. This kind of aristocracy brought with it culture and dignity of bearing. Dominion dignifies a man just as it did in the days of the centurion who said, "I say unto this man go, and he goeth, and to another come, and he cometh." Dominion is the pride of a man—dominion over something. A negro is proud if he owns a possum dog, and can make him come and go at his pleasure. A poor man is proud if he owns a horse and a cow, and some razor-back hogs. The thrifty farmer is proud if he owns some bottom land and a good horse and top buggy, and can take the lead in his country church and country politics. The big boy loves dominion over his little brother, and the father over all. But the old Anglo-Saxon stock aspires to a higher degree of mastery. They glory in owning men, and it makes but little difference whether the men are their dependents or their slaves. The glory is all the same if they have them in their power. Wealthy corporations and railroad kings and princely planters have dominion over their employees, and regulate them at their pleasure. It is not a dominion in law, but is almost absolute in fact, and there is nothing wrong or oppressive about it when it is humanely exercised. In fact, it is generally an agreeable relation between the poor laborer and the rich employer. An humble poor man, with a lot of little children coming on, loves to lean upon a generous landlord, and the landlord is proud of the poor man's homage.

The genuine Bill Arp used to say he had rather belong to Col. Johnson than be free, for he had lived on the Colonel's land for twenty years, and his wife and children have never suffered, crop or no crop; for the Colonel's wife threw away enough to support them, and they were always nigh enough to pick it up.

He was asked one day how he was going to vote, and replied: "I don't know until I ax Colonel Johnson, and I don't recon he can tell me till he sees Judge Underwood, and maybe Underwood won't know till he hears from Aleck Stephens, but who in the dickens tells little Aleck how to vote I'll be dogged if I know."

The dominion of the old aristocracy of the South was not over their own race, as it was at the North, but over another, and it was absolute both in law and fact.

Hence it naturally grew into an oligarchy of slave-owners, and the poorer whites were kept under the ban. There was a line of social caste between them, and it was widening into a gulf, for the poor white man could not compete with slave labor, any more than the farmer or mechanic can now compete with convict labor. This kind of slave aristocracy gave dignity and leisure to the rich; and Solomon says that in leisure there is wisdom; and so these men became our statesmen and jurists and law-makers, and they were shining lights in the councils of the nation; but it was an aristocracy that was exclusive, and it shut out and overshadowed the masses of the common people, like a broad spreading oak overshadows and withers the undergrowth beneath it.

But now there are only two general classes of people at the South —those who have seen better days and those who havent. The first class used to ride and drive, but most of them now take it a-foot or stay at home. Seventy-five per cent. of them are the families of old Henry Clay Whigs. Thirty-five years ago they were the patrons of high schools and colleges, and stocked the learned professions with an annual crop of high-strung graduates, who swore by Henry Clay, and Fillmore, and Stephens, and Toombs, and John Bell, and the Code of Honor. They were proud of their birth and lineage, their wealth and culture, and when party spirit ran high and fierce they banded together against the pretensions of the struggling Democracy. When I was a young man, a Whig girl deemed it an act of amiable condescension to go to a party with a Democratic boy. But the wear and tear of the war, the loss of their slaves, and a mortgage or two to lift, broke most of these old families up, though it didn't break down their family pride. They couldn't stand it like the Democrats, who lived in log cabins, and wore wool hats and copperas breeches.

I speak with freedom of the old Georgia Democracy, for I was one of them. The wealth and refinement of the State was in the main centered in that party known as the old-line Whigs. Out of 160 students in our State University, 45 years ago, 130 of them were the sons of Whigs. I felt politically lonesome in their society, and was just going over to the Whig party when I fell in love with a little Whig angel who was flying around. This hurried me up, and I was just about to go over to that party, when suddenly the party came over to me. I don't know yet whether that political somersault lifted me up or pulled the little angel down—but I do know she wouldn't have me, and at last I mated with a Democratic seraph who had either more piety or less discrimination. She took me, and she's got me yet; she surrendered, but I am the prisoner.

These grand old gentlemen of the olden time were the pioneers in all the great enterprises of their day. They sowed the seed and we are reaping the harvest. They planted the tree and we are gathering the fruit. They laid the foundations of the proud structure of our commonwealth, and we have built upon it. My good old father took $5,000 of stock in the Georgia Railroad before it was built. He kept it for twelve years without a dividend, and when financial embarrassment overtook him the stock was down at its lowest point, and he sold it to Judge Hutchins at $27 a share. There was a gloom over the family that night, but I tried to disperse it, for I told them I had just made a matrimonial arrangement with the judge's daughter, and maybe the stock matter would come out all right; and it did. I got it all back for nothing, and the judge's lovely daughter to boot, and it was the best trade I ever made in my life.

Most of these old families are poor; but they are proud. They are highly respected for their manners and their culture. They are looked upon as good stock, and thoroughbred, but withdrawn from the turf. Their daughters carry a high head and a flashing eye, stand up square on their pastern joints, and chafe under the bit. They come just as nigh living as they used to as they possibly can. They dress neatly in plain clothes, wear starched collars and corsets, and a perfumed handkerchief. They do up their hair in the fashion, take Godey's Lady's Book or somebody's Bazaar. If they are able to hire a domestic, the darkey finds out in two minutes that free niggers don't rank any higher in that family than slaves used to. The negroes who know their antecedents have the highest respect for them, and will say Mas' William or Miss Julia with the same deference as in former days. One would hardly learn from their general deportment that they cleaned up the house, made up the beds, washed the dishes, did their own sewing and gave music lessons—in fact, did most everything but wash the family clothes. They won't do that. I've known them to milk and churn, and sweep the back yard, and scour the brass, but I've never seen one of them bent over the wash-tub yet, and I hope I never will. I don't like to see any one reduced below their position, especially if they were born and raised to it. In the good old times their rich and patriarchal father lived like Abraham, and Jacob, and Job. They felt like they were running an unlimited monarchy on a limited scale. When a white child was born in the family it was ten dollars out of pocket, but a little nigger was a hundred dollars in, and got fifty dollars a year better for twenty years to come.

The economy of the old plantation was the economy of waste. Two servants to one white person was considered moderate and reasonable. In a family of eight or ten—with numerous visitors and some poor kin—there were generally a head cook and her assistant, a chambermaid, a seamstress, a maid or nurse for every daughter and a little nig for every son, whose business it was to trot around after him and hunt up mischief. Then there was the stableman and carriage driver and the gardener and the dairy woman and two little darkies to drive up the cows and keep the calves off while the milking was going on. Besides these there were generally half a dozen little chaps crawling around or picking up chips, and you could hear them bawling and squalling all the day long, as their mothers mauled them and spanked them for something or for nothing with equal ferocity.

But the good old plantation times are gone—the times when these old family servants felt an affectionate abiding interest in the family, when our good mothers nursed their sick and old helpless ones, and their good mothers waited so kindly upon their "mistis," as they called her, and took care of the little children by day and by night. Our old black mammy was mighty dear to us children, and we loved her, for she was always doing something to please us, and she screened us from many a whipping. It would seem an unnatural wonder, but nevertheless it is true, that these faithful old domestics loved their master's children better than their own, and they showed it in numberless ways without any hypocrisy. Our children frolicked with theirs, and all played together by day and hunted together by night, and it beat the Arabian Nights to go to the old darkey's cabin of a winter night and hear him tell of ghosts and witches and jack-o'-lanterns and wild cats and grave-yards, and we would listen with faith and admiration until we didn't dare look round, and wouldn't have gone back to the big house alone for a world full of gold. Bonaparte said that all men were cowards at night, but I reckon it was these old darkeys that made us so, and we have hardly recovered from it yet. When I used to go a-courting I had to pass a grave-yard in the suburbs of the little village, and it was a test of my devotion that I braved its terrors on the darkest night and set at defiance the wandering spirits that haunted my path. Mrs. Arp appreciated it then, for she would follow me to the door when I left and anxiously listen to my retiring footsteps. But now she declares she could hear me running up that hill by the grave-yard like a fast-trotting pony on a shell road.

It was a blessed privilege to the boys of that day to go along with the cotton wagons to Augusta, or to Macon or Columbus, and camp out at night and hear the trusty old wagoners tell their wonderful adventures, and it was a glorious time when they got back home again, and brought sugar and coffee and molasses, and had shoes all 'round for both white and black, and the little wooden measures in them, with the names written upon every one. They had genuine corn shuckings in those days, and corn songs that were honest, and sung with a will that beat a camp meeting chorus—and they had Christmas, too, for white folks and black folks. Little red shawls and head handkerchiefs, and jack knives, and jewsharps, and tobacco, and old-fashioned pipes were laid up for the family servants, who always managed to slip up about break of day with a whisper of "Christmasgif" before the family were fairly awake. But it's all over now—and they are gone. Like Job of old these proud old masters have all been put upon trial. They lost their noble sons in the army, and their property soon after. The extent of their afflictions no one will ever know, for the heart knoweth its own bitterness, but they have long since learned how to suffer and be strong.

I have now in mind a proud old family, living in quiet obscurity—

the children of one of Georgia's noblest governors, a statesman of national reputation. They are poor, but they are not subdued. Their children work in the field and milk the cows and chop the firewood, but they have never forgotten or dishonored their grand old ancestor from whom they sprung. I recall another one who, forty-five years ago, represented us in the National Congress—who was for many years almost a monarch in his rule over hundreds of employees, and whose draft was honored for thousands of dollars. With tottering gait and trembling fingers he now bargains for a nickel's worth of soda, but still is grand and noble in his poverty. Always cheerful, he welcomes those who visit him with the same kindness and dignity which characterized him in his better days.

I believe the day of prosperity is coming back, and the children of the present generation will yet reap an inestimable blessing from what seemed to be a great calamity.

"Hard indeed was the contest for freedom and the struggle for independence," but harder still has been the struggle of these old families to live up to the good old style with nothing hardly to live upon. Society is exacting, and then there were the long-indulged habits of elegance and ease which are hard to be broken. The young can soon learn to serve themselves, but the middle-aged and old found it no labor of love to begin life anew on an humble scale.

What a change it was to the refined and dignified housewife when the chambermaid withdrew and set up for herself, and the good old cook, who had grown fat and greasy with service, departed from the old homestead in search of freedom, and the good lady, who was well versed in the theory of cooking, had to take her first lesson in its practice. The times have wonderfully changed since then—some things for better, some for worse. The grand old aristocracy is passing away. Some of them escaped the general wreck that followed the war, and have illustrated by their energy and liberality the doctrine of the survival of the fittest—but their name is not legion. A new and hardier stock has come to the front—that class which prior to the war was under a cloud, and are now seeing their better days. The pendulum has swung to the other side. The results of the war made an opening for them and developed their energies. With no high degree of culture, they have nevertheless proved equal to the struggle up the rough hill of life, and now play an important part in running the financial machine. Their practical energy has been followed by thrift and a general recuperation of our wasted fields, and fenceless farms and decayed houses. They have proved to be our best farmers and most prosperous merchants and mechanics. They now constitute the solid men of the State, and have contributed largely to the building up of our schools and churches, our factories and railroads, and the development of our mineral resources. They are shrewd and practical and not afraid of work. The two little ragged brothers who sold peanuts in Rome in 1860 are now her leading and most wealthy merchants. Two young men who then clerked for a meagre salary are now among the merchant princes of Atlanta. These are but types of the modern self-made Southerner—a class who form the most striking contrast to the stately dignity and aristocratic repose of the grand old patriarchs and statesmen, whose beautiful homes and long lines of negro houses adorned the hills and groves of the South some thirty years ago.

But the children of the old patricians have come down some and the children of the common people have come up some and they have met upon a common plain and are now working happily together both in social and business life. Spirit and blood have united with energy and muscle, and it makes a splendid team—the best all-round team the South has ever had.

But there is one feature about the new order of things which has surprised and bewildered the most philosophical minds, and that is the disposition which this generation has to educate their daughters. In the old ante bellum times the sons were the special objects of the parents' care. They gave to both a first-class education if they could, but if either had to be neglected it was always the daughters. The female colleges were few, while the male colleges abounded all over the land, both North and South, and were thronged with the sons of wealthy and aristocratic Southerners. But now the rule is reversed, the boys are sacrificed and the girls are sent to college.

This is all very well, I reckon, and if it is not, I don't see how we are going to help it. The trouble is to find out who these college girls are going to marry. I don't suppose they will marry anybody until somebody asks them, but it's natural and very proper for man and wife to be pretty much alike, mentally and socially. They should, as it were, class together, like the cotton buyer classes his cotton, or the merchant his sugar, or the farmer his cattle, or the geologist his strata of rocks. I don't allude to property at all, for that is about the last consideration that secures real happiness in wedded life, though I wouldn't advise any poor man to marry a poor girl just because she is poor, and I hope none of these girls will ever refuse a rich man because he is rich. Money is a right good thing in a family, and no sensible girl will turn up her nose at it. Money is a social apology for lack of brains or education or graceful manners, but it's no apology for lack of honesty or good principles. Money enables a man to step up higher in the social circle than he could do without it. Hence, we see a rich man without culture ranks pretty well with a poor man with culture. Hence it is that lawyers and doctors and teachers and preachers and editors, however poor, move in the same strata with bankers and merchants, however rich. The difference is that money may be lost, but education and culture cannot be; and when an uneducated man loses his money he loses caste, and must step down and out. The value of a man's money depends, however, upon the manner in which he obtained it. Shoddy fortunes don't amount to anything. They may shine for a while in gilded coaches and splendid halls, but they will not last. If the possessor does not lose it his children will spend it, and leave the world as poor as their father came into it. A fortune gained in a year rarely sticks to anybody. Five years is not secure. But one gained by the pursuit of an honorable calling for ten, twenty or thirty years brings with it that high social position which justly entitles a man to be called one of the aristocracy. It is a great mistake for anybody to desire a fortune to come suddenly. It would embarrass him. A big pile of surplus money will make a fool of most anybody on short acquaintance. It takes a man several years to learn its best uses, and to handle it with becoming dignity. If a man never rode in a phæton behind a spanking team it takes him a good while to get used to that. He doesn't know exactly what to do with his hands or his feet, whether to lean complacently back or cautiously forward. If the vehicle crosses a sudden rise, he doesn't rise with it in graceful undulations, but humps himself awkwardly and imagines that everybody is observing his conscious embarrassment. Money-making sense is very good sense, but I know a wealthy young man without culture who was made to believe that an ostrich egg which he saw in a museum was laid by a giraffe. I know a nabob in Atlanta who subscribed for Appleton's Cyclopedia, and when they came said that he didn't know there was but one volume and refused to pay for any more. And there is another one there whom I have known since his boyhood when he plowed barefooted in a rocky field over treadsafts and dewberry vines at ten dollars a month. He now swims in shoddy luxury and lucky wealth. He took me through his new and elegant mansion. He talked gushingly about his liberry room. He showed me a beautiful piece of furniture in the dining room and when I said it was *unique* he said no it was a sideboard. When I inquired after the health of his wife he said she had a powerful bad pain in her face and the doctor said it was newralogy but he believed she had an ulster in her nose.

But what troubles me is that these girls are climbing up where there are no boys, or very few at most. Mental culture begets mental superiority, and that raises one socially and puts him or her in a higher strata. There are, I suppose, not less than ten educated girls in the South to every educated young man; but where are the boys? They are in the stores or the workshops or on the farms. It did not use to be so, but the bottom rail is now on the top. I don't know that it can be helped, for the war left our people so poor they can't send all their children off to college, and so they send the girls and put the boys to work to pay for it. The consequence will be that these girls when they go home can't find anybody good enough for them. A nice, clever, country girl graduated last year, and when she came home and asked her farmer brother to name his fine colt Bucephalus, after Alexander's famous horse, he said, "Why, I didn't know that Tom Alexander had any horse."

Well, now, you see a college girl is not going to marry a man like that—that is, not right away quick, on the first asking. She will wait a year or so at least for some chevalier Bayard or some first honor man to come along, but by and by she will get tired waiting, for he won't come, and then, in a kind of desperation, she will mate with some good, honest, hard-working youth, and educate him afterwards. Maybe this will all work out very well in the long run; for it's the mother who makes the man, and if she is smart, so will her children be. Of course it will delay and put off these early marriages, which our wives and mothers say are all wrong. I have been very intimate with a lady for thirty-five years, who was married at sweet sixteen, but she thinks it would be awful for her daughters to do likewise unless the offer was a very splendid one in all respects. I recon that was the reason why she went off so soon.

I did not marry my first love, but Mrs. Arp did—bless her heart—and she now declares I took advantage of her innocent youth and gave her no chance to make a choice among lovers. That is so, I reckon, for I was in a powerful hurry to secure the prize and pressed my suit with all diligence for fear of accidents. Once before I had loved and lost, and I thought it would have killed me, but it dident, for I never sprung from the suicide stock. I had loved a pretty little school girl amazingly. I would have climbed the Chimborazo mountains and fought a tiger for her—a small tiger. And she loved me, I know, for the evening before she left for her distant home I told her of my love and my devotion, my adoration and aspiration and admiration and all other "ations," and the palpitating lace on her bosom told me how fast her heart was beating, and I gently took her soft hand in mine and drew her head upon my manly shoulder and kissed her. Delicious feast—delightful memory. It lasted me a year, I know, and has not entirely faded yet, for it was the first time I had ever tasted the nectar on a school girl's lips. I never mention it at home—no, never—but I think of it sometimes on the sly—yes, on the sly. I never saw her any more, for she never came back. In a year or so she married another feller and was happy, and, in course of time I married Mrs. Arp, and was happy too. So it is all right and no loss on our side.

But what are the college girls going to do when they graduate and settle down in the old homestead? It will be right hard to descend from the beautiful heights of astronomy, the enchanting fields of chemistry and botany, the entertaining grottos of history and geology, and the charming chambers of music and social pleasures down to the drudgery of washing dishes, scouring brass kettles, making little breeches, and doing all sorts of household and domestic work. It will take a good strong resolution and common sense and filial respect to do it, and do it gracefully and cheerfully, and be always ready to brighten up the family hearth with her educated smile. Such girls are not only happy in themselves, but they make others happy, and that is the highest, purest and noblest of all ambitions.

Be content, then, with your lot, young ladies, and enjoy what you have got; and if you haven't got anything, then enjoy what you haven't got, and be contented still.

I know every true man wishes from his heart it was so that the dear creatures did not have to work, only when they felt like it. I never see ladies of culture and refinement doing the household drudgery but what it shocks my humanity, and I feel like Mr. Bergh ought to establish a society for the prevention of cruelty to angels. The burden of bearing children and raising them is trial enough, and involves more of the wear and tear of the sinews of life than all the men have to endure. Mothers are entitled to all the rest and indulgence that is possible, and those who have brought up eight or ten children ought to be retired on a comfortable pension from the Government. There is an old gander at my house who for four weeks stood guard by his mate as she set on her nest. She plucked the down from his breast and covered her eggs, and when she left them for food he escorted her to the grass and escorted her back with a pride and a devotion that was impressive. My respect for geese has been greatly enlarged since I made their more intimate acquaintance.

But after all there need be no serious or gloomy apprehension concerning the future of the sons and daughters of the South. If the boys cannot go to college they will gather culture by absorption and association, and acquire property by diligence and industry. Our young men have learned that it is best to remain in the land of their birth, and few emigrate to another clime; and indeed the attachments of the Southern people to their neighbors and kindred and country are stronger than those of our Northern brethren. Our society is not made up of a mixture of all races. We have a common ancestry, and have assimilated in thought and habits and customs and languages and principles. Added to this we have the influence of a genial climate, mild winters, fertility of soil, lovely sunsets, variegated scenery, with fruits and flowers abounding everywhere to sweeten and make glad the rosy days of our childhood. We have more latitude and longitude. Our homes are more spacious, and our manhood is comforted with the memories of our youth, when we roamed over the fields and forest and hunted the deer and turkey by day and the coon and 'possum by night. It is a hard struggle for our young men to emigrate from the homes of their childhood, and when they do, a resolution to return at some future day lingers with them like a sweet perfume and comforts them on their weary way.

Not so with the sons of New England, or the remote, inclement North. Their earliest training is to go—go West—go anywhere for business. They snap the cord that binds them to home and State and kindred as they would snap a thread. I do not know a people upon earth who have less emotional love or veneration for home and the local memories of childhood. I speak respectfully of the descendants of the Puritans. I speak advisedly, for I have mingled with them and know them, and have many dear relatives in the old Bay State. I had three male cousins in one family, and they were off almost as soon as they were out of their teens—one to Australia, one to California, and the other to Nevada. They are at home in every land but ours. We have been calling them kindly ever since the war. We have tendered the olive branch, and gave cordial welcome to those who did venture among us. We have sold them cotton, and sugar, and rice, and tobacco, and bought their patent medicines, and flytraps, and picture papers, and Yankee notions, and gimcracks, and go to all their circuses and monkey shows. I know we whipped them pretty bad during the late war—that is, at first and all along the middle, but at last they got the best of it, and it looks like they ought to be satisfied, and make friends. We used to think slavery was the cause of all this alienation, but slavery has been abolished 28 years. Now, the Yankee is an Anglo-Saxon, and has many admirable traits of character, some of which we have not, but need, and we have been living in the hope that he would come down and live with us, and teach us economy and contrivance, and mix up and marry with us, and give us a cross that would harmonize the sections, but he will not. The last census shows that there are 180,000 more females than males in the New England States. Before the war their educated young ladies used to venture South and teach school, and our young men and widowers married them, and they made good wives and good mothers; but they don't come now, and their young men keep going off, and the poor girls up there are in a bad fix. I have been trying to persuade some of our poor and proud young men who seem so hard to please at home, to go up there and take the pick of the lot, and bring them down here, and they say they would if the girls would send them the money to travel on.

My good father was born in Massachusetts. He came South just seventy years ago, with a cargo of brick, and never returned. Well, he couldn't return, for he was shipwrecked, and lost his cargo, and had nothing to return on. My good mother was born in Charleston, and was hurried away from there to Savannah during the yellow fever panic of 1814. She went to school to my father, and he married her. When I was old enough to understand my peculiar lineage, I wondered that I could get along with myself as well as I did. When a small chap, I used to bite myself and bump my head against the door; but my good mother always said I couldn't help it, for it was South Carolina fighting Massachusetts. It was a storm that lost my father's cargo, and caused him to settle down in Savannah. It was a fearful pestilence that hurried my mother away from Charleston when she was an orphan child. So I was the child of storm and pestilence and two belligerent States—how could I behave. But for these remarkable combinations, I reckon my father would have lived and died in the old Bay State, and my mother in Charleston; but what would have become of me? But fifty years' residence made my father a good Southern man, and the Palmetto Cross made me a high-strung rebel, and on the eve of secession, I loaded my pen with paper bullets and shot them right and left. We soon found out it would take some other sort to whip them in fight, and I joined the army, and succeeded in killing about as many of them as they of me. But we have all made friends again after a fashion, and now love one another's money with a devotion that is unaffected and supreme.

In recurring to the grand old days that are past, I sometimes feel sad because our children know so little of what the South was in the good times, say from thirty to forty years ago—nothing of the old patriarchal system—nothing of slavery as it was—nothing of those magnificent leaders and exemplars of the people, such as Clay and Calhoun and Berrien and Crawford and the Lamars and Styles.

They and their illustrious companions moulded manners and sentiment and chivalry and patriotism, and stood up above the masses like the higher heads overtop the rest in a field of golden grain. But the diffusion of knowledge is now bringing the masses up to the standard of education which these noblemen created. The field of grain is coming up to a uniform and unbroken level. The chances of men for fortune and for fame are more generally diffused and more nearly equal than they have ever been, and the rise of a man from the humblest walks of life is no longer considered a miracle.

The pendulum is always swinging. Generations play at see-saw—up to-day and down to-morrow—but still the pivot on which they play is rising higher and higher at the South. Then let us not complain about that which we cannot help, for whether we are up or down we have a goodly heritage. Let us all stand fast—stand fast by our land and our people and by the blessed memories of the past. Let patriotism begin at home by the fireside and then stretch its wide arms and take the whole nation in its embrace.

CHAPTER XLI.

THE OLD SCHOOL DAYS.

It was about the close of a bright and happy day. We were all sitting in the broad piazza and Mrs. Arp had laid aside her spectacles and was talking about the old Hog mountain that she had been reading about in Joel Harris's pretty story, "At Teague Poteets." "Why," said she, "that Hog mountain is in old Gwinnett, away up north towards Gainesville, and I went to school there when I was a child. Old Aunty Bird taught us, and she was a sweet old soul. I know she is in heaven if anybody is. I wonder if it is the same Hog mountain —but I don't remember any of the Poteets."

Good, honest, clever Tom Gordon who lives a few miles above us passed along as we were talking, and Mrs. Arp's memories took a fresh start as she remarked: "He was a good boy, Tom was. I went to school with him to Mr. Spencer, and I know his speech right now," and she rose forward, and assuming an anxious, excited countenance, she said as she stretched forth her hand, "Is the gentleman done? Is he completely done?" Mrs. Arp is mighty good on a speech, and her memory is wonderful, and so to toll her along I said, "and Charley Alden, what was his speech?" and without a moment's hesitation she took a new position and made one of those short neck bows and cleared her throat, and repeated with slow and solemn voice,

"'On Linden, when the sun was low,
All bloodless lay the untrodden snow,
And dark as winter was the flow
Of Iser rolling rapidly.'"

Then she put her other little foot forward, and brightened up as she continued:

"'But Linden saw another sight,'"

And when she got down to the thick of the fight it was thrilling to hear her and to see her heroic attitude as she screamed:

> "'Wave, Munich—all thy banners wave,
> And charge with all thy chivalry.'"

And she waved an imaginary flag all around her classic head.

We all cheered and clapped our hands, for the girls had never seen their mother in that role before.

"And poor Thad Lowe," said I, "what was his speech?"

"So from the region of the north," said she.

"And Rennely Butler," said I.

"At midnight in his guarded tent," and she gave us a whole verse of Marco Bozzaris. She likes that and we begged her to go on, and she went through that fighting verse where the Greeks came down like an avalanche, and her martial patriotism was all aglow as she said:

> "Strike for the green graves of your sires,
> Strike for your alters and your fires,
> God and your native land."

Goodness gracious, what a soldier she would have made.

It was my turn now, and so I put in on Jim Alexander's speech at my school.

> "Make way for liberty, he cried.
> Make way for liberty and died."

Jim was always a cruising around for liberty, and the speech suited him mighty well. But Tom, his brother, had a liking for the law and spoke from Daniel Webster, "Gentlemen, this is a most extraordinary case." And there was Gib Wright, the biggest boy in school, who carried his head on one side like he was fixing to be hung, and he came out on the floor with a flourish and made big demonstrations, fixing his No. 13 feet, and you would have thought he was going to speak something from Demosthenes or Ajax or Hercules or the rock of Gibralter, when suddenly he stretched forth his big long arm and said:

> "How doth the little busy bee
> Improve each shining hour."

We never thought he would get to be a big lawyer and a judge, but he did.

And General Wofford was there too, and his speech was the speech of an Indian chief to the pale faces, and most every sentence began with "brothers," and he whipped a big sassy Spaniard by the name of Del Gardo for imposing on us little boys, and then went off to fight the Mexicans for imposing on Uncle Sam, and ever since he has been fighting somebody or imposing on somebody, and I think he had rather do it than not.

And there was Jim Dunlap who used to spread himself and swell as he recited from Patrick Henry's great speech: "They tell us, sir, that we are weak, but when shall we be stronger? Will it be the next week or the next year?" and he just pawed around and shook the floor as he exclaimed, "Give me liberty, or give me death!" Jim didcnt carry as much weight before him as he carries now, but he was a whale and had a voice like a bass drum with a bull frog in it. Jim was called on during the late war to choose betwixt liberty or death, and he sorter split the difference and took neither, but he pulled through all right.

After this effort, which sorter exhausted me, Mrs. Arp recalled Melville Young's speech about "King Henry of Navarre," and Charley Norton's speech to the eagle, "Great bird of the wilderness, lonely and proud," and Charley Rowland's solemn dirge to Sir John Moore, "Not a drum was heard, not a funeral note," and then I was called on for my own speech and I had to stand up and advance forward and make a bow and say: "My name is Norval—on the Grampian hills my father fed his flocks."

I remember it took my teacher two weeks to keep me from saying "my name is Norval on the Grampian hills," and he asked me what was my name off the Grampian hills; and finally I got the idea that I must put on the brakes after I said Norval and then make a new start for the hills.

Mrs. Arp then branched off on the composition and recitations of the girls, and recited sweet little Mary Maltbie's piece on the maniac: "Stay jailer, stay and hear my woe," and Sallie Johnson's composition on "Hope."

"Hope! If it was not for hope man would die. Hope is a good invention. If it was not for hope, woman would mighty nigh give up a ship."

And that reminded me of Mack Montgomery's prize essay on money.

"Money! Money is a good invention. The world couldn't get along much without money. But folks oughtent to love money too good. They oughtent to hanker after other folkses money, for if they do its mighty apt to make 'em steal and rob. One day there was a lonesome traveler going along a lonesome road in the woods all solitary and alone by myself, without nobody at all with him, when suddenly in the twinkling of an eyeball out sprang a robber and shotten him down, and it was all for money."

Mrs. Arp's thoughts seemed away off somewhere as she tenderly repeated:

> "When I am dead no pageant train
> Shall waste their sorrows at my bier."

"That was my dear brother's speech," said she "and it all came true. He was killed at Chicamauga. The cruel bullet went in his brain and he fell with his face to the foe and there was no pagent train; no kindred; no sorrows wasted; no time for sorrow; no loving hand; no burial for a long time. Oh, it is so sad, even now, to think about the poor, dear boy. He was so good to us and we loved him."

Our school-mates are few and far between now. Death has carried most of them away and those who are left are widely scattered. How the roads of life do fork—and some take one and some another. We are all like pickets skirmishing around, and one by one get picketed off ourselves by the common foe. I had liked to have got picked off myself a day or two ago. The wagon had come from town with a few comforts and one was a barrel of flour. Mrs. Arp and the children always come to the south porch when the wagon comes, for they want to see it unloaded and feel good for a little while, and so when the hind gate was taken off and Mrs. Arp had wondered how we would get out the flour, I thought I would show her what a man could do. I rolled the barrel to me as I stood on the ground and gently eased it down on my manly knees. My opinion now is that there is a keg of lead in that barrel, for my knees gave way and I was falling backwards, and to keep the barrel from mashing me into a pancake or something else, I gave it a heave forward and let her go, and it gave me a heave backward and let me go, and I fell on a pile of rocks that were laid around a cherry tree, and they were rough and ragged and sharp, and tore my left arm all to pieces and raked it to the bone. The blood streamed through my shirt sleeve and I was about to faint, for blood always make me faint, when Mrs. Arp screamed for camphor, and the girls run for it, and before I could stop 'em they had campfire and turpentine fire poured all over my arm, and I went a dancing around like I was in a yaller jacket's nest. It liked to have killed me, shore enuf, but after while I rallied and went to bed. I havent used that arm nor a finger on that hand till now, and go about sad and droopy. But I have had a power of sympathy, and Mrs. Arp is good—mighty good. I'm most willing to tear up a leg or two by and by, for they are all so good. And now I'm in a fix—for I can't shave but one side of my face and company is coming tomorrow.

Well, I used to could let down a barrel of flour—I used to could—but rolling years will change a man—anno domini will tell. I reckon by the time I get my neck broke I will begin to realize that I'm not the man I used to be, but as Cobe says, "if I could call back 20 years I'd show 'em." The next time a barrel of flour comes to my house I will get two skids twenty-five feet long and let it roll out, see if I don't. But it's all right, and I've had a power of sympathy, and sympathy is a good thing. I would almost die for sympathy. I shall get well slowly—very slowly. But Mrs. Arp asked me this morning if I couldn't pick the raspberries for dinner with one hand—said she could swing a little basket round my neck. What a thoughtful, ingenious woman.

CHAPTER XLII.

Old School Days.

The older we grow the oftener do we reverse the telescope and look back. How distant seem the scenes of our youth. If I did not know better I would say it has been a hundred years since I was a little boy trudging along to the first school I ever attended. The old school days are a notable part of everyone's life. My wife and I frequently indulge in these memories, for we went to school together, though I was six years her senior. We tell over to the children all the funny things that happened, and discuss the frailties and the virtues of our school mates and magnify the teachers, and she tells them as how I was a smart boy and stood head in the spelling class for a month at a time, and she remembers the speeches I spoke, and with a pretended regret she says: "Children, your father was a very handsome boy, with black, glossy hair, and he had plenty of it then. The girls used to cast sheep's eyes at him then, but I didn't, for I was too young to be a sweetheart then, but he had them. Yes, he was smart and good-looking too, and he knew it. Yes, he knew it. He had a fight once at school about his sweetheart. Her name was Penelope McAlpin and another boy called her Penny-lope, just to tease your pa, and he hit him right straight and they fought like wild cats for awhile. When he was a young man and I was in my teens, he was the dressiest youth in the town and wore the tightest boots. Oh, my! I had no idea he would ever notice me, and I don't know yet what made him do it."

Well, you see, the like of that called for a response, and so I had to put in and tell what a beautiful, hazel-eyed creole she was—what long raven hair that fell over her shoulders in waving tresses, and what beautiful hands and feet, and how fawn-like she locomoted about and about, and how shy and startled she was when I began to address her, and what juicy lips that seemed pouting for a lover, and then her teeth—her pearly teeth—that were almost as pretty as those she has now. I told them how hard it was to win her until she found out I was in earnest, and then how suddenly she surrendered with tumultuous affection, and I recited with tender pathos those beautiful lines of Coleridge:

> "She wept with pity and delight,
> She blushed with love and virgin shame,
> And like the murmur of a dream
> I heard her breathe my name.
>
> She half enclosed me in her arms,
> She pressed me with a meek embrace,
> And bending back her head looked up
> And gazed upon my face."

Just then Mrs. Arp stopped sewing and gazed at me sure enough, as she said: "Was there ever such a story-teller? Why, you know I didn't do any such thing. You ought to be ashamed of yourself."

"I was just telling how Genevive did," said I, "and how Coleridge won his 'bright and beauteous bride.' She had hazel eyes, too."

Young man, you had better not try to flirt with a pair of hazle eyes. It is a waste of time and dangerous. They are less susceptible than the blue, and when once deceived do not pine away in grief, but rally for revenge and take it out in scorn. If you tackle them you had better go in to win or leave the country. And while I think of it, I'll make another remark: When you woo and win and wed, you had better keep on wooing and winning afterwards or leave the country. It takes a power of love to do them.

We little chaps used to go to school to female teachers—to Yankee school marms, who were well educated and smart. But they never taught school very long, for our widowers married them about as fast as they came. You see, our high-strung blooded girls wouldn't marry widowers, for they could always get young men to their liking, but a well-to-do widower had a fancy for a settled woman, who was raised to economy, and would be so grateful for having bettered her condition in life. Of course they did not all marry widowers, but they married, and they made good wives and good mothers, and their descendants are all over the sunny land, and have proved a splendid cross from Southern blood and Northern energy.

The first teacher I ever went to was a Yankee woman, and she had a dunce block set up in the middle of the room for the lazy scholars to sit on. The mischievous ones were made to stand on the table or in the corner with face to the wall. She never whipped us, and was a kind motherly woman. Jim Wardlaw "fit" her once and she laid him on her lap and tried to spank him, but he bit her on the knee and she screamed "mercy" and let him go.

The other day I chanced to be one of a party of assorted gentlemen and they took it by turns telling of their schoolboy frolics and adventures. One said, "while I was going to school to old Greer I picked a lot of wet mud off my shoe heels and made it into a ball and thought I would just toss it over and hit Ed. Omberg, who sat on the other side of the school room. Old Greer was on that side, too, and right between me and Ed., but I thought I could flip it over his head while he was leaning over his desk setting copies, but somehow dident flip it hard enough and it came down on old Greer's head kerflop and flattened out like a pancake. I never saw a man more astonished in my life, and I was scared mighty nigh to death. I ducked down to my book and dident dare to look up. My ducking down was what caught me, for the other boys were looking up in wonder, and they would look at old Greer and then look at me, and a pointer dog couldn't have spotted a bird any better. 'Come here,' said he. 'Come here; come here; come right along here;" and he met me half way and gave me about twenty-five that lasted and lingered for a whole week.

"Jim Jones was a stuttering boy, and chock full of mischief. Early one morning he fastened the historic pin in old Greer's split-bottom chair, and when he came in and called the roll and then took a seat in his accustomed seat, he didn't stay there long, but rose up with great alacrity. His eyes flashed fire as he gazed around the room, and he caught Jim in the same way he caught me, and seizing a long, keen, supple hickory said: 'Come up here, sir, you villainous scamp. I'll show you—come along, sir.' Jim approached trembling and slow. 'Come along, I tell you, sir.' Jim stopped and stuttered with pitiful accents: 'Ger-ger-ger-gwine to wh-wh-wh-whip me?' 'Come along, I tell you, or I'll—' 'Ger-ger-ger-gwine to wh-wh-whip me hard.' Old Greer started towards him, but Jim had lost confidence, and wheeling suddenly made tracks for the door with old Greer after him. Jim bounced over two benches to get there first, but Greer had to turn a corner around the benches, and in doing so tripped and fell broadcast and rolled over besides, and we boys just cackled. He bounced up as mad as Julius Cæsar, and said in a towering passion: 'I'll whip every boy that laughs. Now laugh again, if you dare.' And we dident dare."

Well, it is curious that most every devilish boy in every school is named Jim. The very name seems to make a boy devilish. They generally make notable men, and some of them climb very high. There is James Madison and James Monroe and Polk and Buchanan and Garfield. And Jimmy Blaine is cavorting around and thinks he ought to be president just because his name is Jim. If there is any other good reason I don't know it. And I went to school with Jim Wilson and Jim Alexander and Jim Wardlaw and Jim Linton and Jim Walker and they were a sight. There is another thing to be noted about school boys. They always call their teachers "old." They called Dr. Patterson "old Pat," and Professor McCoy "old Mack," and Professor Waddell "old Pewt," and there was old Nahum and old Beeman, and old Fouch and old Isham.

We were talking about old Isham, and one of our party said: "I went to school to him, and sometimes he would slip up on a boy as slyly as a cat upon a rat, and catch him making pictures on his slate. He would hover over him for a moment, and then pounce down upon him like a hawk upon a chicken, and catch him by the ears and shove his face down on the slate and wipe out the pictures with his nose. One day Jim Harris was up at the blackboard blundering along and making all sorts of mistakes, and old Isham got mad and, seizing him under the arms, lifted him up bodily and mopped the blackboard with him and rubbed out all his figures, and set him down again and sent him to his seat.

I went to school to old George, said another, and there was a fireplace at one end of the long room, and when it was cold weather the small fry were allowed to sit up near the fire and the big boys had to do the best they could at the other end. Tom Jackson was a big, strapping, freckle-faced boy, who was everlastingly hungry. One morning he brought a big, long sweet potato to school and so he pretended to be very cold and said "Mr. George, mayn't I go up to the fire to warm?" "Go along, sir," said George. Tom took the shovel and pretended to be punching the fire, but he was slyly opening a hole in the ashes and suddenly dropped the potato in and covered it up. Some of the little boys saw him and whispered: "Gimme some, Tom; when its done gimme some." "Hush," said Tom, "and I will." In about half an hour Tom got very cold again and asked to go up and warm. "Go along, sir," said George, "you must be very cold this morning." Tom warmed awhile and took the shovel and pulled out the potato and put it in his pocket. "Gimme some, Tom; gimme some," was whispered all around as he marched backed to his seat. "Gimme some or I'll tell."

The little boys began to snicker and point at Tom as he was peeling and blown' his "tater" behind his desk. "What are you boys making all that racket about?" said old George, as he approached them with his hickory. "We was laughing at Tom Jackson over yonder eatin' his 'tater.' He roasted it here in the fire and promised to give us some if we wouldn't tell, but he didn't." "Aha," said old George, "come up here, Tom Jackson, you sly, deceitful rascal. That is what you were so cold about. What is that sticking out of your pocket?" "A tater, sir." "Give it here, sir. I'll have you to know this school house is no cook kitchen. You are so cold I think a little warming up will do you good, sir." And he gave him about a dozen over his shoulders and lower down, and then divided the tater among the little boys.

These school boy tales would fill a book, and I wish that "Philemon Perch" would write another.

CHAPTER XLIII.

ROASTING EARS AND THE MIDNIGHT DANCE.

I once heard of a grumblin' old farmer who made a big crop of very fine corn and on being congratulated about it, said: "Well, yes; my corn is all mighty fine, but I don't know how I'll get along without some nubbins to feed the steers on."

It's a raining now every day, but it came a little too late, and we'll all have plenty of steer food this year. I reckon we will make some tolerable corn on the bottoms, and the late planting is coming out smartly. If misery loves company we can take comfort like the darkey did that Mr. Stephens told about in his speech, for poor crops are a pretty "general thing" in this naborhood.

But maybe it's all right—for we did make an abundance of wheat, and it aint too late to make a right smart cotton and git 15 cents a pound for it. A man ought to be reconciled to what he cannot help, that is unless he owes a little passel of money he can't pay and is reminded of it once a month on a postal card. That's bad, aint it? Or unless he has got a lot of sickly no account children. I tell Mrs. Arp we ought to be mighty thankful for there's nary one of the ten that's cross-eyed or knock-need or pigeon-toed or box-ankled or sway-backed or hump-shouldered or lame or blind or idiotic and the grandchildren are an improvement upon the stock, and I don't believe any of 'em will ever git to the poor-house or carry a pistol or go to the legislature and have some feller offer 'em a hundred dollars for his vote.

A sound, healthy body is a great blessing, and a fair set-off to most every kind of bad luck that can happen to a man. Mr. Beecher was right when he said the first rule to insure good health was to select good, healthy parents to be born from. My ruminations on this subject have been quite luminous of late, for I've been powerful sick. The fact is, I like to have died the other night, and all of a sudden. You see I had overworked myself a fixing up a turnip patch, and got wet besides, and didn't stop for dinner, and was sorter hungry and bilious to start on and we had roasten ears for supper and buttermilk and honey, and takin' it all together I took the green corn dance about midnight and the small of my back caved in and from then until daybreak I never sot up, nor lay down, nor stood still a minute. Doubled up and twisted and jerked around with excruciatin' pains, I cavorted all over one side of the house, for we had some Atlanta company on the other, and my groanings were worse than a foundered mule. It was just awful to behold and awfuller to experience. Spirits of turpentine, camphire, hot water, mustard plaster, mush poultice, paregoric, Jamaica ginger were all used externally and internally, but no relief. I trotted around and paced and fox-trotted and hugged the bed-post and laid down and rolled over on the floor like a hundred dollar horse, and my wife, Mrs. Arp, she trotted around too, and dosed me with this thing and that thing and had the stove fired up and hollered for hot water forty times before she got it.

"I told you not to work so hard in the hot sun," said she. "Oh, Lordy," said I.

"I asked you to change your clothes as soon as you came to the house and you didn't do it." "Oh, my country," said I.

"Don't wake up the company," she continued. "And you would eat them roasten ears for supper—did ever anybody hear of a man eating roasten ears for supper and then wash 'em down with buttermilk and honey." "Oh, my poor back," said I.

"Do you reckon it's your back—aint it further round in front?" "Oh, no," said I, "it's everywhere, it's lumbago, it's siatiker, it's Bright's disease, it's Etna and Vesuvious all mixed up. Oh, I'm so sick—can't nobody do nothin'."

"Poor fellow, poor William, I'm so sorry for you, but you will wake up the company if you don't mind—I'm doing everything I can. You've taken enough things now to kill you. I declare I don't know what to do next, and all this comes from moving to the country five miles from a drug store or a doctor. I told you how it would be—plumbags and skyatiker and a bright disease, and the Lord knows what, and I would'nt be a bit surprised if you had the yellow fever to boot—caught it a trampin' around Memphis, and it's just broke out on you. Poor man, if he does die what will become of us? But if he gets well he'll go and do the same thing over again. Don't grunt so loud. I declare you make enough noise to wake up a grave-yard.

THE GREEN CORN DANCE.

I never saw such a man. Here, try this mush poultice. I thought that water never would get hot. Does it burn you?"

"Oh, yes; it burns, but fire is nothing now, let it burn. Oh! I'm so sick. Bring me the paregoric, or the laudanum, or something, I can't stand it ten minutes longer," said I.

"There aint a drop left. You've taken it all. There's nothing left but chloroform, and I'm so afraid of that, but maybe it will relieve you, William. My poor William, how I do hate to see you suffer so, but you will never do as I tell you. Do please don't wake up the company!"

Well, I took the chloroform and went to sleep—to the happy land—all-blessed relief, and when I waked I was easier, and in due time was restored to my normal condition. In my gyrations my mind was exceedingly active. I ruminated over my past life, and could find a little comfort in what Lee Hunt wrote about some Arab who was admitted to heaven because he loved his fellow-men, that is, except some. Just so I have loved mine, that is, except some. I thought about money in comparison with health and freedom from pain, and I felt such an utter disgust for riches; it made me sick at the stomach, I would have given a house full of gold for two minutes' cessation of those internal hostilities.

Well, I kept this numerous and interesting family in a very lively state for a few long hours, and it taught me a useful lesson. I'm going to take care of myself; I am going to do everything Mrs. Arp tells me, for she has got sense—she has. She takes care of herself—not a gray hair in her head, and is as bright as the full moon; and when she gives an opinion it is an opinion. From that horrible night's experience I am more than ever satisfied she loves me as well as ever, and wouldn't swap me off for nobody. When I stand up before her and say "juror look upon the prisoner—prisoner look upon the juror," she always says "content." And then she has such a considerate regard for her "company."

CHAPTER XLIV.

Open House.

In the good old patriarchal times most every family of wealth kept what was called 'open house' and all who came were welcome. There was no need to send word you were coming for food and shelter were always ready. The generous host met his guests at the gate and called for Dick or Jack or Cæsar to come and take the horses and put them up and feed them. There is plenty of corn and fodder in the barn—plenty of big fat hams and leaf lard in the smoke house—plenty of chickens and ducks and turkeys in the back yard—plenty of preserves in the pantry—plenty of trained servants to do the work while the lady of the house entertained her guests. How proud were these family servants to show off before their visitors and make display of their accomplishments in the kitchen and the dining room and the chamber. They shared the family standing in the community and had but little sympathy for the "poor white trash" of the neighborhood.

Some of us try to keep open house yet but one can't do it like we used to. The servants are not trained and they come and go at their pleasure. Sometimes the larder gets very low and the purse looks like an elephant had trod on it. But still we do the best we can. We "welcome the coming and we speed the parting guest."—

During the last summer we had a great deal of company at our house and some of them stayed a good long time, for most of them were from a lower latitude and imagined that the yellow fever or some dread pestilence was about to invade their low country homes. And so they were easily pursuaded to protract their visit. When they had all departed I was glad, for I knew that Mrs. Arp was tired—very tired. I was glad too because the supplies were well nigh exhausted and the cook had given notice of a change of base. Our recess had just begun when I received the following appalling epistle:

SAVANNAH, GA.

My Dear Cousin William:

It is about time that we were paying you that long-promised visit. [The way he came to be our cousin was his step-father's aunt married my wife's great uncle about 40 years ago.] It is awful hot weather down here. The thermometer is away up to an 100. It makes us long for the rest and shade of some quiet, cool retreat in the mountains of North Georgia, where we can get on the broad piazza of a country home and enjoy the fresh mountain air and the cool spring water. Our children are all at home now. Our eldest son has just returned from college, and our eldest daughter is now spending her vacation, and they need a good frolic in the country—and there are, as you know, just six others of all ages and sizes and they continually talk of your springs and your branches and the fish pond that you write about so charmingly in your Sunday letters. So if you have room for us we will all be up in a few days. Our second boy has a favorite dog to whom he is much attached. If you have no objections we will bring the dog. He is well behaved and will give you no trouble. The third boy has a pair of fancy goats that are trained to work in harness, and I know your children will like to frolic with them. We will bring the goats. Our nurse will come with us. Now don't give yourselves any anxiety on our account for we are just coming to have a free and easy time and enjoy the air and the water. We will bring our fishing tackle along. YOUR LOVING COUSIN.

It was with great hesitation that I read this letter to Mrs. Arp, but she was equal to the occasion, for her hospitality never surrenders. "Well, write to them to come along," she said with a sigh. "I expect their children are tired of that hot city, and would be happy to get up here and play in the branch. Their poor mother has had a time of it just like I have—a thousand children and no negroes. Born rich and had to live hard, and will die poor I reckon. But write to them to come along and enjoy the air and the water, for there is not much else here now."

"But, my dear," said I, "there isent anything else, and I don't see how we can take them. The truth is I am plum out of money and I am ashamed to go to town and ask for any more credit. Two months ago when our company began to come we had 3 or 4 hundred chickens running around the lot, and before the company left I was buying twenty a day. It is just awful, and we can't get another cook anywhere."

"Well, it don't matter," said she, "we can't refuse them—it would be bad manners. Write to them to come along, and we will do the best we can. You can pick up something, I know; I never knew you to fail."

So under conjugal pressure I indited the following reply:

My dear Cousin: Your letter delighted us beyond expression. Our end of the line is all fixed up, and when you telegraph us that you are coming we will meet you at the depot. We have a double buggy and a farm wagon, and if they will not hold all and the baggage and livestock, the boys and the dog and the goats can walk out and peruse the country. It is only 5 miles, so come along and be happy and enjoy the air and the water. There is plenty of room now, for we shipped the last of 18 visitors yesterday. They have run us down to air and water, but there is still abundance of that and you are welcome to it. We don't care anything about your dog, but we have one here that I am afraid will eat his ears off in two minutes. Country dogs never did have much consideration for a town dog. The only trouble is about feeding your dog with palatable food, for we have no scraps left from our table now, and our dog has got to eating crawfish. This kind of food makes a dog hold on when he bites.

I think you had better bring the goats, for we would like to have a barbacue while you are here, and we are just out of goats. You needent bring your fishing tackle as we have plenty, but fish are awful scarce in our creek since the mill pond was drawn off. Couldent you bring some salt-water fish as a rarity to our children. Huckleberries are ripe now and your children will enjoy picking them. Ticks and red bugs are ripe, too, and your children will enjoy picking them about bed time. Scratching is a healthy business in the country and is the poor man's medicine. Town folks can take Cuticura and Sarsaparilla and S S S and B B B but a poor man just has to scratch —that's all.

I wouldent mention it to my wife, but it has occurred to me that as you are about to break up for a season you might just as well bring your cow along, for ours are about played out. It would do your cow good to enjoy the air and the water. And this reminds me that my wife scraped the bottom of the sugar barrel yesterday. It does take

a power of sweetning for these country berries. A hundred pounds or so from your store wouldent come amiss. I suppose your nurse wouldent mind sleeping in the potato shed. It is a good cool place to roost at night. We have no musketoes but snakes are alarmingly frequent in these parts. Carl killed a rattle snake in the garden yesterday but he had only six rattles and we think we can soon train your children to dodge them. So come along and enjoy the air and the water. It is well worth a visit up here to see the blue mountains and watch the young cyclones meander around. A cyclone came in sight of us last spring and unroofed nabor Munford's house and killed seven mules and three negro children and went on. It is a grand and inspiring sight to see a cyclone on an excursion. Our crab apples are ripe now. I read the other day a very sad account about three children dying of crab apple colic in one family. Our cook has given us notice that she will leave us next Sunday and my wife says she has tried all over the naborhood to secure another but failed. May be you had better bring up a cook with you but if you cant why then we will all try and get along on the air and the water. I can cook pretty well myself on an emergency but don't fancy it as a regular job. But the greatest trouble now is that we have nothing to cook. But come along and enjoy the air and the water.   Your cousin
                                                                 WILLIAM.

Well he dident come. The next time I saw him he said he was just a joking, and I told him I was too.

CHAPTER XLV.

The Old Tavern.

Some time ago my business called me to an old venerable town that is still a score of miles from a railroad, and consequently has not made much progress in its business or its architecture. Forty years had passed since I visited the place, and there was but little change. The same old hotel was there, one of those big old-fashioned barns that used to prevail in almost every town, and had a swinging sign-board that creaked and swayed with the wind and said, "Entertainment for Man and Beast." They used to have a plantation bell swung up on a frame close by, and a rope attached to ring the guests to fried chicken and ham and eggs and beat biscuit and bacon and greens and sausage and lye hominy and cracklin' bread. The judge and the bar rode the circuit then—not in railroads nor one at a time, but all together in buggies and gigs and sulkies. It was quite a cavalcade, and attracted wonder and awe and attention like a travelling circus. The judge's room was always the biggest and best, and every night the lawyers would gather there and talk and tell anecdotes and exchange their genial wit and humor, and it was a rare treat to a young man to be admitted to a corner and listen to them. It was a feast to me I know, and I still treasure the memory of those delightful evenings at Gainesville and Jefferson and Monroe and Watkinsville and Clarkesville, when Howell Cobb and Tom Cobb and Hillyer and Dougherty and Overby and Hutchins and Peeples and Jackson and Hull and Underwood were the luminaries of the western circuit. What a galaxy was there—all notable men in their day, and all honorable. There was no trickery in their practice, for they scorned it, and they loved to meet each other on these semi-annual ridings, and each one was expected so come laden with a new batch of anecdotes wherewith to cheer the night. Book agents were unknown; newspapers were neither numerous nor newsy, and hence it was a great comfort to the people to catch the sparks of genius as they scintilated from the lawyers and the politicians on the stump and in the forum. Stump politics were a big thing with the people. The two great parties of whigs and democrats were pretty equally divided. Sometimes one was in power and sometimes the other, and the contest went on from year to year and never ceased to create excitement. It is not so now at the South, for there is practically but one party and it takes two to get up a fight.

But this venerable town had memories and its moss covered hotel with its steep stairs and narrow passages carried me back to those good old primitive times, and I felt like painting a head board and nailing it up somewhere with the inscription "Sacred to the memory of"———

A friend said that it was a pity the old house would not catch fire and burn up. But no. I wouldent have it so. Let it stand if it will stand. It will never rot for the timbers are all heart and hewed and honest. I felt like taking off my hat to it and saying

>Good friend, let's spare that barn,
>   Touch not its mossy roof—
>Its walls heard many a yarn
>   In its historic youth.
>
>Under the weight of years
>   Its back has crooked grown;
>Look at the creaking doors,
>   See how the stairs are worn.
>
>Oft in each hall and room,
>   Lye-soap and sand were thrown,
>And many a home-made broom
>   And many a shuck have gone.
>
>Full many a chick was killed,
>   And died without a tear,
>And many a guest was filled
>   With comfort and good cheer.
>
>No, no; let's keep the inn,
>   Though it has lost the sign—
>Keep it for what it's been—
>   Keep it for auld lang syne.

A good old matron is keeping it now, and her table abounds in generous old-fashioned fare.

The other day Judge Milner and Col. McCamy and I were lamenting that Judge Underwood, the last of that splendid galaxy of lawyers had passed over the river, and we exchanged many delightful recollections of him, for he was a genial gentleman, and his presence always brought sunshine. He was a notable man—notable as a judge, as a lawyer, as congressman, and as a wit. We recall the famous Calhoun convention, when Judge Wright and General Young and General Wofford and Lewis Tumlin and some others were candidates for the nomination to congress, and no man had enough votes to elect, and all were stubborn, and the balloting went on all day and part of the night, and the delegates were getting mad and furious and were about to break up in a row, and Judge Underwood, who was not a candidate, volunteered to make a conciliatory, harmonizing speech, and he did it in such a delightful affectionate manner, and praised up all the candidates in such eloquent tributes that when he closed one man got up and waved his hat and moved for three cheers to Judge Underwood, and they were given with wild enthusiasm, and right on top of it another delegate moved that he be nominated for congress by acclamation, and he was. Never was there such a surprise to everybody except to the judge, though he always denied that it was a preconcerted scheme.

"Oh, rare Judge Underwood! Colonel McCamy remarked that the judge did not have a very high regard for that picture of justice which makes her blindfolded and holding the scales equally balanced in her hand. So far as crime was concerned he claimed the right to see, and he did see the criminal with open, unfriendly eyes, and he sought to convict him and gave the solicitor general so much aid and co-operation that the lawyers used to say the judge and the solicitor were in partnership. His charge to the jury in a criminal case was always fair and strictly legal, for he was a great lawyer; but woe be unto the lawyer who asked for more than he was entitled to. On one occasion a big rough, malicious, young man was indicted for striking a smaller youth with a brickbat and inflicting a terrible wound. The small boy had been imposed upon by him, and seizing a stick he struck him and ran. Bill Glenn was defending the young man who used the brick, and after the judge had given a very fair charge to the jury, he said: "Now, gentlemen, if I have omitted anything that you think should be given in the charge, I will be glad to be reminded of it." Bill Glenn rose forward and said, "I believe your honor omitted to charge the jury that a man may strike another in self-defense."

"Yes, gentlemen of the jury," said the judge, with great sarcasm, "Yes, there is such a provision in the law, and if you believe from the evidence that this great big, double-jointed, long-armed, big-fisted young gentleman was running after that puny, pale-faced boy with that brickbat, and because he couldent catch him threw it at him with all his force, and struck him on the back of the head and knocked him senseless, and that he did all this in self-defense, then you can find the defendant not guilty. Is there anything else, Brother Glenn?"

"Nothing, I believe, sir. Your honor has covered the ground," said Glenn, biting his lips.

"I was always afraid," said McCamy, "to ask the judge to charge anything more than he chose to—especially in a criminal case."

CHAPTER XLVI.

The Old-Time Darkeys.

A merchant or a lawyer or any outsider who never farmed any has got an idea that farming is a mighty simple, and easy, and innocent sort of business. They think there is nothing to do but plow and hoe and gather the crop, and there is no worry or complication about it, except you can't get a rain every time you want it, and the crop is short in consequence. I had pretty much that sort of a notion myself, but I know better now. I've been farming for five years, and I like it better and better; I like the freedom of it, its latitude and longitude and its variety; but there is a power of little worries, and not a few big ones, that a man has to encounter and provide for that these outsiders never dreamed of. When a man is running hired labor it takes about half his time to watch 'em and keep 'em from wasting things, and losing things, and doing things wrong. I went down in the field yesterday and stumbled on the monkey-wrench in the grass by the turn row, and it had been there for a month, and I had hunted for it all over the premises, and nobody could tell anything about it; but now the darkey "members takin' it down dar to screw up de taps on de cultivator." Not long ago I found the hatchet in the edge of the bushes where one of the boys had cut poles to lay off by. I can pick up scooters and dull plows all about the farm, in the corners of the panels and on the stumps where they put 'em when they changed 'em. My log chain is missing now, and the little crow-bar and one of the hammers, for sometimes I have to leave home for a few days, and although these niggers and my yearlin' boys do their level best to surprise me with doin' a power of work while I was gone, they don't notice little things; they lose at the bung-hole while stopping up the spigot, or vice varcy, as the saying is. They bore the auger bit against a nail, or dull the saw in the same way, and let the old cow get into the orchard, or the hogs into the tater patch. I've got good workin' boys and right industrious darkeys, but it takes a man with a head on and his eyes

HOW THE CYCLONE DONE HIM.

well open to keep up with 'em and watch out for little things—little damages that aggravate a man and keep him in a fret, that is if he is but human and can't help fretting when things go wrong. A nabor borrowed my brace and bit, and the bit came back with one corner off; another one borrowed my cross-cut saw, and it came back awful dull, and will cost me a new file. They don't like it if I don't lend them my mower to cut their clover, though they never have cleaned up the rocks in their field.

A darkey will work a mule sometimes for two hours with the hames out of the collar and never see it, and he thinks it mighty hard if you won't lend him a mule to ride to meetin' of a Sunday. But I won't do that. They beg me out of a heap of things but they shan't ride my stock of Sundays, for I hate to do it myself, and when a darkey gets on a mule and out of sight he is like a beggar on horseback, he'll ride him and run him as long as he can stand up. I like the darkeys, I do, but I haven't got much hope of 'em ever being anything but the same old careless, contented, thoughtless creatures they always were. I've got one who took a notion he would lay up half of his wages in spite of himself, and he told me to put it in the contract that I wasn't to pay him but five dollars a month and keep the other half till the end of the year. And now he tries to beg me out of the other five at the end of every month, but I won't pay it, and he goes off satisfied. Nabor Freeman came home the other day and found his nigger tenants right smart behind with their crops, and they had all been off to a three days meeting and an excursion besides, and so he got mad and hauled up Bob, and says he: "Bob, what in the dickens are you all goin' to so much meetin' for? What is the matter, is the devil after you with a sharp stick, and a bug on the end of it?"

"Well now, Boss," says Bob, "I'll tell you how it is. We niggers have been seein' for a long time dat you white folks done got dis world, and so we is gwine to meetin' and fixin' up to get de next one as soon as we git dar; dat's all;" and Bob stretched his mouth and showed his pearly teeth, and laughed loud at his own wit.

I love to hear these old time good natured darkeys talk. John Thomas was in the ragged edge of a cyclone the other day, and said I, "John what did you darkeys do when the cyclone struck you?" "Good gracious, boss, I tell you—dem niggers just frow themselves down on de groun', sir, and holler "Oh, Lordy—good Lord hab mercy on a poor nigger. Nebber be a bad nigger any more, oh Lordy, good Lordy"—and de old slycoon pay no tention at all, but jes' lif 'em up and twis 'em all roun and roun and toss 'em ober de fence into de red mud hole, and Gim, my soul I wish you could hab seen Gim, for as he was gwine ober de fence he struck a postis that was stickin up, and he gethered it wid both arms and held on and hollerd wus than eber, "Oh, Lordy—oh my good Lord. Bless de Lord, hab mercy on a poor nigger;" and about that time the old slycoon twis he tail aroun and lif Gim's feet way up over he's head and his holt broke and he bounced off on the groun and den took another bounce off on the groun and den took anoder bounce into the mud hold, and dar de consarn lef him.

Atter de slycoon gone clean away I run up to Gim, and says I, "Gim, is you dead or no." Gim lyin dar in de mud hole wid nuffin but his head out. Gim neber spoke nary word, and his eyes was swelled like a dead steer, and says I agin, "I say Gim, is you done gone clean dead," for you see I thought if Gim dead no use in my wading in de mud after him, and Gim he grunt and wall one eye at me and whisper "wha is he." "Whar's who," said I. "De debbil," said he. "Done gone," said I—"gon clean away." "Git up trom dar—git up, I say." Gim gib a groan and say, "I can't, I'm done dead." "Git up I tell you," said I, but Gim neber move.

Bymeby I frow up my hands and look down de big road and say, *"my good Lord Almighty, ef dat old slycoon aint a comin right back here."* Neber see a nigger come to life like Gim. He bounced outen dat mud hole and start off up de road a runnin' and hollerin' for a quarter of a mile. White folks come along and stop him and look all ober him and nebber find a scratch. When he got back we was all cuttin' away de timbers from offen de mules, and it was a half an hour before we could git Gim to strike ary lick. Tell you what boss, we was all mighty bad skeered, but I neber see a nigger as onready for judgment as dat same nigger, Gim. When de old debil do git him he raise a rumpus down in dem settlements, shore."

"Dident the cyclone take of the roof of your cabin, John?"

"Of course he did, boss. He take de roof off along eberywhere he go. Look like ebery house he come to he dip down and say take your hat off, don't you see me comin', and aint you got no manners, and zip he strike 'em and take it off hisself. He take de roof offen de colored school and offen de white school all de same. He no respekter of pussons, bless God. Tell you, boss, what I tink about dis old slycoon, I tink he nuffin but de old debil on a scursion, yah, yah, yah," and John cackled at his own ideas.

Bob came over last Sunday to see us. He used to be a tenant of mine, and we liked him because he had a big mouth and was always happy. He was a good worker and not afraid of the weather, but he was careless and left his tools most anywhere and barked my young apple trees when plowing the orchard. I loaned him a new shovel to work the road and he lost it, but I couldn't stay mad with Bob long at a time. We never supposed that he could get mad enough to have a fight with anybody, but he was not on good terms with a neighboring darkey, and so one Saturday when they both came from town and had taken a drink or two of red eye they undertook to settle the old feud and Bob killed him. It was a willing fight and a bad case all round and Bob got two years and would have got ten but for his good character, all his previous life. He has served out his term, and honestly feels that he has paid the debt, if he ever owed it.

"How did they treat you, Bob?"

"Well, sir, dey treat me purty well, purty well; I can't complain. No, sir, I can't complain. For de fust six mont I didn't like it very well, for, you see, me and de gyards hadn't got 'quainted. Bimeby, when we all got 'quainted, dey took a liken to me and tell de capen to take off my shackles, and he take 'em off. De best way is to make friens wid de gyard fust, jes like when a man wants to make a frien of another man he muches up de chillun fust, and dat gits de old man and de old 'oman, too. Den de next bes way is ter pervide by de laws as nigh as you kin. De capen tell us dat de fust day—sez he, boys, you must pervide by de laws. Den he tell us de laws. Dere wasent but three or four of 'em, and I lissen wid both years wide open, and I say to myself, Bob Smith, you mus pervide by de laws, and shore enuf I did, and atter we git 'quainted like, we gits sorter intimat and I never had any trouble. Dey like me so well dey shorten my term three months and three days, and when I cum away de capen say 'Bob, I am sorry to see you go—can't you finish out your visit?' And I say 'capen, I likes you mighty well, but dis is de longest visit I eber made anybody in my life, and if we ever meet again, you will have to come to my house.'

"Did they work you very hard, Bob?"

"No, sir, not overly hard—got to do a full day's work, though, and dey knows prezactly what dat is. Can't fool 'em, and can't play sick unless you is sick, and hardly den. I neber lose but four days in all my time. Heap times I thought I was sick, and if I had been home I would have laid up shore, but dey said I wasent, and dey looked like dey knowed and I didn't know and so I went to work, and shore enuf I was all right agin by dinner. Colonel Towers he come along every week or so and look roun, and he ax me if I had any complaint, and I say 'no, sir, sepen I would like some poun cake,' and he say he forgot to bring it. I tell you what, Boss, de very best thing for a man to do when he gets dar is not to go dar —not to do nuffin to go dar for, and den when he gets dar de nex bes thing is to pervide by de laws. Dere is some folks in dar jes as mean an no count as folks outen dar. Dere is mean niggers and mean white folks everywhere you go. Some folks cum in de worl mean and dey stays mean all de time; but I say dis, dat if a man, when he goes dar, will haive hissef and pervide by de laws he kin git along and hav a tolable easy time.

"De last six mont I stay dar I dident have to work any. Dey made me a trusty and I have charge of de dogs—de track dogs— and when de niggers get away de boss he holler for Bob mighty quick. We had two track dogs; one of 'em was a big, long-eared houn dog— could track mighty fast—de oder was a small dog, sorter like a fice, but he mighty shore on de scent of a run-away. One mornin' about daybreak de boss holler, 'Git up, Bob, git up quick, bring de dogs, two niggers got away.' So I brings de dogs and we put 'em on de track, and away dey went cross an old field and into de woods and was barkin' every step. I throws de saddles on de mules in a hurry, and I got on one and de boss on toder and away we went after de dogs. De run-aways dident have more'n half an hour start and de track was powerful warm. And so de dogs run and de niggers run and we run, and bimeby after we gone about four miles we hear de old houn change his tune like he treed sumfin, and de boss say, 'Bob, old Sheriff have got 'em.' And shore enuf when we got dar de run- aways was up in a white oak tree a settin on a limb, and de old houn dog was a settin on de groun wid his head up a lookin' at 'em and a barkin', and every time he open his mouf he say, 'Too-ooo of 'em, too-ooo of 'em, too-ooo of 'em.' And de little dog was a settin' back on his tail and he say, 'dats a fak, dats a fak, dats a fak.' Yah, yah, yah. Boss make dem niggers come down from dar quick and march 'em back to de stockade and give 'em forty lashes apiece, cos you see dey dident pervide by de laws."

Bob asked me one day if a man's soul could be split in two. "What do you mean," said I, "What kind of a fool question is that?" Bob spread his big mouth and said: "My boss was tryin' to devil me one day 'bout gwine to meetin' so much and he say: 'Bob, don't you know dat a nigger ain't got no soul?' And den I ax him if a white man got a soul, and he say, 'of corse he had.' And den I say, ''Sposin' a colored man is a mellater and is jes half and half, how's dat?" He study awhile and say he 'low a mellater have jes half a soul. And den I say, 'Look a here, Boss, what kind of a thing is dat, dat half of a soul? Can you split a soul in two?' He turn off and laugh and say, 'Damfino,' and I tell him I's gwine to ax you about it." And Bob showed his pearly teeth and laughed tumultuously.

When the prohibition election came off in our county the negroes were generally on the side of whiskey, more whiskey and better whiskey, but Bob came up as a temperance darkey and made a speech to the darkeys of his church. A whiskey man in the crowd interrupted him and said, "Sho as you are bornd, Bob Smith, effen you vote whiskey outen Cartersville de grass will grow waist high in dem streets." "'Sposin it do?" said Bob, "'Sposin' it do? Den we'll raise more hay and less hell, and dats what's de matter wid Hannah. Yah! Yah!"

CHAPTER XLVII.

OWLS, SNAKES AND WHANG-DOODLES.

Most every night about half-past eight,
A screech owl mourneth at the outside gate.

The sweet little katydids sing all the day long. Earlier in the season they were happy only at night, but now the woods are full of their music by day. It is not a song from the mouth, but they rub the bars of their wings together and puff out their bodies for sounding boards, and if a man could sing as loud in proportion to size, I suppose he could be heard across the Atlantic ocean, and his voice would make an earthquake and shake down the stars, and so that wouldn't do at all, and he wasn't made that way. But these little screech owls are a nuisance, and are enough to make a nervous woman have fits or hysterics or something. I shot one on the gate post one night while he was complaining about something we had done to him, but another one came back and set up his mournful wails. I wonder what makes 'em stay away off in the woods all day and come screeching around the house at night like they wanted to haunt us. There is some excuse for superstition about owls, for they love darkness rather than light, and the ancient philosophers said they were the sentinels and forerunners of evil spirits, and the scriptures classed 'em with demons and all sorts of trouble and misery. The Prophet Isaiah cursed Babylon and said the owl should dwell there, and satyrs should dance there. And then they look so wise out of their big eyes and twist their heads 'round and 'round watching you, and you can't scare 'em nor tame 'em. Well, they were made for something; but I don't know what it is, and I have frequently thought that when the flood covered the earth it was a mighty good time for Father Noah to have left out of the ark all such disagreeable varmints as owls, and snakes, and whang-doodles that mourn for their first born.

Gen. Black told me that if I wanted to get rid of screech owls to put the shovel in the fire when one of 'em was a screechin' and he would leave forthwith. The general said the fire contracted with the oxide in the iron and deluminated an odoriferous that was disagreeable to the delicate oil factories of the bird. Jesso! Well, I tried it, and he dident leave worth a cent.

That screech owl is sitting on the gate-post singing a funeral dirge. It's a bird of bad omen, and I would shoot him, but my wife says an old African witch told her grandmother there would be a death in the family if you killed one of 'em, shore. It always seemed to me that in the fitness of things they belonged to a graveyard or a haunted house or a dismal swamp or a country meetin' house that the hogs slept under and nobody preached in. I don't like 'em, especially at this juncture of home concerns, for my wife saw the last new moon through a bushy tree-top right over her left shoulder, which she dident mean to do by no means. Things don't move on serenely, and the old horse-shoe over the kitchen door has lost its influence. I havent seen a pin on the floor that dident pint away from me, and the other day a rabbit run across the road right before me, and soon after I come to a snake track, which they say is mighty bad if you don't rub it out with your face towards the snake, but I couldn't tell whether the snake that made the track was going north or coming back, and so had to rub out by guess, and now while I'm a-writin' Mrs. Arp has got a hummin' in her right ear, and she says it sounds like an Eolean harp, or a musketer away off, and that's another funeral sign—and last night a black pet chicken came in the family room while we was at supper, and went to roost on top of a picture that hung over the clock on the mantel-piece, and nobody knowd it until we had put the light out and went to bed, when it chuckled a little and Mrs. Arp chuckled a good deal until I struck a light, and now she says Mr. Poe had a raven that done the same thing and he died soon after.

The weather is sad. It mists and weeps and stays cloudy all the time, and that makes everybody gloomy. There hasent been a dry day in three weeks that we can plow. The grass grows as fast as the cotton and the seed will scatter all over the open bolls and the cotton-buyers will dock us a cent for trash. Things are not working right for us farmers, but we can't help it. The flies take shelter in the house and so do the bugs and the grand-daddies and the bats.

Here, William, quick, I say—here's a grand-daddy on me; don't you see; why don't you take him off. Lord a mercy, did I ever see a man as slow as your are. Do please take the thing off."

Well, you see it takes a long time to find the thing, and when you do he's a crawlin' on the floor a gettin away as fast as he can, and she declares that's another one and I have to hunt all over her for five minutes.

"There's one of those contemptible bats in here again. Get the broom, William, I wouldn't have it to get on me for a thousand dollars. Mercy on me! I do believe the house will be run over with vermin. Don't break the bureau glass. Why don't you stand on the table? Why, you don't come in a yard of him! It does seem to me if I was a man I could knock a bat down."

"He has gone out," said I, meekly.

"How do you know—did you see him? Bet anything its on my bed somewhere. Move the pillows and bolster. I'll dream about the thing all night."

It looks like I'll perish to death for want of some good warm vittels. I'm juicin' away. You see when Mrs. Arp was a cookin' the other day in the basement an innocent chicken-snake crawled out from behind the meal-chest. Such a scream was never heard since the Injuns scalped my great uncle. I run for my life and was pickin' her up in my arms when she rallied and said, "kill the snake first;" and I killed it. He was a lovely snake—all speckled with dark green and white and had just swallowed a mouse. But, alas! the kitchen is purty much deserted and all regular cooking abandoned. When they cook now I have to take a gun and stand guard. I march forrerds and backwards like a sentinel. I've had to move the meal tub and the stove wood, and everything else fourteen times, for she declares its got a mate, and the mate is there somewhere. "Maybe its a bachelor snake," said I.

"Oh, of course, you don't believe there's another snake in the wide world—and I've found out you killed one last week under the hearth and you told the children not to let me know anything about it; didn't you?"

"It was a very little one," said I, "and I dident want you troubled about it."

"Yes, I suppose it was a little one, but snakes are snakes, and where there's little ones there's big ones. I do believe the whole plantation is haunted with 'em, and everywhere else, for I can't take up a newspaper without seeing where somebody was bitten."

"Men and boys," says I; "I havent seen any mention of a woman being bitten nowhere—fact is, I don't believe they bite females. You know that old mother Eve was mighty friendly with 'em."

"Yes, that's always the way—you turn everything into ridicule. Well, you may hire a cook; I'm not going to risk my life nor the children's in this old haunted kitchen."

But I think she is getting over it, and with a little encouragement things will resume their natural condition in a few days. The greatest trouble I have in this connection is Freeman—my nabor Freeman. I reckon he don't mean any harm by it; but just as soon as my wife, Mrs. Arp, told him about the snake, he up and told her about killin one over in his field as long as a fence rail, and how it had its den in a rock pile, and would run out after him and the niggers, and then retreat; and they were all fightin' and runnin' and runnin' and fightin for two hours, until they wore him out; and he brung down the rattles of a rattlesnake and rattled 'em around, and told about finding a spring lizzard in the water pail, and had like to have swallered him alive in the gourd. And now my wife, Mrs. Arp, won't drink out of anything but a glass goblet; and when she walks out in the front yard she has one eye for flowers and the other for snakes and lizzards, and shakes her clothes tremendious when she comes back. I wish that one would bite Freeman.

CHAPTER XLVIII.

THE AUTUMN LEAVES.

The earliest fires of the fall
  Have brightened up the room,
The cat and dog and children all
  Have bid old winter come.
The wind is running at the nose,
  The clouds are in a shiver;
By day we want more warmer clothes,
  At night we want more kiver.

When a farmer has laid by his crop and the seasons have been kind and the corn and cotton are maturing, and the sweet potato vines have covered the ground, what an innocent luxury it is to set in the piazza in the shade of evening with one's feet on the banisters, and contemplate the beauty and bounty of nature and the hopeful prospect of another year's support. It looks like that even an Ishmaelite might then feel calm and serene, and if he is still ungrateful for his abundant blessings he is worse than a heathen, and ought to be run out of a Christian's country. Every year brings toil and trouble and apprehension, but there always comes along rest and peace and the ripe fruits of one's labors.

Persimmons and 'possums are getting ripe. The May-pops have dropped from the vines. Chestnuts and chinkapins are opening, and walnuts are covering the ground. Crawfish and frogs have gone into winter quarters—snakes and lizzards have bid us adieu. All nature is preparing for a winter's sleep—sleep for the trees, and grass and flowers. I like winter; not six long months of snow and ice and howling winds, but three months interspersed with sunny days and Indian summers. The Sunny South is the place for me, the region of mild and temperate climate, of lofty mountains and beautiful valleys, and fast-flowing streams. The region where the simoon nor the hurricane ever comes, and the streams do not become stagnant, nor the mosquito to sing his little song. I don't want to be snow-bound in winter, nor to fly from a fiery hurricane in summer; and it's curious to me that our Northern brethren don't bid farewell, a long farewell, to such a country and settle down in this pleasant land.

> "The cricket chirrups on the hearth
> The crackling fagot flies."

The air is cool and lively. The family have peartined up, and everything is lovely around the farmer's comfortable fire. How invigorating is the first chilling breeze of coming winter. The hungry horses nicker for their corn; the cattle follow you around; the pesky pigs squeal at your feet, and this dependence of the brutes upon us for their daily food makes a man feel his consequence as he struts among them like a little king. The love of dominion is very natural. It provokes a kindliness of heart, and if a man hasn't got anything else to lord it over it's some comfort to love and holler at his dog. I've seen the day when I strutted around among my darkies like a patriarch. I felt like I was running an unlimited monarchy on a limited scale. And Mrs. Arp felt that way too. Sometimes in my dreams I still hear the music of her familiar call, "Becky, why don't you come along with that coal-hod?" "I'se a comin', mam." "Rosanna, what in the world are you doing; havent you found that needle yet?" "I'se most found it, mam." Poor thing; patient and proud, she hunts her own needles now, and the coal-hod falls to me.

But we still live, thank the good Lord, and are worrying through the checkered life as gracefully as possible. What's the use of brooding over trouble when you can't help it? Sometimes, when a rainy day comes and all out-doors is wet and sloppy, and the dogs track mud in the piazza, and the children have to be penned up in the house, and everything is gloomy, we get sad and look on the dark side, and long for things we havent got. When the little chaps play hide and seek till they get tired, and shove the chairs around for cars and engines, and look at all the pictures, and cut up all the newspapers, and turn summersets on their little bed, and then get restless and whine around for freedom, Mrs. Arp opens her school and stands 'em up by the buro to say their lessons.

"Now, Carl, let me see if you can say your psalm. Put your hands down and hold up your head."

"The Lord is my shepherd. I shall not want. He—he—he—"

"Let that fly alone, and put your hands down. He maketh me to lie down—"

"He maketh me to lie down in green pastures. He, he."

"Quit pulling at that curtain. He leadeth me—"

"He leadeth me. La, mamma, yonder comes a covered wagon. I speck it's got apples."

"Carl, stand away from that window. If I take a switch to you I"ll make you look after apple wagons. He leadeth me."

"He leadeth me—in the house of the Lord forever."

"Bless my soul, if he hasn't skipped over to the very end. Where are you going now?"

"Mamma, I want a drink of water—mamma, please give me and Jessie an apple."

"No, sir, you shan't smell of an apple. Every time I try to teach you something you want water, or an apple, or go to catching flies. I wish I had that switch that's up on the clock."

"I'll get it for you," said I.

"No you needent, either. Just go on with your writing. I wish you would let me manage the children. All the learning they ever get I have to ding dong it into 'em. When I want the switch I can get it. Here, Jessie, come and say your verses."

And Jessie goes through with "Let dogs delight" like a daisy.

Oh, she's smart as a steel trap—just like her mother. I wish you could see Mrs. Arp's smile when some other woman comes along and norates the smart sayings of her juvenile.

"Aint it strange," says she to me, "how blinded most mothers are about their children. Mrs. Trotter thinks her Julia a world's wonder, but Jessie says things every day a heap smarter, and I never thought anything about it."

"Jesso," says I; "children are shore to be smart when they have a smart mother. Their meanness all comes from the old man."

But the rainy days don't last forever. Sunshine follows cloud and storm and darkness. In the journey of life the mountains loom up before us, and they look high and steep and rugged, but somehow they always disappear just before we get to them, and then we can look back and feel ashamed that we borrowed so much trouble and had so much anxiety for nothing. What a great pile of miserable fears we build up every day. It's good for a man to ruminate over it and resolve to have more faith in providence, and I am ruminating now, for I went to town to-day to attend a little court that had my tenant's cotton money all tangled up by the lawyers, and I never expected to get my share, but I did and I feel happy. Mrs. Arp had told the children she would like to go and do some shopping for them but she knew that I was so poor and they would have to do without.

So when I came home and found her stitching away with a sad expression on her countenance, I pulled out the 22 dollars of cotton money, and assuming a pathetic attitude exclaimed:

"Turn, Angelina, ever dear,
My charmer, turn to see
Thine own, thy long-lost William here,
Restored to Heaven and thee."

And I laid the shining silver in her lap. In about two minutes everything was calm and serene, and we had music that night and Mrs. Arp played on the piano and sang some of the songs of her girlhood. It's most astounding what a little money can do.

CHAPTER XLIX.

Uncle Tom Barker.

Uncle Tom Barker was much of a man. He had been wild and reckless, and feared not God nor regarded man, but one day at a camp-meeting, while Bishop Gaston was shaking up the sinners and scorching them over the infernal pit, Tom got alarmed, and before the meeting was over he professed religion and became a zealous, outspoken convert, and declared his intention of going forth into the world and preaching the gospel. He was terribly in earnest, for he said he had lost a power of time and must make it up. Tom was a rough talker, but he was a good one, and knew right smart of "scripter," and a good many of the old-fashioned hymns by heart. The conference thought he was a pretty good fellow to send out into the border country among the settlers, and so Tom straddled his old flea-bitten gray, and in due time was circuit riding in North Mississippi.

In course of time Tom acquired notoriety, and from his strong language and stronger gestures, and his muscular eloquence, they called him old "Sledge Hammer," and after awhile, "Old Sledge," for short. Away down in one corner of his territory there was a blacksmith shop and a wagon shop and a whisky shop and a post-office at Bill Jones's crossroads; and Bill kept all of them, and was known far and wide as "Devil Bill Jones," so as to distinguish him from 'Squire Bill the magistrate. Devil Bill had sworn that no preacher should ever toot a horn or sing a hymn in the settlement, and if any of the cussed hypocrites ever dared to stop at the crossroads, he'd make him dance a hornpipe and sing a hymn, and whip him besides. And Bill Jones meant just what he said, for he had a mortal hate for the men of God. It was reasonably supposed that Bill could and would do what he said, for his trade at the anvil had made him strong, and everybody knew that he had as much brute courage as was necessary. And so Uncle Tom was advised to take roundance and never tackle the crossroads. He accepted this for a time, and left the people to

I SEE TOM BARKER RISIN' OF THE HILL.

the bad influence of Devil Bill; but it seemed to him he was not doing the Lord's will, and whenever he thought of the women and children living in darkness and growing up in infidelity, he would groan.

One night he prayed over it with great earnestness, and vowed to do the Lord's will if the Lord would give him light, and it seemed to him as he rose from his knees that there was no longer any doubt—he must go. Uncle Tom never dallied about anything when his mind was made up. He went right at it like killing snakes; and so next morning as a "nabor" passed on his way to Bill's shop, Uncle Tom said:

"My friend, will you please carry a message to Bill Jones for me? Do you tell him that if the Lord is willin', I will be at the crossroads to preach next Saturday at eleven o'clock, and I am shore the Lord is willin'. Tell him to please 'norate' it in the settlement about, and ax the women and children to come. Tell Bill Jones I will stay at his house, God willin', and I'm shore he's willin' and I'll preach Sunday, too, if things git along harmonious."

When Bill Jones got the message he was amazed, astounded, and his indignation knew no bounds. He raved and cursed at the "onsult," as he called it—the "onsulting message of 'Old Sledge'"—and he swore that he would hunt him up, and whip him, for he knowed that he wouldn't dare to come to the crossroads.

But the "nabors" whispered it around that "Old Sledge" would come, for he was never known to make an appointment and break it; and there was an old horse-thief who used to run with Murrel's gang, who said he used to know Tom Barker when he was a sinner and had seen him fight, and he was much of a man.

So it spread like wild-fire that "Old Sledge" was coming, and Devil Bill was "gwine" to whip him and make him dance and sing a "hime," and treat to a gallon of peach brandy besides.

Devil Bill had his enemies, of course, for he was a hard man, and one way or another had gobbled up all the surplus of the "naborhood" and had given nothing in exchange but whiskey, and these enemies had long hoped for somebody to come and turn him down. They, too, circulated the astounding news, and, without committing themselves to either party, said that h—ll would break loose on Saturday at the crossroads, and that "Old Sledge" or the devil would have to go under.

On Friday, the settlers began to drop into the crossroads under pretense of business, but really to get the bottom facts of the rumors that were afloat.

Devil Bill knew full well what they came for, and he talked and cursed more furiously than usual, and swore that anybody who would come expecting to see "Old Sledge" tomorrow was an infernal fool, for he wasn't a-coming. He laid bare his strong arms and shook his long hair and said he wished the lying, deceiving hypocrite would come for it had been nigh on to fourteen years since he had made a preacher dance.

Saturday morning by nine o'clock the settlers began to gather. They came on foot and on horseback, and in carts—men, women and children, and before eleven o'clock there were more people at the crossroads than had ever been there before. Bill Jones was mad at their credulity, but he had an eye to business, and kept behind his counter and sold more whiskey in an hour than he had sold in a month. As the appointed hour drew near the settlers began to look down the long, straight road that "Old Sledge" would come, if he came at all, and every man whose head came in sight just over the rise of the distant hill was closely scrutinized.

More than once they said, "Yonder he comes—that's him, shore." But no, it wasn't him.

Some half a dozen had old bull's-eye silver watches, and they compared time, and just at 10:55 o'clock the old horse thief exclaimed:

"I see Tom Barker a risin' of the hill. I hain't seed him for eleven years, but, gintlemen, that ar' him, or I'm a liar."

And it was him.

As he got nearer and nearer, a voice seemed to be coming with him, and some said, "He's talkin' to himself," another said, He's a talkin' to God Almighty," and another said, "I'll be durned if he ain't a praying," but very soon it was decided that he was "singin' of a hime."

Bill Jones was soon advised of all this, and, coming up to the front, said: "Darned if he ain't singing before I axed him, but I'll make him sing another tune till he is tired. I'll pay him for his onsulting message. I'm not a-gwine to kill him boys. I'll leave life in his rotton old carcass, but that's all. If any of you'ens want to hear 'Old Sledge' preach, you'll have to go ten miles from the road to do it."

Slowly and solemnly the preacher came. As he drew near he narrowed down his tune and looked kindly upon the crowd. He was a massive man in frame, and had a heavy suit of bark brown hair; but his face was clean shaved, and showed a nose and lips and chin of firmness and great determination.

"Look at him, boys, and mind your eye," said the horse thief.

"Where will I find my friend, Bill Jones?" inquired "Old Sledge."

All round they pointed him to the man.

Riding up close he said: "My friend and brother, the good Lord has sent me to you, and I ask your hospitality for myself and my beast," and he slowly dismounted and faced his foe as though expecting a kind reply.

The crisis had come and Bill Jones met it.

"You infernal old hypocrite; you cussed old shaved-faced scoundrel; didn't you know that I had swored an oath that I would make you sing and dance, and whip you besides if you ever dared to pizen these crossroads with your shoe-tracks? Now sing, d—n you, sing and dance as you sing," and he emphasized his command with a ringing slap with his open hand upon the parson's face.

"Old Sledge" recoiled with pain and surprise.

Recovering in a moment, he said:

"Well, Brother Jones, I did not expect so warm a welcome, but if this be your crossroads manners, I suppose I must sing;" and as Devil Bill gave him another slap on his other jaw he began with:

"My soul, be on thy guard."

And with his long arm suddenly and swiftly gave Devil Bill an open hander that nearly knocked him off his feet, while the parson continued to sing in a splendid tenor voice:

"Ten thousand foes arise."

Never was a lion more aroused to frenzy than was Bill Jones. With his powerful arm he made at "Old Sledge" as if to annihilate him with one blow, and many horrid oaths, but the parson fended off the stroke as easily as a practised boxer, and with his left hand dealt Bill a settler on his peepers as he continued to sing:

"Oh, watch, and fight, and pray,
The battle ne'er give o'er."

But Jones was plucky to desperation, and the settlers were watching with bated breath. The crisis was at hand, and he squared himself, and his clenched fists flew thick and fast upon the parson's frame, and for awhile disturbed his equilibrium and his song. But he rallied quickly and began the offensive, as he sang:

> "Ne'er think the victory won,
> Nor lay thine armor down—"

He backed his adversary squarely to the wall of his shop, and seized him by the throat, and mauled him as he sang:

> "Fight on, my soul, till death—"

Well, the long and the short of it was, that "Old Sledge" whipped him and humbled him to the ground, and then lifted him up and helped to restore him, and begged a thousand pardons.

When Devil Bill had retired to his house and was being cared for by his wife, "Old Sledge" mounted a box in front of the grocery and preached righteousness and temperance, and judgment to come, to that people.

He closed his solemn discourse with a brief history of his own sinful life before his conversion and his humble work for the Lord ever since, and he besought his hearers to stop and think—"Stop, poor sinner, stop and think," he cried in alarming tones.

There were a few men and many women in that crowd whose eyes, long unused to the melting mood, dropped tears of repentance at the preacher's kind and tender exhortation. Bill Jones's wife, poor woman, had crept humbly into the outskirts of the crowd, for she had long treasured the memories of her childhood, when she, too, had gone with her good mother to hear preaching. In secret she had pined and lamented her husband's hatred for religion and for preachers. After she had washed the blood from his swollen face and dressed his wounds she asked him if she might go down and hear the preacher. For a minute he was silent and seemed to be dumb with amazement. He had never been whipped before and had suddenly lost confidence in himself and his infidelity.

"Go 'long, Sally," he answered, "if he can talk like he can fight and sing, maybe the Lord did send him. It's all mighty strange to me," and he groaned in anguish. His animosity seemed to have changed into an anxious, wondering curiosity, and after Sally had gone, he left his bed and drew near to the window where he could hear.

"Old Sledge" made an earnest, soul-reaching prayer, and his pleading with the Lord for Bill Jones's salvation and that of his wife and children reached the window where Bill was sitting, and he heard it. His wife returned in tears and took a seat beside him, and sobbed her heart's distress, but said nothing. Bill bore it for awhile in thoughtful silence, and then putting his bruised and trembling hand in hers, said: "Sally, if the Lord sent 'Old Sledge' here, and maybe he did, I reckon you had better look after his horse." And sure enough "Old Sledge" stayed there that night and held family prayer, and the next day he preached from the piazza to a great multitude, and sang his favorite hymn:

"Am I a soldier of the Cross?"

And when he got to the third verse his untutored but musical voice seemed to be lifted a little higher as he sang:

"Sure I must fight if I would reign,
Increase my courage, Lord."

Devil Bill was converted and became a changed man. He joined the church, and closed his grocery and helped to build a meeting house, and it was always said and believed that "Old Sledge" mauled the grace into his unbelieving soul, and it never would have got in any other way.

CHAPTER L.

BILL ARP ON JOSH BILLINGS.

Josh Billings is dead, and the world will miss him. He was a success in his way, and it was not a bad way. He did no harm. He did much good, for he gave a passing pleasure and gave it frequently, and left the odor of good precepts that lingered with us. He was Æsop and Ben Franklin, condensed and abridged. His quaint-phonetic spelling spiced his maxims and proverbs, and made them attractive. It is curious how we are attracted by the wise, pithy sayings of an unlettered man. It is the contrast between his mind and his culture. We like contrasts and we like metaphors and striking comparisons. The more they are according to nature and everyday life, the better they please the masses. The cultured scholar will try to impress us by saying "*facilis decensus averni*," but Billings brings the same idea nearer home when he says, "when a man starts down hill, it looks like everything is greased for the occasion." We can almost see the fellow sliding down. It is an old thought that has been dressed up fine for centuries, and suddenly appears in every day clothes. Wise men tell us that the people do not think for themselves, but follow their leaders in politics and religion. That is true, and it is tame and old. But when I asked the original Bill Arp how he was going to vote he said he couldn't tell me until he saw Colonel Johnson, and Colonel Johnson wouldn't know until he talked to Judge Underwood, and Judge Underwood wouldn't know until he heard from Aleck Stephens. "But who tells Aleck Stephens how to vote?" "I'll be dogged if I know." Well, that was the same old truth, but it was undressed, and therefore more forcible. The philosophic theory has come down to a homely fact.

Some years ago I met Mr. Shaw in New York, at Carleton's book store. I did not know that he was Josh Billings. In fact I had forgotten Billings' real name, and I thought this man was a Methodist preacher. He looked like one, a very solemn one. His long hair was parted in the middle and silvered with gray. His face was heavily bearded, his eyes well set and his mouth drooped at the corners. We sat facing each other for a few moments, when suddenly he leaned forward and said: "Friend Arp, say something." I knew then that Mr. Carleton had surprised me and that this was Billings, for he had told me that his friend Billings was going to call. We soon got friendly and familliar, and suddenly he inquired, "how is my friend Big John?" "Dead," said I. "And how is that faithful steer?" said he. "Dead," I replied. With a mock sorrow he wiped his eyes and remarked, "hence these tears." (Steers.)

While we were talking, a lad of the house came back and said there was a man in a balloon and we could see him from the front. We all went forward and we watched the daring æronaut soar away until he was out of sight and we took seats near the door. Billings heaved a sigh and said, "I feel very bad, my friends. That sight distresses me." We asked him why, and he said, "It carries me back to the scenes of my early youth, and reminds me of a sad event." We waited a moment for him to recover from his depression, and he said: "I was an indolent, trifling boy. I wouldn't work and I wouldn't study at school. I had a longing to get away from home and go West. Most everybody was going West, and so one morning my father said to me: "Henry, I reckon you had better go. You are not doing any good here." And so he gave me ten dollars and a whole lot of advice, and my mother fixed me up a little bundle of clothes and I started. That money lasted me until I got away out to Illinois, for I worked a little along the way to pay for lodging and vittels, but at last it was all gone, and my shoes were worn out, and when I got to a little village one afternoon I was homesick and friendless, and I didn't know what to do next. I noticed that the people were all going one way, and they told me they were going out to the suburbs to see a man go up in a balloon. So I followed the crowd and when I got there I saw a little dirty Italian sitting down on an old dingy balloon, and there was a fellow going around with a hat in his hand trying to make up ten dollars. The little Italian said he would go up for that money. But the fellow couldn't make it. He counted the money and had only six dollars and a half, and so he gave it up, and was about to give the money back when I thought I saw my opportunity.

I was sorry for the Italian and sorry for myself, and so I whispered to him and asked him if he would give me all over ten dollars that I could make up and he said 'yes, all over eight dollars.' Well, I had the gift of speech pretty lively, and I went round and round among the folks and told them how this poor, little, sunburnt son of Italy came three thousand miles from his home to minister to their pleasure and put his life in peril, and it was a shame that we couldn't make him up the pitiful sum of ten dollars. I soon got the crowd in good humor, and in about five minutes I had made up eighteen dollars. I felt proud and happy, and said: 'Now, my friend, fire up,' and I helped him to fire up. The old balloon was patched and leaky, and I thought it would burst before we got ready, for we piled the gas in heavy. Before long the little chap was in the basket, and we cut the ropes and away she went. It was a calm, still day in June—not a breath of air to drift the balloon from a perpendicular. Up, up, she went, growing smaller and smaller, until finally she was but a tiny speck in the zenith. We nearly broke our necks looking at it, and sure enough, in a few minutes more she was gone. Not a spy-glass could find it. We watched all the evening for the little fellow to come back in sight, but he never came. The shades of night come over us but no Italian. The crowd dispersed one by one until all were gone but me, for I was his friend and treasurer, you know. Next morning he still was missing and all that day we made inquiries from the surrounding country, but no Italian and no balloon, and from that day to this good hour he has never been heard from. I have felt a heavy weight of responsibility about him, for I fear I put in too much gas. My hope is that he went dead straight to heaven. I have his money in my bank, and it is drawing interest."

And Josh wiped away another pretended tear of grief.

He was a companionable man and talked without a strain. When he visited our little city of Rome our people gave him glad welcome, for he had been long ministering to their pleasure and in all his great and curious utterances he had never written a line that showed prejudice or malignity to our people or our section.

Peace be to his ashes and honor to his memory.

CHAPTER LI.

THE CODE DUELLO.

They are the funniest things—these duels. They are both funny and fantastic. They beat a circus—that is to say the newspaper pictures of them beat the circus pictures, and it is reasonable to suppose that the antics of the performers are more ludicrous than the clown and the monkeys and the trick horse combined. I would like to be up in a tree and see a duel—no I wouldent either. It would be safer to be in front of one of the performers. Sometimes I think that these little affairs of honor are just gotten up to amuse the public, and they are a success in that way. They beat Sullivan and Kilrain in the wind up, and the ouly objection is we don't know about it until the show is all over. We don't have a chance to take sides and bet on anybody, and if we did we wouldent win or lose, for it is always a draw—nobody hurt, wonderful pluck, amazing heroism, magnanimous conduct, noble bearing, amicable adjustment, but nobody hurt; that's what's the matter. When it leaks out that a great show is coming, the people want it to come. If a hanging is advertised, it is an outrage if somebody don't hang. If a duel has to be fought to preserve honor, the public want some blood. Honor or death, honor or crippled, honor or hit somewhere. But this sidewiping around and fixing up the thing on a wood-pile, or, "I'll retreat if you'll retreat," or, "I dident mean what you thought I meant," don't satisfy the public.

Some years ago one of our notable men called another notable man a thief and he got challenged for it, and we thought there was blood on the moon, but mutual friends interposed and he retracted by saying he dident mean that he was a personal thief but an official thief, and that was satisfactory and the affair was honorably adjusted.

When an affair of honor is settled now-a-days we can't find out who whipped the fight—who was right and who was wrong. The whole matter is left so mystified that the stakeholders won't pay the money.

In fact it is sometimes hard to tell from the newspapers who were doing the fighting, the principals or the seconds, or an amateur performer who recklessly rushed in where angels feared to tread.

"The combat thickens—on ye brave,
Who rush to glory or the grave."

Awful scene—terrific beyond expression. It reminds me of a little Frenchman who was prancing around the hotel in St. Louis and had a little impudent terrier dog following him about. The dog gave just cause of offense to a big whiskered Kentuckian who was talking to a friend, and with a sudden swing of his boot he sent the animal a rod or two out in the street. Quick as lightning the Frenchman danced up to Kentuck, and with violent gesticulations exclaimed: "Vat for you keek mon leetle tog? Vot for me say? Here is mine card. I demand de sateesfacsheon of de shenteel mon." The Kentuckian seized him gently by the nap of the neck and lifted him bodily to the door and gave him a kick outward, and then walked back and resumed his conversation.

The Frenchman spied an acquaintance who was passing, and rushing up to him poured out this history: "Vot you call des American honeur. He keek mon leetel tog and I geeve heem mine card and demond de sateesfacshun of de genteelhomme, de sateesfacshun of de sword or de peestole—dear to de Frenchman's heart. You tinks he geeve him to me. No sare—no time, but mon Dieu he leef me up by de collare—he speen me roun and roun like I was von tom top and keek me more harder than de leetle tog. Vot you calls dot, American honeur? Bah! I go pack to La belle France and hoonts up some American and fights him. I will have de satisfacshun—begor."

If retractions are to be made they should be very explicit. It is related of John Randolph that he expressed his contempt of a man by saying of him that he wasn't fit to carry—offal to a bear. A *retraxit* was demanded or a fight, and he promptly responded that he would now say that the gentleman was fit to carry—offal to a bear. This proved satisfactory and goes to show how small a *retraxit* will satisfy wounded honor. But it seems to be a matter of great nicety as to the time when the *retraxit* shall be made. Among all gentlemen it is admitted that an apology should be made just as soon as the gentleman has discovered he has done another gentleman an injury or has, without just cause, wounded his feelings; but these mysterious affairs of honor are very slow about such things, and the *retraxits* are not allowed to be made until a challenge has passed and the seconds chosen and the pistols loaded and everything got in readiness for a fight. Then the *retraxit* is in order and the honorable adjustment. The whole thing is methodical, to say the least of it. It is like a bill in equity that has nine parts, and there is the accusation and the rejoinder and the surrejoinder and other mysteries. The fact is, considering the funny and fantastic and harmless character of most of the modern duels, I think that justice's court would be the best tribunal wherein to settle such matters. The first case I ever had, was a case in justice's court, where I was employed to defend a man who was sued for thirty dollars worth of slander because he had accused his nabor of stealing his hog and changing the mark from an underbit in the right ear to a swallow fork in the left. After the joinder and the rejoinder and the surrejoinder the jury retired to a log and eventually brought in this verdict: "We, the jury, find for the plaintiff two dollars and fifty cents unless the defendant will take back what he said." I have always thought that was a just verdict, and if ever any fool sends me a challenge I shall propose to leave the matter to a jury in a justice court. They always give a man a chance without his having to practice with pistols on a tree. It is a strange thing how a man can hit the bull's eye on a tree every pop but can't hit a man one time in five, and yet be perfectly cool and calm and serene all the time.

The books say that duelling originated in the superstitious ages when it was believed that the fates or the gods were on the side of truth and justice, and always avenged the man who had been wronged. The philosophers declared that there was a mysterious connection between honor and courage and between courage and the nervous system, and that when a man was in the wrong his courage wavered, and his nerves became unsteady, and so he couldn't fight to advantage and was easily overcome by his adversary. There may be something in this, but not a great deal, for we do know that the professional duelist is generally in the wrong and generally whips the fight. In fact, the wrong man has most generally been killed in all the fatal duels of modern times. During the past century duelling has had its chief support from the army and the navy where chivalry seems to have centered. They talk about chivalry as though they belonged to some knightly order like unto the olden times when Don Quixote mounted his flea-bitten gray and sallied forth and charged a windmill with a lance about twenty feet long. The word chivalry comes from 'cheval," a horse, and so if a man was not mounted there was no chance to be chivalrous. A seat in a buggy won't do at all. It won't churn up heroism like the canter of a horse. That was called the "fantastic age of famished honor," for honor was said to be always hungry for a fight with somebody, and the knights started out period ically to provoke difficulties. Happy for us that this age has passed away and the knights are unhorsed, but unhappily for us, like the comet, a portion of its tail still lingers in the land, and ever and anon some valiant knight shows up and strikes his breast and exclaims: "Mine honor, sir, mine honor!" Right then I want to rush to his relief and give him a sharpened pole and mount him on some "Rosinante' and escort him to one of these modern windmills that are built to pump water and tell him to charge it until his honor is satisfied. Most of these chivalric gentlemen have a very vague, indefinite idea of what honor is and where it is located. Hudibras throws some light upon the seat of honor when he tells of a man who was "kicked in the place where honor is lodged," and he says:

"A kick right there hurts honor more
Than deeper wounds when kicked before.

This locates honor in the back ground where we will leave it.

Honor is like the chamelion. It takes any color that suits its surroundings. Aaron Burr challenged Hamilton in order to preserve his honor, and yet he was a traitor, an enemy of Washington, a libertine and boasted of his amours and his intrigues. If a man is going to fight for his honor he should be sure that he has not tarnished it by his own dishonorable conduct. If a man is a thief or a swindler or an extortioner or a libertine or a black mailer, he has no right to challenge a man for calling him a liar. Honor is a very broad quality and does not split up in parts. It makes up the complete gentleman in all his conduct, though a man may not have told a lie, yet he may have no honor to defend, for he had lost it all in other vices. When a man can look his fellow-men in the face and say, "Whom have I defrauded or whom have I wronged or from whom have I taken a bribe?" then let him fight for his honor if he wants to.

But the average man who has made his money by ways that are dark and tricks that are vain or who has used deceit, dishonesty, hypocrisy or oppression in gaining his ends, has no right to send or accept a challenge to mortal combat. He must stand fair and square before the people if he expects their sympathy. If he fights of course it is out of respect to public opinion, for no two men would fight if they were on an island by themselves. And this proves the duelist a coward, the worst kind of a coward, for he has more regard for public opinion than he has for himself or his family or his friends or his Maker. He knows that a duel proves nothing and settles nothing and yet he deliberately lets public opinion outweigh his wife and his children and worse than all he puts his soul in reach of the devil. From every moral standpoint he is a fool and a coward and could be convicted of lunacy in any court, and ought to be. Lord, help us all—when will this foolishness stop? The law is against it. Public opinion is against it. Common sense is against it and so is humanity and morality. Public opinion says that every such case lowers our moral standard at home and belittles us abroad. Public opinion doesn't care a snap for the duel or the duelist. Duels prove nothing. They establish no man's character for truth or integrity. They give him no better credit in bank, no more friends in business. Among decent peaceable people he is looked upon as a partial outlaw, and they shrink from his society for fear of offending him. His code of morals and his peculiar sense of honor is a silent insult to them as though he had said: "I move in a higher plane than you common folks. I am a man of honor—a gentleman." He has been engaged in a dishonorable business and he knows it, for he has had to skulk around in the night and hide and dodge like a thief. He does not dare to fight on the genial, loving soil of his own State, for that would disfranchise him and so he seeks some other. In fact, the whole thing would be as funny as a farce if nobody was concerned but the principals and their seconds. But there are parents and wives and children and friends and hence the deep concern. Then let us have more peace and less foolishness. Let a man take part in no show that he has to keep secret from his wife or his children. Let him undertake no peril that his preacher couldn't approve with a parting prayer and benediction. In fact, I have always wondered why the preacher was not taken along as well as the surgeon, for where the devil is, the man of God ought to have an equal chance to capture an immortal soul.

CHAPTER LII.

"BILLY IN THE LOW GROUNDS."

Write, my child—write something to *The Constitution*. I don't care what. I am too nervous. I can't think my own thoughts. It is perfectly horrible—awful, but I reckon it's all right. I reckon so. I wish there was not a tooth in my head. When they come, they come with pain and peril, and keep the poor child miserable, and when they go they go with a torture that no philosophy can endure. Oh, my poor jaw—just look how it is swollen. I am a sight. A pitiful prospect. I look like a bloated bond-holder on one side of my face and no bonds to comfort me. I wonder what would comfort a man in my fix. I have suffered more mortal agony from my teeth than from everything else put together. Samson couldn't pull them, hardly, for they are all riveted to the jawbone. I have been living in dread for a month, for I knew that eyetooth was fixing up trouble; and so yesterday morning it sprung a leak at the breakfast table, and I jumped out of my chair. The shell caved in, the nerve was touched, and in my agony I gave one groan and retired like I was a funeral. Five miles from town and no doctor. Don't put down what I suffered all that day, and the night following, for you can't. Mush poultices and camphor and paregoric and bromide and chloroform and still the procession moved on, and the jumping, throbbing agony sent no flag of truce—no cessation of hostilities. What do I care for anything? Don't tell me about Hendricks being in Atlanta. I don't care where he is. Yes, I do. He is a good man, but I've got no time to think about him now. Please give me some more of that camphor. I've burned all the skin off my mouth now but it is a counter-irritant and sorter scatters the pain around. If I had some morphine I would take it for I want rest. I am tired. Oh, for one short hour of rest.

Write something, my daughter—write to *The Constitution* and explain. Tell them I am "Billy in the low grounds." I am suffering and want sympathy. Write a note to the doctor, and tell him to come, come quick. I can't go through another night. Oh, my country. Let me try that hot iron again. I'll cook this old fat jaw outside and inside. I wish I had no tongue, for I can't keep it from touching the plagued tooth. Just look at my gums, they have swelled up so you can hardly see the old tooth. Give me a knife and a hand glass. I'll see if I can't let some blood out of these strutting gums. I am so nervous I can't hardly hold the knife, but here she goes. Oh, my country, now give me the camphor and I'll let it burn in a new place.

Just write a line to *The Constitution*, I don't care what—say I am sick. I wonder if the doctor will come. He will kill me I know. It is awful to think of cold steel clamping this tooth and being jammed away up on these gums. I'll take chloroform, I reckon, for I can't stand it. I am afraid he will come. I want him and I don't want him. The last tooth I had pulled I went to the dentist's office like a hero and I was glad he wasn't in—glad his door was locked—and for two more days I endured my agony, and then had to have it pulled at last. And he pulled me all to pieces, and the chloroform left me before he got done, and I had an awful time. The memory of it is excruciating, and yet I have got to go through the same thing again. "Oh, the pity of it, Iago, the pity of it." What has a man got teeth for, I would like to know. It is the brute that is in him, the dog, or the old Adam that evoluted from the monkeys. There is nothing Godlike about teeth. They bite, that is all. They are called "canines." I saw a man bite another man's nose off, once—the teeth did it. The eye is God-like, angelic, beautiful, harmless. The ear is a good thing, too, for it takes in the harmonies of nature, and makes music sweet —music, that is the only thing common to angels and to men. The nose is gentle and ornamental, but is not of much consequence except to blow off a bad cold, and tell the difference between cologne and codfish. But, the teeth—well, I think that false ones are better than the genuine, for they never ache. I don't care for any now. I am tired. These women can have eight or ten pulled at one time—just to get a new set. How in the world do they stand it? Pride, I reckon; womanly pride, womanly nature. Her love of the beautiful. But we men can wear a moustache, and hide a whole set of rotten snags. If women had beard, the dentists would perish.

There she goes again, and then boom! Let me try some more paregoric and camphor. Maybe I can go to sleep, after a while, if I will keep dosing. I wish I had just a small grain of dynamite behind that tooth, just at the end of the roots; I would explode it if it killed me.

The doctor coming, you say! Merciful heavens! Well, let him come. In the language of Patrick Henry, "I repeat it sir, let him come." "Lay on, McDuff"—cold steel forceps, wrenching, twisting, crushing, gouging. I don't believe I have got a friend in the world. I almost wish I was dead. Teeth are a humbug—a grand mistake—a blunder—an eye-tooth, especially, that sends its root away up under the eye and makes an abscess there. They say a child is smart when it cuts the eye-tooth. I believe I had rather do without and be a fool. I have had rheumatism, and all sorts of pains, but I will compromise on anything but the toothache. I've a great respect for dentists, for they do the best they can to relieve mankind from this most miserable agony.

"Good morning, doctor. I suppose I am the unfortunate individual you have come to doctor. I am ready for the rack. Get out your chloroform, and your steel-jawed grabs; I am ready for the sacrifice. Is that a dagger that I see before me?"

Father is in his little bed. He is asleep, now. The long agony is over. For nearly one hour we all wrestled with him, for the chloroform gave out. He had taken so many things before the doctor came that chloroform failed to subdue him. It only made him delirious, and when we could not hold him we called in our blacksmith, and even then he pulled us all over the room, and the doctor had to take him on the wing. The old shell crushed and the roots had to be dug out in fragments. It was pitiful to hear him beg to go home. He has morphine now, and will be all right in the morning. He told me to write you something, and I have written.   BILL ARP, Per M.

Just now he waked up and wanted to know who whipped that fight —the parrot or the monkey.   M.

CHAPTER LIII.

WILLIAM GETS LEFT.

It is home where the heart is, and we are all happy now. Here is the big old family room and the spacious fireplace is crowded with the big back logs and the front logs and the top logs, and the cheerful, genial blaze leaps out at every opening and makes us all sit back in the family circle. I sit near the good old window and look out upon the same pleasing prospect of fields and distant hills and am comforted. The dogs are in the family ring and the canaries are singing in their cage, and the maltese cat is purring in Jessie's lap. There is a lively chattering of happy voices all around me, for the long spell is broken and the broken family almost united. I say almost, for the sick boy and his mother are in town at his sister's, and these children have not yet seen them. It was too cold to bring him five miles over a frozen road, and so I came out alone to give them pleasure in broken doses. I hoped to surprise them and peep in at the window, but they were on the look out down the road, and have nearly looked a hole through the window pane in anxious expectation. With a scream and a shout they all came flying down the hill to meet me, and such a time as we all had, hugging and kissing and dancing around with joy. They loaded me down and I could hardly wag along for their embraces. I don't believe that folks are any happier in heaven, and I don't know that I wish to be.

We left Sanford last Tuesday, took the boy on a cot over the long wharf that stretches away out into the lake and put him aboard the beautiful steamer, the "City of Jacksonville." We set him down in an easy chair, and when the warning bell was rung we bade a sweet good-by to kindred and friends and soon the engines were unloosed and the big wheels turned and the boat moved down the lake with quivering throbs. The anxious mother watched her boy with watery eyes as he looked out greedily upon the bright waters and feasted his eyes once more upon scenes outside of a sick chamber. The boy has no use of his lower limbs and has to be carried in arms from place to place, and it was no small trouble to get him through narrow doors and up and down the stairs and into the cars, but next morning we got him safely on a sleeper at Jacksonville and then breathed easier, for it was the last transfer until we got to Macon.

Waycross. I see Waycross now. I expect to see Waycross in visions by day and in dreams by night for years to come. I have memories of Waycross. I like Waycross, for it is a bright and pleasant town, and has good hotels and pleasant homes, and is kept lively with moving trains, but I had an awful time at Waycross. Our train stopped there and had to wait for a train on another road, they said, and I got out with other passengers and walked the broad platform, but keeping an eye upon our sleeper and within easy reach of it. There were two sleepers behind ours that belonged to the train, and so I meandered along down to where a newsboy was selling Savannah morning papers. I gave him a quarter and was quietly waiting for the change when suddenly I heard a darkey say: "Macon is just a slippin' and a slidin' off." I looked around instantly to see what he meant, and sure enough she was already a hundred yards away moving like a black snake over the ground and getting faster with every moment. The two rear sleepers had been cut off and I did not know it. I will never forget the concentrated misery of that moment when I realized that my wife and helpless boy were gone and I was left. My heart sank down, my voice left me, and all my philosophy was gone. I grew weak and faintish, and sat down on a bench to collect myself and consider the awful situation. What will they do? When will they find out that I am not somewhere on the train? The boy will soon want me, I know, and his mother will send the porter to hunt me up. The conductor will soon call for our fare, and I have the passes, and my wife no money. By and by she will learn that I am not on the train, and then, ah! then. I could see the tears in her eyes and the quivering lips, and the nervous restlessness of the boy, and there was no help. Arousing myself, I hurried to the telegraph that was clicking near by and asked hurriedly for a dispatch to be sent to Jesup so that the operator there might tell the conductor or my wife that I was safe, and would overtake them at Macon. My anxiety was intense, but I got no sympathy. The youth said all right, and I waited for an assurance from the operator at Jesup that he would attend to it. I called three times for an answer from him, but got none. When, for the third time, I asked and almost begged for him to ask for a reply, he said with uncivil indifference: "I have got no time, sir; I am busy." Well, he was very busy—smoking a cigar and chatting with a friend. He was not at the instrument. A gentleman near by noted the incivility and told me I had better go up to the Western Union if I wanted attention. This was news to me, for I had thought all the time that this was the Western Union, but suddenly found that it was only a railroad office. I had paid him for a dispatch to Mr. Brown, of Macon, that called for an answer, and two hours had passed and none had come. So I went to the Western Union and repeated to Mr. Brown and soon had a reply that he would meet my wife and boy and take care of them. Her desolation and distress was complete when she learned that I was missing—nobody called on her or the conductor at Jesup. The train rolled on and passed Eastman before her fears began, and from there to Macon she imagined I had fallen from the platform or in some way had met my death, and when at last she reached Macon, and Mr. Brown came in the sleeper and told her I was all right, she and the boy both cried with joy. The Brown house gave them kind welcome and every attention. They had a good night's rest and were only aroused by a vigorous knock at the door at four o'clock next morning. That was me. The poet says:

"One glorious hour of crowded life
Is worth an age without a name."

And just so we can sometimes live longer and live more in a minute than at any other time in a month. I dident blame her for slipping off and leaving me, and she didn't blame me for stopping at Waycross, but now that the long agony is over, we can smile at our mutual woes and fears. My kind and considerate wife has not told told it on me but fourteen times up to this date, and I don't expect to hear of it any longer than I live. She gently hinted yesterday that she didn't suppose that I would ever mention Waycross in my Sunday letter, for it was most too personal and was not of a character to interest the public. So you perceive I have taken the hint and told it all just as it was. As General Lee said at the battle of Gettysburgh: "It was all my fault. It was all my fault."

I shall step off no more trains to buy a paper, and I now warn all travelers to stand by the car the wife is in and not go fooling down the line. Dick Hargis hollers "All aboard" like a fog horn when his train is ready to move, and you can hear him a quarter of a mile, but Dick can't run all the trains and so ever and anon some poor fellow like me is bound to be left.

Farewell, Waycross. I found some pleasant friends there before I left, and they comforted me, especially the host of the Grand Central, who was an old Gwinnett boy, and we revived many recollections of of our youthful days. But still when I think of Waycross, it is with feelings somewhat like those we have when we visit an old-time battle-field, where we fought, bled and died for liberty.

CHAPTER LIV.

PLEASURES OF HOPE AND MEMORY.

We see that Dr. Curry, that great and good man, is writing the reminiscences of his youth. How lovingly he proceeds with his work! How gushingly he tells of his old school days, and the halos and rainbows that gilded his childhood! How reverently he writes of the grand old men of the olden time, for there were giants in those days! How feelingly he records his companionship with the family negroes —the servants of the household who were contented and happy and trusting, and who loved and honored every member of their master's family, and were loved by them! Oh, the tender and teary recollections of 'possum hunts and coon hunts and rabbit hunts and corn shuckings, and eating watermelons in the cotton patch and sometimes finding them while pulling fodder in the hot and sultry cornfield! What frolics in going to mill and going in washing and jumping from the springboard into ten-foot water! What glorious sport in playing town-ball and bull-pen and cat and rolly-hole and knucks and sweepstakes. Base-ball has grown out of town-ball; it is no improvement. The pitcher used to belong to the ins and threw the best ball he could, for he wanted it hit, and knocked as far away as possible, but now he belongs to the outs and wants it missed. We used to throw at a boy to stop him running to another base, and we hit him if we could, but these modern balls are hard and heavy and dangerous, and many a boy goes home with a bruised face or a broken finger. We used to take an old rubber shoe and cut it into strings and wind it tight into a ball until it was half grown, and then finish it with yarn that was unraveled from an old woolen sock. Our good mothers furnished everything and then made a buckskin cover and stitched it over so nice. Oh, my, how those balls would bounce, and yet they didn't hurt very bad when hit by them. They were sweet to throw and sweet to catch. I heard lying Tom Turner say he had one that bounced so high it never came down till next day, and then his little dog grabbed it, and it took the dog up, and he had never seen the dog nor the ball since. I used to believe that but I don't now. When we played town-ball some of the outs would circle away off 200 yards, and it was glorious to see them catch a ball that had nearly reached the sky as it gracefully curved from the stroke of the bat. We had an hour and a half for recess, and most of it was spent in town-ball or bull-pen. Bull-pen was no bad game, especially when the ins got down to two and the juggling began. I used to be so proud because I could stand in the middle of the pen and defy the jugglers to hit me for I was slender and active and could bend in or bend out or squat down or jump up and dodge every ball that came, but I couldn't do it now, not much I couldn't, for alas! I can neither squat nor jump and a boy could hit my corporosity as easy as a barn door. Oh these memorys, how sweet they haunt us.

> "I remember, I remember
> The house where I was born;
> The little window where the sun
> Came peeping in at morn."

Of course I do—everybody does. The other night there were ten of our school board in session, and the special business was whether to give a longer recess at noon or not, and it was curious to hear the various opinions on the subject. Our president listened patiently to all and then made a speech for himself, and said that the children should have more time to go home and get a good warm dinner. "Cold dinners," he said, "are unhealthy. The laws of hygiene teach us that the processes of digestion are much more easily carried on when the food is warm and fresh from the oven. More than half of the pupils take their dinners to school shut up in tin buckets or wrapped up in baskets, and they get cold and clammy, and are crammed into the stomach in a hurry, and the children go to playing before digestion begins, and of course the stomach rebels and won't do its work, and after school is out they go home and cram in a lot of cake and jelly and pickle on top of the cold, undigested dinner, and the first thing you know the boy or the girl is sick and has to stay at home a day or two to recuperate. I am decidedly in favor of a longer recess and warm dinners."

That was a good speech and a sensible argument, but it hurt my feelings so bad that I rose forward and in trembling accents told how I went to school three miles from home for three long and happy years, and carried my dinner in a bucket, and how I enjoyed those cold dinners that my good mother so carefully prepared and how I had often tried to write a poem to that little tin bucket—such a poem as Wordsworth wrote about "The old oaken bucket that hung in the well." My poem began just like his, but always ended with,

>That dear little bucket,
>That bright, shining bucket,
>That little tin bucket I carried to school.

Oh those delightful cold dinners that were so nicely arranged! The tender and luscious fried chicken, with the liver and gizzard and all; the hard-boiled eggs, with the little paper of pepper and salt close by; the home-made sausages, linked sausages, that, in the language of Milton, were "linked sweetness—long drawn out;" the little bottle of syrup and the round, hand-made biscuit that were beaten from the dough and had no soda in them—and last of all, the good, old-fashioned ginger cakes and the turn-over pies. Ah, those rights and lefts, those delicious juicy pies that were made of peaches that my mother dried.

Just then there was a racket behind me and Will Howard was seen falling over in his chair, with his hands clasped below the belt and his eyes rolled up to heaven. He gasped piteously as he whispered: "Hush, Major, hush, for heaven's sake." Martin Collins shouted, "Glory!" and Judge Milner heaved a troubled sigh and murmured, "Oh, would I were a boy again."

For fear of a scene I suspended my broken remarks, and our worthy president gracefully subsided. Major Foute wiped his eyes with his empty sleeve and moved for an adjournment, and so the recess hour remains unchanged.

I believe it is best for children to walk a mile or two to school, especially if there are other children to walk with them a part of the way. Every step of that three-mile way is dear to me now, and I love to recall the boyish frolics as morning and evening we meandered along, playing tag or mad dog, or running foot races, or jumping half-hammond, or stopping at the half-way branch to wade in the water, or dam it up, or catch the tadpoles, or drive the little minnows into their holes. It was there that I saw for the first time a tadpole turning to a frog, and it was there we killed a water moccasin, with a frog in his throat, and saw his frogship kick out backwards and hop away. I can go now to the very gully that had a vein of red chalk, and another one that had white. I know every persimmon tree and chestnut and hickory, and where the red haws were, and the black haws and the fruitful walnut that we climbed in its season and rattled the nuts to the ground and stained our hands and clothes in hulling them. All such things are around me now, not far away, but there is no charm, no fond memory about them, for they were not mine. All these are for another generation—another set of boys and girls. By and by they will be looking back at theirs as I am looking back at mine. In a few more years they will reverse the telescope. Until I was past thirty I looked through the little end and saw life expanded and magnified before me, while the distant things were brought almost within reach, and I was nearing the goal with my hope and my ambition, but alas! I havn't reached it, and by degrees hope weakened and ambition became chilled, and with a sad humility I began to look backwards—I reversed the telescope and saw my life away back in the distant past. The picture was far—very far away, but it was beautiful, and now as the years grow short, I find myself looking through the large end almost altogether. The memories of the past grow sweeter as the years roll on. The capital stock of the young is hope—but the treasure of age is memory.

CHAPTER LV.

ARP'S REMINISCENCES OF FIFTY YEARS.

A sweet little girl from Marietta writes me a nice letter and begs me to write something for the children—just for the children.

I never look upon a flock of happy, well-raised children without wondering if they know how well off they are—how much better off than their grandparents were some fifty or sixty years ago. I would like to see old Father Time set his clock back a half a century just for a week and put everything like it was then, and I would walk around and have lots of fun out of those little folks. I don't believe they could stand it a whole week, but it would do them good to try. In the first place, they would have to get out of their comfortable houses with plastered walls and large glass windows and coal grates, and get into smaller houses with about two rooms in front and a back shed room, that had no fireplace and no ceiling and a window with a wooden shutter, and in that shed room they would have to sleep, and the wind would come slipping in all night and kiss their faces ever so nice. They would have to take off all their pretty clothes, and wear country jeans and linsey, and they would have to go to the shoemakers and have some coarse, rough shoes made of country leather and no high heels nor box toes nor buttons. But they would be good and strong, and two pairs would last any boy or girl a whole year—one pair would do them if they greased them now and then and went barefooted during summer as we used to do. All the store stockings would have to be dispensed with, and the elastic too, and they would put on some good warm ones that were knit by hand, and be tied up with a rag. No nice hats from the milliners, with pretty flowers and ribbons gay flying, but the girls would have to put on home-made bonnets, nicely quilted, and the boys have to wear home-made wool hats or seal-skin caps that would last two or three years, and stretch bigger as the heads grew bigger. There would not be found a store in the whole State where ready-made clothing could be found—not a coat nor a pair of pants, nor a shirt, nor a skirt, nor a doll, nor hardly a toy of any kind. I suppose that some few things for children might be found in Augusta, or Savannah, or Macon; but the country stores wouldent have anything, not even candy or oranges or a box of raisins. A boy could find a dog knife or a barlow, and be allowed about one a year, but the little girls couldent even find a thimble small enough nor a pair of scissors. Children were not of much consequence then, especially girls.

I would like to see the clock set back for one week and see the boys cutting wood and making fires, cutting wood half the day Saturday for Sunday, and Sunday morning sitting down to learn some more of the shorter catechism about justification, and sanctification, and adoption and some more verses in the Bible, and that poetry in the primmer about—

>"In Adam's fall
>We sinned all.
>The cat doth play
>And after slay.
>Xerxes must die
>And so must I.
>Zacheus, he
>Did climb a tree
>His Lord to see."

I would like to see one of these boys wake up some cold morning and when he tried to make a fire and stirred around among the ashes to find a coal, he couldent find one, and what then? Not a match in the wide, wide world, for there was none invented. Wouldent he be in a fix! Well, he would have to run over to the nabors, if he was a town boy, and borrow a chunk. If he was a country boy he would have to walk a mile or so, maybe, and nearly freeze to death before he got back, and if it was raining his chunk would be apt to go out on the way. I would like to see these boys and girls studying their lessons by the light of one tallow candle. No gas, no kerosene, no oil of any sort—only one flickering light of a candle, or maybe only a lightwood blaze in the fireplace. I reckon they would study hard and study fast and go to bed soon and get up early in the morning and try it again. I would like to see them sit down to write a letter and find nothing but an old goose quill for a pen—not a steel pen in in the world. I would watch the poor fellow as he tried to make a pen out of a quill, and after he had cut it to a point see him try to split it in the middle with his knife, and split too far or not far enough, or on one side and then throw it away in despair.

It would all be fun to us old folks, but it wouldent be fun for the boys or the girls to be set back. But there are old people living now who do the same old things and live the same old way. Colonel Campbell Wallace still uses the quill pens and makes them himself, and I wish you could see how nicely and how quickly he can do it. Our school teachers had to make the pens for all their scholars, and it took about half their time, for they had to mend them oftener than make them. When the first split wore out he had to split it again and trim it down to a new point. His knife was always open and ready. Poor man! He died before the steel pens were invented and never got the good of them.

But we were used to these ways and never thought hard of them. Judge Lester used to run over to our house of a cold morning and say to my mother: "Please mam, lend me a chunk of fire," and I used to go over to his house and do the same thing. But we didn't let it go out often. We knew how to cover up fire in the ashes so as to keep it till morning. I remember going over to Forsyth county once when an old Indian lived there by the name of Sawnee. He didn't go off with the rest of the Indians, but lived on a mountain called Sawnee's mountain, and he had some grandsons about our age. George Lester and Cicero Strong were with me, and we gave an Indian boy some money to show us how they got fire when their fire went out. He took two dry hickory sticks about a foot long and as large as my thumb and a little bunch of dry grass, and started off on a run, and rubbed the sticks together so rapidly that you could hardly see them, and the friction made fire and caught the grass, and he came back in half a minute with a blaze in his hand. I used to go down to the store at night with my father, and he had a tinder box nailed up by the door and would strike the steel with the flint and make a spark and let it fall on a piece of punk and light it, and then he would light his candle from the punk. But matches came along after awhile and stopped all that. I remember the first matches that came to our town. They were called Lucifer matches for some folks thought that the "old boy" had something to do with them and wouldent use them. They smelled strong of brimstone and were sold at twenty-five cents a box. Now ten times as many sell for a nickle. But about lights. Dipping the candles was one of the notable events of the year. It was almost as big a thing as hog killing. The boys prepared the canes or reeds, about sixty in number, as large as the little finger and nearly a yard long. They were smoothed at the joints and put away in a bundle to dry. When the time come, the first cold weather in the fall, our mother would get out the candle wick and wind it around a pair of cotton cards, end ways, and after a good deal was wound would cut one end with the scissors and that made the wicks when doubled just long enough for a candle. Three or four canes were then interlaced through the back of an old-fashioned chair to keep them steady while she looped the wicks around them and twisted their ends together. Seven wicks were put on each cane and when the cane was taken out and held horizontal the wicks hung down and were about two inches apart. When all the canes were full they were laid upon a table ready for dipping. The tallow was melted in a big wash pot. Some beeswax was added and a little alum. Old plank were placed on the floor where the dipping and dripping was to be. Two long poles or quilting frames were placed parallel on the backs of chairs and were wide enough apart to let the candles between and hold up the canes. The big pot had to be kept nearly full all the time. A cane of wicks was let down slowly in the pot, until the cane rested on its edges. Then it was lifted up and allowed to drip awhile and then placed as number one between the long poles where, if it dripped any more it was on the old plank. The first course was long and tedious, for it took the loose cotton wick some time to absorbe the tallow. After that the process was rapid. Tallow would harden on tallow quickly, and at every dipping the little candles got larger until after awhile they were large enough at the bottom ends to fill a candlestick, and that ended the job. They were left on the poles over night and then slipped off the rods and placed in the candlebox or an old trunk.

Seven times sixty made 420 candles, and that was the year's supply. Only one candle was usual for the table in the family room. The reading and sewing was all done by that. The boys were allowed a piece of one to go to bed by. Nobody sat up until midnight then. The night was believed to be created for sleep and rest, and the day for work. There were no theaters nor skating rinks—no reading novels half the night and lying in bed until breakfast next morning. The rule was to go to bed at nine o'clock and get up with the chickens. But now we couldn't read by candle light. It takes at least two lamps, and one lamp is equal to ten candles. But we got along pretty well. All the substantial things were as good as they are now. Good water, good air, good sunshine and shower, good health, good warm clothes, good bread and meat and milk and butter, good peaches and apples, good horses to ride, good fishing and swimming and hunting. We dident have railroads and telegraphs and telephones and sewing machines, and so forth, but we didn't need them. We need them now, for the world is so full of people that the old ways wouldent feed and clothe them. The right thing always comes along at the right time. If the clock was set back I wonder how this generation would manage about the cooking business. Fifty years ago there were no cooking-stoves. The ovens and skillets and spiders were big heavy things that had to be lifted on and off the fire with a pair of pot-hooks. They had heavy lids, and the cooking was done by putting coals underneath and coals on top. It took bark and chips to make coals quickly, and our old cook used to say, "Now git me some bark, little master, and I gib you a bikket when he done." There was no soda, or tartaric acid, or baking powder. The biscuit were made by main strength. The dough was kneaded by strong arms, and sometimes it was beaten with the rolling pin until it blistered. When the dough blistered it was good and made good biscuit. I can't say that we have any better cooking now than we had then; but the stove makes it a great deal easier to cook.

The boys had no baseball, but they had bullpen and cat and townball and roley hole and tag and sweepstakes and pull over the mark and foot races and so forth, and they thought there was nothing better. They had the best rubber balls in the world, and made them themselves. Some of them could bounce thirty feet high. They were made by cutting an old rubber shoe into strings and winding the strings into a ball and covering it with buckskin. But after awhile the rubber shoes were not made of all rubber. They were mixed with something that took some of the bounce out, and our balls degenerated. There was an old man living near us who was called "Lying Tom Turner," and he told us boys one day that when he was a boy he had a rubber ball that he was afraid to bounce hard for fear it would go up out of sight and he would lose it. We asked him what became of his ball, and he said he bounced it one day most too hard and it went up into the clouds and was gone half an hour, and when it came down his little dog grabbed it in his mouth, and it rebounced and carried the dog up with it out of sight, and he had never seen the ball nor the little dog since.

Well, I don't know which times are the best—the old times or the new. It is very nice to have a nice house and nice furniture and nice clothes and lots of nice story books and to ride on the cars, but in the old times people didn't hanker after such things, and they were easy to please, and were in no hurry to get through life, and there were no suicides, and very few crazy folks, and no pistols to carry in the hip-pockets. Nowadays there is a skeleton in most every house. I don't mean a real skeleton, but some great big trouble that throws a dark shadow over the family. There were not any exciting books to read— no sensation novels that poison the mind, just like bad food poisons the body. There were but half a dozen newspapers in the whole State, and they didn't have whole columns full of murders and sui- cides and robberies and awful fires that burned up poor lunatics and all other horrid things to make a tender heart feel bad. There was nobody very rich and nobody very poor, and we had as great men then as we have now.

If the clock was set back, and the little girl who wrote to me wanted to go to Augusta with her grandpa to visit her kinfolks, she would have to get in the mail coach and jog along all day and all night at four miles an hour and pay ten cents a mile, and it would take two days and nights, and she would be tired almost to death and so would her grandpa. Well, they just couldn't go. But now they can go as cheap as to stay at home, and do it in less time, as the Irish-man said.

But the clock will not be set back, and so we must all be content with things as they are, and make them better if we can.

CHAPTER LVI.

WILLIAM AND HIS WIFE VISIT THE CITY.

The old carpet in the family room has been down and up and up and down for seventeen years. It has been the best carpet we ever had. It used to be the parlor carpet, but was reduced to a lower rank a long time ago. Time and children and dogs and cats and brooms have worked on it until it is faded and slick and threadbare. The colors are gone and so are the figures and the fuz and the nap, but it is a carpet still. It has been taken up and hung on the fence and beaten with thrash poles about seventeen times, and yet there is not a hole in it. In its aristocratic days it bore the burden of aristocratic shoes and fancy slippers, and music and song and love making, and the parlor dance, and the family weddings. Its downy flowers treasured many a secret and many a joy. But in course of time it ceased to be the pride of the family, and became its servant. We have raised children on that carpet—rough boys and romping girls. We have raised dogs and cats. It has been the mudsills of a nursery and a menagerie and a schoolroom and a circus. As its colors disappeared in the middle and around the hearthstone Mrs. Arp would take it up and change corners and bring to the front a brighter portion that lay hidden under the bed and the bureau and the sofa. She has done this so often that there is little difference now. Every part has traveled the grand rounds over and over again.

Mrs. Arp has been hinting about a new carpet for some time. "We could do without it if I couldn't afford it," she said, "and I must have a talma cloak anyhow, and the children needed so many things, but she didn't want anything for herself." Of course she didn't. I didn't give her a chance. I keep her supplied. I never said anything—I just looked into the fire and ruminated. She knows my weakness. It's all honey and sugar and a little flattery thrown in. When it comes to driving and bulldozing I am an austere man,

I am, and she knows it. She said last week that she had promised Ralph to go down to Atlanta and see him, and while there she could get a cloak and some little things for the children for Christmas. "I'll go with you," said I. "I wish to see Ralph, too, and keep him encouraged. I think he will make a pretty good doctor in ten or fifteen years, if he keeps on studying and cutting up stiffs and holding the candle for Dr. Westmoreland. He uses powerful big words now for a boy of his size. He talks about anesthetics and antiskeptics, and the like." It wasn't much trouble to get her off, and she never said nary time that she had nothing to wear. She has got past that at last. We took one of the girls along as a chaperone, for my wife and I haven't kept up with city style and street behavior and how to shop and look at fine things like we were used to them. We had hardly got off the cars when she met an old friend and hugged and kissed her, and they got to talking about old times and somebody that was dead, and my wife she got full in the throat and watery in the eyes, and they blocked up the sidewalk and everybody had to walk around them, and so to prevent a scene our chaperone dissolved the interview and we hurried on to Whitehall. It has been built up wonderfully since Mrs. Arp was there, and the show windows are just beautiful beyond description. She stopped squarely before the first jewelry store and feasted her hazel eyes in rapturous amazement. "Did you ever in your life? Isen't that perfectly lovely? Do look at that little cherub swinging to that clock for a pendulum. I wonder if those are real diamonds in those brooches. Oh my! see that beautiful breastpin. Wouldent Jessie love to wear that. Poor thing, she has never had a nice pin." The chaperone began to take on a little, too, and the passsing crowd had to go round us again, and some of them looked back and smiled, and that made me mad, and so I took my women folks away from there and remarked: "I wouldn't stop to look at everything. People will think you never saw anything pretty or fine in your life." Mrs. Arp prouded up her head and said: "What do I care for people. The merchants put their finest things in the windows to be looked at, and I am going to look just as much as I please," and she stopped squarely against another window and began the inspection of those lovely ladies' shoes. Mrs. Arp goes perfectly daft on fine shoes—No. 2s. Daft is the word she uses on me sometimes, but I don't know what it means. She says I promised her thirteen pair a year before she married me. One pair a month and one pair over. Maybe I did, but I've forgotten all those things. They were not said in a lucid interval. "Now buy your shoes," said I, "and let us move on to the carpet store; it will be dinner time directly." She looked at me in sweet surprise and followed me like a lamb, for I hadent mentioned the carpet before. We went to the carpet store, and there were so many beautiful patterns that she couldent decide on any. The carpet men unrolled piece after piece, and sent the rolls whirling away down the room and then back again, and they kept getting lovelier and lovelier, and the price higher and higher, until my wife sighed, and said: "Well, let us go now; we will come back again after awhile." I followed them around meekly, and, as we passed a French clock, I pointed to the hour, and it was 2 o'clock p. m. "Only an hour and a half longer to stay," said I, "and we have had no dinner." They didn't seem to be worried about the dinner, and made a final assault upon another carpet store, and I had to settle it at last and make a choice for them. I always do. I used to be a merchant, and kept the finest and prettiest goods in town. I used to sell Mrs. Arp fine dressing when she was a miss, and she wouldn't trade anywhere else, and it took her a long time to make up her mind, and I had to make it up for her just as I do now. She never traded much at any other store, and, to my opinion, there is about as much courting done over the counter by day as in the parlor by night. After we were married she traded with me altogether. Thirty-six yards of carpeting was all that I had bargained for when I left home, but there was a rug and a hassock and two pairs of shoes and some sylabub stuff for ruffles and flounces and a few Christmas things, and by the time we got to Durand's we had only twenty minutes for dinner. We were all happy and hungry, too, and the dinner was splendid, and my wife brought home a basket of fruit for the children, and she told them all about the big day's work, and the beautiful things, and whom she saw, and I reckon it was worth the money that was spent and more too. The carpet came along in due time all ready made, and three of the children were at school, and dident know it, and we hurried up and took everything out of the room and bid farewell to the old one, and cleaned up the straw and the dust, and washed up the floor and the windows, and put down the paper, and the carpet on top of it, and pulled, and stretched, and tugged and tacked until it was all right. Then we put the furniture all back just like it was, and sat down before the fire just like nothing had happened, and in about ten minutes the school chaps came singing up to the back door and walked in upon us before they had time to look down, and it was worth $5 more to hear the raptures and adjectives and adverbs and exclamation points and other parts of speech that they indulged in when their wondering eyes feasted upon the rich brown colors under their feet. If I was rich I would buy another carpet right away just to have another good time with Mrs. Arp and the children.

But we didn't have the pleasure of Ralph's company at last. I found him at Dr. Westmoreland's with his sleeves rolled up, helping the doctor to mend a man's broken arm. They had a little tub half full of plaster paris in solution, and a lot of bandage rolls in it, getting saturated. They set the bones and kept the arm pulled straight, while the bandages were wrapped from wrist to elbow, and elbow to wrist, and wrapped again and again, and the plaster hardened as fast as it was rolled on, and in a few minutes it was hard as chalk and nearly half an inch thick, and the man's arm was in a vice. He was was soon dismissed, and the doctor said "next." Then there was a man whose hand was crushed between the cars, and another who had an awful splinter thrust into his stomach, and a child with a grain of coffee in her lungs, and her throat had to be cut open. It is cutting and mending and sewing up human flesh and bones all the day long, and blood is as common as water. There is no time for sympathy or tender words. It is business—hard, stern business, and the signal word is "next." May the Lord keep us all and preserve us from such calamities.

CHAPTER LVII.

THE BUZZARD LOPE.

I'm going to quit thinking about the race problem, and the tariff, and Speaker Reed, and John Wanamaker, and everything else of a turbulent and transitory nature. I'm going to boycott everything now except domestic affairs. I'm going to attend to my own business. I'm going to stay at home and work, and if I read a paper at all it will be with one eye on the head lines and nothing else.

They say that exercise is a remedy for trouble—trouble of mind or trouble of body. Get up and move around lively. My old father was afflicted with rheumatism, and when the sharp pains began to worry him he would take his long stick and start out over the farm and limp, and grunt, and drag himself along until he got warmed up, and in an hour or so would come back feeling better. A man can mope and brood over his troubles until, as Cobe says, "they get more thicker and more aggrevatiner." He told me that he had tried liver medicine and corn juice and various "ancedotes" for disease, but that a right good sweat of perspiration was the best thing for a man or a beast. He used to cure mules of the colic by trotting them around until the sweat come.

I haven't got the colic nor the rheumatism, but I feel such a constant uxorial goneness that I have to step around lively to forget myself. I feel just like I had lost my tobacco. The sparrows are regailing on my strawberries. The happy mocking birds are singing their tee diddle and too doodle, and the lordly peacock screams and struts and spreads his magnificent tail, and all nature seems gay and joyous, but how can the lord of creation sing a glad song when his lady is far away in a strange land. A letter from there says: "Mamma is having a good time and behaving so nice to everybody." Of course, of course. And I'm nice to everybody here—especially the ladies. Some of them come every day—come to comfort me, they say. I'm having a pretty good time considering. We had some fine music last night—some of the boys came home with Carl to practice for a serenade to the spring chickens. They had a guitar and some harps and a triangle, and were right good singers besides, and I enjoyed it immensely. Jessie is a musician, too, and when she struck the ivory key with some saltatory notes like, "Oh Jinny is your Ash-cake Done," and "The Highland Fling" and "Run Nigger Run," accompanied by the sweet harmonicas and the guitar, I just couldent keep my old extremities subdued, and they got me up and toted me around on light fantastic toes amazing. I was all by myself in the next room, but I had lots of fun. It does a man good sometimes to unbend himself and forget his antiquity. I like a little hornpipe or a pigeon wing on the sly sometimes. It may be original sin, or it may be that there is a time to dance, as Solomon says, but I like it. My beard is growing gray, and there's not many hairs between my head and the cerulean heavens, but I'm obliged to have some recreation, especially when Mrs. Arp is away. You ought to see me caper around to the music with a little grand-child, a three-year-old who chooses me for a partner whenever the music begins. She knows the dancing tunes as well as I do, bless her little heart. My boys have got a new step now that they call the "buzzard lope," that is grand, lively and peculiar. The story goes that an old darkey lost his aged mule, and found him one Sunday evening lying dead in the woods and forty-nine buzzards feasting upon his carcass. Forty-eight of them flew away, but the forty-ninth, whose feathers were gray with age, declined to retire. Looking straight at the darkey, he spread his wings about half-and-half, like the American eagle on a silver dollar, and tucked his tail under his body and drew in his chin and pulled down his vest and began to lope around the dead mule in a saltatory manner. He was a greedy bird and liked his meat served rare, and rejoiced that he now had the carcass all to himself, and so he loped around with alacrity. The old darkey was a fiddler and dancer by instinct and inspiration. He had danced all the dances and pranced all the prances of his naborhood for half a century. He had played prompter for the white folks at a thousand frolics, and knew every step and turn and fling of the heel-tap and the toe, but he had never seen such a peculiar double demi-semi-quiver shuffle as that old buzzard loped around that mule. He stood aghast. He spread his arms just half-and-half, and bent his back in the middle, unlimbered his ankle joints, stiffened his elbows, and forgetting both the day and the place, he followed that bird around that mule for four solid hours and caught the exquisite lope exactly. At dusk the tired buzzard souzed his beak into one of dead mule's eyes and bore it away to his roost, while the old darkey loped all the way home to his cabin door, feeling ten years younger for his masterpiece. The buzzard lope suits an old man splendid, for it is best performed with rheumatism in one leg and St. Vitus dance in the other, and it is said to be a sovereign remedy for both.

Some folks don't care much about music—some don't care anything about dancing, but some folks like both because it is their nature and they can't help it. It is just as natural for children to love to dance to the harmony of sweet sounds as it is for them to love to play marbles or jump the rope, or any other innocent sport. The church allows its members to pat the foot to music, but condemns dancing because it leads to dissipation and bad company; but we shouldn't let it lead the young folks that way. The church condemns minstrel shows and minstrel songs, but has lately stolen from them some ot their sweetest tunes, and set them to sacred verse, and is all the better for it. Who does not appreciate the "Lilly of the Valley" that is now sung to the "Cabin in the Lane?" Puritanism, and penance, and long faces, and assumed distress are passing away. The Methodist discipline that forbade jewelry, and ornaments, and fine dressing has become obsolete, for it was against nature. What our creator has given us to enjoy, let us enjoy in reason and in season and be all the more thankful for His goodness.

I believe in music. Joseph Henry Lumpkin, our great chief justice, said there was music in all things except the braying of an ass or the tongue of a scold. I believe in the refining influences of music over the young, and if an occasional dance at home or in the parlor of a friend will make the young folks happy, let them be happy. I read Dr. Calhoun's beautiful lecture that he delivered before the Atlanta Medical college—a lecture on the human throat as a musical instrument—and I was charmed with its science, its instruction, and its literary beauty. I read part of it to those boys who were practicing for the serenade—about the wonders of the human larynx, that in ordinary singers could produce 120 different sounds, and fine singers like Jenny Lind could produce a thousand, and Madam Mora, whose voice compassed three octaves, could produce 2,100 different notes;

and about Farinelli, who cured Phillip V., king of Spain, of a dreadful malady by singing to him, and after he was fully restored he was afraid of a relapse and hired Farinelli to sing to him every night at a salary of fifty thousand francs, and he sang to him as David harped for Saul. Music fills up so many gaps in the family. The young people can't work and read and study all the time. They must have recreation, and it is better to have it at home than hunt for it elsewhere. If the old folks mope and grunt and complain around the house, it is no wonder that the children try to get away. And they will get away if they have to marry to do it. I have known girls to marry very trifling lovers because they were tired of home. This reminds me of a poor fellow who was hard pressed by a creditor to whom he owed forty dollars. He came to employ us to get a homestead for him so as to save his little farm. "Are you a married man?" said I. "No, I aint," said he. "Well, you will have to get married before you can take a homestead. Is there no clever girl in your naborhood whom you have a liking for?" He looked straight in the fire for a minute or more, and then rose up and shook his long, sandy hair, and said: "Gentlemen, the jig are up. I'll have to shindig around and get that money, for I'll be dogond if I'll get married for forty dollars. Good mornin'."

We are working hard, now, renovating and repairing the home inside and outside. We have whitewashed the fence all round, and the barn and coal-house, and chicken house, and all. We have paint- the gates a lovely red, and striped the greenhouse, and Carl wanted to stripe the calf with the same color, as a meandering ornament to the lawn, but he couldn't catch him. I have planted out Madeira vines and Virginia creepers and tomato plants, and we have declared war against the English sparrows that destroy more strawberries than we get. We will have things fixed up when the maternal comes home. I reckon she will come sometime—come home spoiled like I do as when I take a trip off and am petted up by genial friends. It will take us a week to get her back in the harness, but it won't take her half that long to get us back. We've got two picnics on hand, and a fishing frolic, and there are five pretty girls from Cement coming here tonight, and on the whole I don't think I am as lonesome as I think I am.

"So here's a health to her who's away."

CHATPER LVIII.

UP AMONG THE STARS.

I was talking to the children the other night about astronomy, and I said: "I am a traveler—a great traveler. I have traveled forty thousand million of miles in my life. I was born traveling. I can beat railroads and telegraphs. When I travel I make 68,000 miles an hour, and don't exert myself a bit. I can make over 1,500,000 miles in a day, and turn a summerset 8,000 miles high in the bargain— I turn one every day when I am on the road. I traveled nearly 600,-000,000 miles last year."

And so I made the children figure it all up so as to impress upon them the immensity of space and the mighty power of God. I know an old man—a lawyer—who didn't believe in any of these things. He said it was not according to scripture. He didn't believe the earth was round or that it turned over. He said the scriptures spoke of the ends of the earth, and the four corners of the earth, and that Joshua commanded the sun to stand still just like he did the moon, and they both stood still. We used to argue with him, and tell him that navigators had sailed all around the earth, but it was no use, and we gave him up.

I know lots of sensible people who don't believe that astronomers know anything about these immense distances and orbits and weights of the planets. They say it is all guess work, pretty much, and that it is impossible to tell how far it is from one place to another, or one planet to another without measuring it with a chain or a rod-pole or a string or something. And here is where a higher education comes in and broadens the mind and elevates it to a higher plane. There is no science so exact and so fully established as astronomy. The distance from here to Atlanta is not so accurately known as the earth's orbit around the sun. A great astronomer like Herschel or Newton or La Place can look through the telescope at Jupiter's moons when they are in an eclipse, and then mix up a few logorithms and fluxions and parallaxes and tell how fast light travels and how far it is to the remotest planet in the universe.

The children wanted to know why the new year began with January, and I couldent tell them. Christmas would have been a better day. The new era should have begun with the birth of Christ instead of a week later; or the year should begin with the birth of spring—the 21st of March—when nature is putting on new garments. Those old philosophers got things awfully mixed up anyhow. Their years used to be measured by the moon, and they had thirteen months, but that dident fit, and so they fell back to ten months of thirty-six days each, and that dident fit, and next they put in two more months and had no leap year, and at last Pope Gregory fixed the measure all right—just as we have it now. It was only in the last century that the civilized nations adopted the new time. Russia hasent adopted it yet; but I don't know whether she is civilized or not.

January was a right good name for the first month. He was a watchful old fellow and had two faces, and could look before him and behind him at the same time. It is a good idea for a man to look back over the year that has gone and review his conduct, and then look forward and promise to do better. But most of the months were named for heathen gods who never existed, and so were the days of the week. I wish the school children would read about them and be able to answer what March means, and April and Wednesday and Thursday, and the other names. Gather knowledge as you go along —useful knowledge—and store it away. If you havent got the books borrow them from somebody and read. I asked two young men yesterday how far it was to the sun, and they had no idea.

1891! There is a meaning in those figures. Every time they are written on a letter head or a ledger or a bank check or a note or a hotel register, or printed on a newspaper, they mean something. The pens of Christians and infidels and skeptics and agnostics and Jews and Gentiles are all writing it visible and indelible upon the paper. Every day, every hour, every minute, it is being written all over the world, and every mark establishes a fact—a great fact—that 1891 years ago there was a birth—a notable birth—and old Father Time began a new count and called it Anno Domini. What a wonderful event it must have been that closed the record of the ages and started time on a new cycle. How in the world did it happen? The Greeks had their calendar and the Romans had theirs, and the Jews had one that was handed down by Moses, but all of them were overshadowed by the one that a handful of Christians set up, and for 1400 years the Anno Domini has given a date to every birth and death and event in the civilized world. It seems to me that if I was an infidel I would not place these figures at the top of my letters. I would not dignify the birth of a child that way; I would rather write 5894 as the date of the creation. But, no, if I did not credit Moses and the prophets, I couldent choose that date, and so I would have no date—no era to begin with. The Greeks had their Olympiads to date from, and the Romans the birth of their ancient city, and the Mohammedans the flight of Mohamet, but a modern agnostic has nothing. If he was an American, I suppose he might begin with the Declaration of Independence, and say January 114. The Jew is better off, for he has a faith—a faith as strong as the ages—and his era goes back to Moses and the prophets, but even he has to conform to the Anno Domini of the Christian in all his business relations with mankind. If he was to date a business letter or make out a bill of goods according to his faith it would be returned to him for explanations. What a wonderful thing is this date—these four simple figures. We write them and write them, but we seldom ponder on what they prove.

On New Year's night I was talking to the children about these things, and about the long journey we had taken since the last New Year. We have gotten back to the same place in the universe and have traveled nearly three hundred million of miles. Talk about your cannon ball trains and your lightning express! Why, we have been running a schedule of thirty thousand miles an hour and never stopped for coal or water, and never had a jostle nor put on a brake nor greased a wheel. Other trains have crossed our track, and we have crossed theirs, but there was no danger signal, no sign board, no red flag, no watchman. Was there ever an engineer so reckless of human life? Fifteen hundred millions of passengers aboard, and they sleep half the time. Did ever passengers ride so trustingly? And what is more wonderful still, our train has a little fun on the way, and every day turns a summersault twenty-five thousand miles round just for the enjoyment and health of the passengers. Turns over as it goes, turns at a speed of a thousand miles an hour and never loses an inch of space or a moment of time. Wouldn't it be big fun if we could stand off away from the train and see it roll on and turn as it rolled and see the passengers all calm and serene? It seems to me that if I was an infidel or an agnostic I would want to get off this train—a train without an engineer—a train that has got loose from somewhere and is running wild at the rate of 500 miles a minute. Talk about your Pullman sleepers and vestibule and dining-room cars! Why, this train carries houses and gardens and fruit trees and everything good to eat. It is a family train, and the family goes along with their nabors and the preacher and the doctor and the graveyard is carried along, too, so that if anybody dies on the way the train don't have to stop for a funeral. It is well that it don't, for the passengers are dying at the rate of a hundred a minute, and the train would never get anywhere if it had to stop to bury the dead.

Then we children got to talking about the centuries away back, when the months and the years were unsettled, and nobody seemed to know how long a year was or how to divide it; when the changes of the moon were a bigger thing than going round the sun; when there were only ten months in a year, and a year was only 360 days, and so January kept falling back until it got to be summer instead of winter; when there were no weeks, except among the Jews, and the month was divided by the Greeks and Romans into three decades of ten days each; when Julius Cæsar tried to regulate the calendar and made the year 365 days and gave a leap year of 366. But that didn't work exactly right, for it made leap year eleven minutes too long, and so, as the centuries rolled on, it was found in 1582 that old Father Time had gained twelve days on himself, or on the sun or something else, and Pope Gregory concluded to set the old fellow back a peg or two, and he did. If a pope could make us all twelve days younger when he pleased to do it he would be a very popular man, I reckon. But the calendar is all right now, and the civilized world has adopted it. It is eleven minutes fast every four years, but as the year 1900 is not to be a leap year the gain will be canceled when that year comes Leap year used to double the sixth day of March instead of adding a day to February, and so it was called the bis-sextile year. It is well for the children to know these things for they are worth knowing.

CHAPTER LIX.

Oh! These Women!

Oh, these women, these women—they make me so tired. But it is a sweet service. Here I've been working in the harness for forty years, and I don't reckon I would be happy if the harness was off. I I know I wouldn't for sometimes when Mrs. Arp goes off to spend the day I don't feel natural about the house. I want somebody to order me around in a sweet, feminine way: "William, that stick that was between the sash has fallen out and is down there on the ground—don't you feel the cool air coming in? William, the clock needs cleaning very bad—it stopped twice yesterday—hadn't you better take it down to Mr. Baker's? William, I wish you would get a little paint and give the old mantlepiece a coat—you have scraped so many matches on it to light your old pipe that it is a sight. A little can of prepared paint won't cost much. And that old grate needs a coat of polish—oh! I did see some of the loveliest grates down at the exposition, and those tiles for hearths were exquisite. I don't mean for you to buy any, but I am just telling you. Somehow, whenever I tell you about the beautiful things I see, you look like you didn't have a friend in the world. Of course I don't mean that I want you to buy them. William, what am I do with the flowers—the geraniums, and verbenas, and all the potted plants? The winter is coming on, and I do wish we had a little pit somewhere. It will be a pity to lose them. Hattie has had a pit dug, and says it didn't cost but two dollars—and she is going to cover it with a cloth frame. Sam Pitts digs pits," she continued—"Sam Pitts digs pits," said I. And so I sent for Uncle Sam and marked off the place, six by ten, and squared it according to rule, and he had been digging a few minutes when Mrs. Arp raised the window and said she thought it was a little too far that way, and so I moved the marks a couple of feet and began to dig again. In a little while she came out and said it was too far this way, and so I moved it back where it was at first, and she said it was about right now. She thinks that I split the difference, but I didn't. The next day she asked me in a gentle voice how much a brick wall around the top would cost—a brick wall about three feet high on one side and a foot high on the other. "And sash with glass for a cover," said I, for I knew she was thinking about it. She smiled sweetly and said: "Yes." I scratched a match on the mantle and lit my pipe and ruminated. That was yesterday. Mr. White is making those sash today, and the brick mason is building the wall, and I am still in the harness. Alek Stephens said he wanted to die in the harness, and he did; but he never knew anything about matrimonial breeching, or he would have wanted to live and not die at all. What would become of a man if he didn't have a woman to keep him lively? When we were in Atlanta the other day, my wife asked me for five dollars to buy a pair of shoes. "Have shoes gone up?" said I, as I handed her the money. No, but I have," she said—"I want a fine pair—shoes that are as soft as kid gloves; you owe me lots of shoe money; you promised me before we were married that you would give me thirteen pair a year—don't you remember?" "Yes," said I, "and you have had them and more too. How can a woman raise ten children on less than thirteen pair a year? But I would have promised you anything then. I would have climed the Chamborazo mountains and fought a tiger for you then—a small tiger—but I would fight a big one now. Here, take another five and buy you some fine stockings to go with the shoes, but don't buy black ones. I despise to see a white woman wear black stockings. It is like a heathen Chinee blacking his teeth." I wish I had the making of the fashions. I see that the bustles have gone out at last, and I am glad of it—I never did like these unnatural humps on a woman's back. They have been in and out a dozen times since I was a boy, and so have hoop-skirts. It is funny to see a new fashion come in and go out. There are women in my town still wearing bustles. They feel sorter shamed to leave them off all of a sudden. But they will fall into line and slim down before long. They have done slimmed at my house. They keep up pretty well. I saw lots of nice ladies at the fair who were behind, and so were their bustles, but they were from the country and little towns, and hadent caught up. It is a good deal of trouble to alter a bustle-dress to a no-bustle-dress, and all the mysterious garments underneath have to be altered, too, and that is why it takes a fashion so long to run out. It costs money and work. Now, if the ladies will cut off about four inches of their skirts and keep out of the winter's mud, they will be all right. Let them show their ankles if they want to. There is nothing prettier than the poetry of motion that is in a lady's foot and ankle when she walks. It pleases an old man mightily.

But the men have passed through some very ridiculous fashions, too. When I was in my teens and had begun to notice the girls and put oil on my hair and cinnamon drops on my handkerchief, the fashion was to wear short pants and straps—leather straps about an inch wide that came under the shoe and fastened to buttons sewed on the inside of the pants. When a feller sat down the whole concern was drawn as tight as an eelskin, and there was a continual strain on the straps at the bottom and the suspenders at the top. Sometimes a button broke or a strap bursted under peculiar circumstances, and then the pants crawled up amazingly. One day I was riding out with my sweetheart and the catastrophe happened as we were running a galloping race up a long hill, and my pants crawled up to my knees and carried the undergarments along, and it was on her side of the horse, and she laughed and laughed until she liked to have fell off, and I had to get down and cut a skewer off of a rail and fasten the strap on again. The mischievous thing told it on me, and I never got even with her until one day her bustle came untied and dropped off as she was passing my store, and I picked it up and handed it to her with a bow as polite as a Frenchman, and said: Miss Mary, your shoe-strap is broken." The bustles of that day were shaped like a new moon and stuffed with bran. They were generally about as large as a hoe-handle and tapered out to a point at each end, but the more style the bigger the bustle. They were all home-made and were considered a very sacred and mysterious article of feminine furniture. Sometimes one of these big ones would rip from long wear and tear, and the bran would leak out as the woman wiggled along, and you could track her all the way home just like the hogs would track a mill boy when there was a hole in his corn sack. I remember when the hoop-skirt of a high-flying woman was three feet across at the bottom, and when she stood up close against the counter, her dress didn't need any shortening behind. It was a sight of trouble to squeeze them in the pews of the churches, and sometimes they behaved in a very unseemly manner when the wind was blowing in a shifty way. I remember when the college boys wore boots according to their politics. The toes were shaped like a duck's bill, and were turned up and over on top of the foot like a skate, and if the boy was a whig he had Clay printed on the toes in large letters, and if he was a democrat he had Polk printed there, and so they walked about sticking their politics into everybody's faces.

But after all, I believe the women of this generation are more reasonable in their dress than for many generations past. Three thousand years ago they were fast, very fast, for Josiah tells about "the bravery of their tinkling ornaments about their feet and their cauls and their round tires like the moon (bustles, I reckon), their chains and bracelets and mufflers, the bonnets and ornaments of the legs and headbands, and tablets and earrings, and nose jewels and changeable suits of apparel, and the mantles and wimples, and crisping pins and hoods and vails." Oh, it took a sight to set up one of those high-flying Hebrew women, and the prophet went for them as fiercely as old Allen Turner used to go for our women a half century ago. "If that young woman with the green bonnet on the back of her head and the devil's martingales around her neck and his stirrups on her ears don't quit her giggling, I'll point her out to the congregation." Yes, we are all doing better—except some. But I must stop; Mrs. Arp is calling me to come and put out some more chrysanthemums, and I'm so tired.

CHAPTER LX.

THE MISCHIEVOUS LITTLE ONES.

There is a wide difference between mischief and meanness. But mischief is close akin to it, when it injures anybody or hurts their feelings, or breaks the rules or the laws. Most all boys love a little mischief. I used to love a good deal. I remember when we thought it ever so smart to slip around at night and change the gates and the signs, or stretch a rope across the sidewalk, or tie a goat in the school house, or put one man's horse in another man's stable. I have worked mighty hard at such things, and I did think it was just as funny as it could be, but somehow or other I don't see a bit of fun in it now. I wonder what is the matter with me. My children inherited mischief, I reckon, and so I have to excuse them, but when my little girl thoughtlessly pulled the chair away just as I was about to sit down, and I came down with a shock that jarred the house, and my feet flew up and knocked the lamp off the table, I was mad, very mad, until I looked at her and saw how frightened she was, for she hadn't counted on such a catastrophe. So I tempered down and picked up the broken fragments and never said a word, and it was a minute before anybody spoke. Mrs. Arp was the first to break the awful silence with an explosion of laughter, and that started the children, of course—all but Jessie, poor little little thing, who come to me and said: "Papa, I didn't mean to do it." I knew that she didn't, but my offended dignity was at stake, and I got me another lamp and went to writing. I wanted to laugh as much as they did, but I wouldn't. That was four years ago, and Mrs. Arp is not done laughing at it yet whenever it is alluded to. I believe it would do her good to see me bump the floor and kick over a lamp about once a week.

I was ruminating about this because my boy came home from school ahead of time and sat down before the fire looking solemn and sad. I was writing by the window and wondered what was the matter. For awhile he never moved or spoke, but suddenly he looked up at me and said, in a pitiful voice: "Papa, was you ever suspended?" "Suspended?" said I. "I don't understand you—suspended how?" "Suspended from school," said he. "Why, no," said I. "What makes you ask that question?" He choked up, and said: "Well, I'm suspended, and so is Tom Milner." "Is it possible?" said I, as I laid down my pen. "What have you been doing?"

Then he told as how he and Tom had got to throwing water at each other while the professor was in the other room, and how he missed Tom and the whole dipper full struck the blackboard and put out the sum and ran down upon the floor, and the professor came in just at the wrong time and asked who did it, and suspended him and Tom and told them to take their books and go home. I felt greatly relieved, of course, for I saw that it was mischief and not meanness, but I never said anything and looked solemn and resumed my writing. Now, it distresses my children to see me distressed, and that is a good sign. As long as a boy loves his parents, and is troubled when they are troubled, there is hope of that boy. After awhile he said: "Papa, what must I do about it?" "I don't know," said I, "until I see the professor. Not long ago we had up a case of suspension, and the board refused to take the boy back. I don't know what they will do with you and Tom. I expect you have been trying the professor's patience for some time. You are not bad boys and are very good scholars, but your disposition to mischief has troubled him and set a bad example. The other boys are talking about you, and say that the professor is partial to you and Tom, and I'm afraid that he is; I am glad that he has stopped your mischief."

But it came out all right. The boys were not suspended, and they went back the next morning and apologized, and now everything is calm and serene. The boys must conform to the rules. If one boy throws water, all the boys have the right to throw water, and that wouldent do, and a sensible boy knows it. Let every boy act upon principle. They may be tempted to tell a story to get out of a little scrape. But it is better to tell the truth. The truth is the thing—the biggest thing I know of If I had a great business that would give employment to a thousand boys, and I had to go about and select them, the first question I would ask would be, "Does he always tell the truth?" I wish the boys and girls could realize how much anxiety they give us. Here are 400 going to school in our little town, and in a few years they have got to take our places and make the laws and do the business and make up society and establish the morals of the community, and upon their conduct the happiness and good name of the people will depend. The young men of this generation will have to solve the race problem and all the other problems, and upon them will depend the existence of the government. We think about this a good deal for it effects our children and grandchildren. It troubles us to think about wars and anarchy and revolution, and about tyrants and bad men getting into power, and about the rich getting richer and the poor poorer. I know that it will be all right if the people will do right—if the children grow up with good morals and good principles. We have got good schools almost everywhere in the South. I know we have in Cartersville. I am proud of the professors and the teachers and the pupils. We are a long ways ahead of Boston. There are no hip pockets in our schools, no kicking of teachers, no bands of forty thieves. We have Christian teachers and the moral training goes right along with the school books. The boy or girl who gets no more education than can be had in our schools has the foundation laid for any beginner in life.

St. Valentine's day has come again and the good old fellow does seem to have some influence upon the bipeds, for our young people are mating and marrying all around us. That is all right, and we love to see it going on, for it is according to nature. Most everybody takes some stock in the marriages of the young folks. Even the old bachelors and old maids wake up and smile and bid them good speed. They are taking a great risk, we know, but it is best to take it, even if the venture is a failure. If it is a failure, it is their fault. I never knew an unhappy marriage that was not made so by one or both of the parties. It is a sad thing to marry in haste and repent at leisure. It don't pay to marry by the month. I never hear of hasty and inconsiderate marriages but what I think of those sad and serious lines of Tom Hood:

> " Oh very, very dreary is the room
>   Where love, domestic love, no longer nestles;
>   But smitten by the common stroke of doom,
>   The corpse lies on the trestles."

The corpse of conjugal love is an awful corpse. Not long ago a married woman asked me for $10. She said her husband had money, but she wouldn't ask him for a dollar if she never got any. There is a corpse in that house. The husband is stingy and tyranical—the wife is proud and sensitive, and so love got sick soon after the marriage and lingered and languished and died. A man ought not to force his wife to ask him for money. It does humiliate a woman. It makes her feel her helplessness, her dependence, and smothers her equality. The husband ought to anticipate her wants if he is able. The money or the bank account ought to be at her disposal at all times, for she will spend less of it foolishly than he will. A very considerate wife told me that it was her greatest trial to ask her husband for money, though he was always kind and never refused. And I suspect there is many a good wife who is humiliated in the same way. It is St. Valentine's season now, and a fit time for the married folks to mate again and renew their promises. What a pity that love should get sick so soon and turn into a corpse—a corpse that cannot be buried but stays in the house by day and by night. From such a corpse, good Lord deliver us.

CHAPTER LXI.

THOUGHTS ON SPRING AND LOVE.

"Hail, gentle spring!" saith the poet. She didn't hail but she snowed and sleeted a little. Another poet says: "Winter lingers in the lap of spring." The old rascal keeps on lingering there—he likes the place. I wish the gentle maiden would shove him off and tell him to go. She seems to like his caresses—I haven't seen an alder tag nor red maple ear drop this year. It is time for the dogwood to bloom and the wild violets to peep out from their wintry beds, and the minnows to play in the branches, and the lambs to shake their new-born tails. Every few days the robins come and the bluebirds sit longingly on the broken cornstalks, but they don't stay long. The plum-tree blooms look sickly, and the peach bud don't know whether to venture out or not. Spring poets are languishing and, languishing do live, and all nature seems waiting and wishing for the grass to spring, and the flowers to bloom, and the birds to sing, and the voice of the turtle dove to be heard in the land.

It is now five long weeks since the good St. Valentine told the birds to mate and the girls and boys to go wooing. St. Patrick has been out and shook his shelalah at the snakes, but still gentle Spring keeps on flirting and fooling with old man Winter and makes him believe she is in love with him. But she isent. May and December never mate, nor March and November. It is against the order of nature. We old people can look and linger and admire, but that is all. We have sailed down the river and encountered its perils, its reefs and rocks and shoals and quicksands, but, strange to say, we give no warning. Maybe it is because we know that warning will do no good; maybe, because misery loves company; maybe, because it is the order of nature, the fiat of the Almighty. Verily, the young people would mate and marry and launch their boat and sail down that river if they knew there was a Scylla and Charybdis at every bend and leviathans and malestroms and cataracts all the way down. Poor, trusting, suffering woman. What perils, what trials, what afflictions does the maternal instinct bring upon you! Close by us, while I write, is a beautiful young mother lingering in the grasp of death—dying that her first-born child may live. There is nothing more touching, more pitiful, more heroic in nature. There is nothing that a man is called upon to endure that compares with the death of a mother in childbirth.

But there is a brighter side—a more charming, comforting picture of life—married life, domestic life—when the good mother is a matron, and looks with pride upon her children and grandchildren as they come and go lovingly before her. What calm serenity hovers over her matronly face. What sweet content, what grateful rest—rest from her labors, her pains, her care and anxiety. Well may she exclaim with Paul: "I have fought a good fight; I have kept the faith; I have finished my course. Henceforth there is laid up for me a crown of righteousness."

To every lad and lassie there is a period of life not always thrilling or tragical, but highly emotional and sensational. Of course, I mean the period of love—young love—or loves young dream, which sometimes runs smooth and sometimes don't. What a luxury it would be to look behind the curtain and see just what love has felt and suffered and enjoyed. Such a kaleidoscope would have a world of eager lookers, for the old are as fascinated with stories of love and courtship as the middle-aged and young. In looking over the daily or weekly paper we may skip the displayed headings of war in Bulgaria or riots in London or murders in Wyoming, but any little paragraph that has love in it, arrests the eye and demands attention. Children go to school to study books, but by the time they are in their teens they begin to mix a little timid, cautious love with their other studies. A sweetheart is a blessed thing for a boy. It straightens him up and washes his face and greases his hair and brushes his teeth and stimulates his ambition to excel and be somebody. Jerusalem! How I did luxuriate and palpitate and concentrate towards the first little school girl I ever loved. She was as pretty as a pink and as sweet as a daisy, and one day at recess, when nobody was looking, I caught her on the stairs and kissed her. She was dreadfully frightened, but not mad. Oh no, not mad. She ran away with blushes on her cheek, and more than once that evening I saw her glance at me from behind her book and wondering if I would ever be so rash again.

And now, Mr. Editor, if a thousand of your patrons peruse these random memories, nine hundred of them can finish up the chapter from their own unwritten book. Who has not loved, who has not stolen a kiss, who has not caught its palpitating thrill and felt like Jacob when he lifted up his voice and wept. Oh, Rachel, beautiful and well favored, no wonder that Jacob watered thy sheep and then kissed thee, for there was no one to molest or make thee afraid. That memorable kiss is now 4,000 years old, and has passed into history as classic and pure, but I have had them, and so have you, dear reader, just as sweet and soul-inspiring, and never said anything about it to anybody. Ours' was a mixed school, and every Friday the larger boys and girls had to stand up in a line and spell and define. My sweetheart stood head most generally, and so I was stimulated to get next to her, and I did, and my right hand slyly found her left, and we both were happy. But time and circumstances separated us, and we both found new loves—she married another feller and was content, and so did I, but neither of us have forgotten the stolen kiss or that tender childish love that made our school-days happy. But love becomes more earnest after awhile—more intense, more frantic—the young man means business and so does the maiden. Like the turtle-doves in the spring of the year, they are looking around for a mate. This is nature, and it is right. God said, "It is not good for man to be alone; I will make a helpmeet for him." And so he made Eve to help meet the expenses, and that is what a wife ought to do now, but a good many of them don't. They help make them, but they don't help meet them, and that is why the young men have almost quit marrying. The rich girls won't have them, and the poor girls are trying to keep up with the rich, and so the turtle-doves mate slowly now-a-days. Folks need to love and court and marry with more alacrity than they do now. It is not vanity to say that I could have married half a dozen nice girls, and my wife could have had choice of a dozen clever, prosperous youths as likely as myself. Cupid just roosted all around those woods and shot his arrows right and left. Sometimes he shoots a young man and then waits days and weeks before he shoots the girl he is after. This keeps the poor fellow on the warpath, and frantic and rampant, and Cupid laughs. But he was clever to me, for as near as I can judge, he let fly both arrows at once and plugged my girl and me simultaneously, and with a center shot. My wife denies this, but I have told it so often I believe it. There was no skirmishing on my part. I never did shoot with a scattering gun. Marrying was cheap in those days. My recollection is that it cost me only about forty-five dollars—twenty-five for clothes, ten for a ring and ten more to the preacher. It didn't cost anybody else anything to speak of, for there were no wedding presents. That tomfoolery wasent invented. We didn't go to Niagara, or anywhere right away, but we went to work. A month or so later, we did take a little trip to Tallulah Falls and look at the water tumble over the rocks, but that didn't cost but a few dollars and made no sensation outside the family. My thoughtful wife had enough nice clothes to last her two years when I married her, and they were long afterwards cut up and cut down for the children and there are some precious fragments hid away in the old trunk now. The old trunk, and of common size, was sufficient then for a traveling wardrobe for a lady of the land. My father and mother and two children made a journey by sea to Boston with one trunk and a valise, and came back to Georgia by land, in a carriage; but not long since I saw a delicate female traveling with two trunks four times as large, and ribbed with iron, and fastened with three massive locks, and still she was not happy. Oh, my country! That girl was too much in love with her clothes to love a man, and nobody but a fortune-hunter would dare to marry her. **Young man, beware of trunks!**

CHAPTER LXII.

BILL ARP PLAYS RINGMASTER.

Mrs. Arp was quietly reading *The Constitution* yesterday while the children were out doors. After awhile she paused, and looking over her spectacles at me, remarked: "I thought that maybe you would have mentioned that little circumstance about the buggy and the ringmaster in one of your letters, but I suppose it does not seem to you to be very interesting matter to write about. Probably if the horse had run away with me, the public would have heard of it." And with that she resumed her reading. Well, that's a fact. I was thinking that the less said about some things the better; and besides, as I told her, I didn't want to make a hero of myself in such a small transaction. She quietly replied: "Oh, no, of course not; but I didn't think there was very much hero about it, and thought you could mention it in a small way without any particular peril—just to fill up, you know." So I reckon I had better tell it.

It was her buggy. One of her boys bought it and gave it to her. It had a nice top, and a phaeton shaped body that she could get into so easy, and the harness were hers, and the whip. Everything was new and nice, and she had taken but two rides in it, and so one day I hinted that I would like to see how it meandered over the country, and as it was all agreeable, I had my young horse hitched in, and sailed around smartly. We had worked that horse in the wagon and in the plow, and considered him pretty well broke, for he came from gentle stock, and we had raised him and petted him, and so had no fears about his behavior. One of the girls had been riding with me, and I let her get out at the front gate and drove on up to the big farm gate at the top of the hill, and opened it and led the black rascal through, and I thought he was serene, and knew he was tired, and so I just stepped back for a moment to shut the gate, and away he went like he was shot out of a gun. He run down to the horse lot gate all right, and I thought would surely stop there; but finding the gate shut, he took a little roundance and went sailing down towards the spring, and jumped over a big log, and the buggy jumped too, for it was doing its level best to keep up, and then he took the grand rounds of the hillside grove, and every time I tried to head and catch him he dodged me, and kept on with the buggy, sometimes on four wheels and sometimes on two. I had the whip in my hand, and Mrs. Arp, my wife, says that when she came to the back door to see what was the racket, I was standing there with the whip a-waving, and looked for all the world like a ring master in a circus, and she actually thought I was making the colt run round just for my own amusement. Well, there's no use in making a long story of it now, for what's done can't be helped. That colt tore that buggy all to pieces, and got away from it before he quit trying. He run it against three trees and over four logs, and left the beautiful top in one place and the wheels in another, and the shafts got bent backwards underneath the running gear, and I can't tell to this day how they got there.

I walked into the house and said nothing for ten minutes, and I didn't want anybody to say anything to me. Mrs. Arp never said nothing, either, but set down to her sewing just as natural, and sorter hummed a piece of a tune. After a spell she looked over at my side of the house, and remarked:

"It was a very pleasant evening for your ride."

"Uncommon," said I.

"I expect it will be good for your rheumatism for you to take a ride every evening," said she.

"They say that walking is better for rheumatism than riding,' said I.

"Well, you will have a good chance for that now," said she; and she laid down her work and laughed at me—and that's the way she broke me of the pouting melancholy. And that's always the way. When I am distressed and low down, she is all serene and lively and cheers me up. Fact is, she gave me such comfort about that buggy business that I am almost glad it happened. But still I am sorter sore about that ring master part of it, and then again, I overheard the children asking Ralph if he wasn't glad that it wasn't him. And Ralph said, "Goodness gracious! I wouldn't have had it happened to me for a hundred dollars."

Well, it is not so bad as it might have been, for I might have been in it and had my wheels and my body and springs all tore up. It will cost about twenty dollars to repair the damage, and she says she will pick it up in the road, or get it somehow, and that I mustn't be bothered.

I was telling my nabor Buford about it yesterday as a great calamity, and he laughed and said: "All we country folks are used to those things and a heap worse. Why," says he, "it was only yesterday morning that I and my brother Alf concluded to go to town, creek or no creek, for we knew it was up mighty high, and so we took roundance for a shallower ford up at Bradley's, and in we went all right till we got to the little deep swimming place, and the horse gave a lunge to jump that and popped the single-tree, and away he went out of the shafts and broke loose the hip straps and got to bank; but me and Alf was in the buggy trying to hold it down, and as I leaned over to catch my overcoat that was floating away, the buggy just careened over and spilt us both in the water, and it turned over on us, and Alf grabbed holt of one wheel and I of another, and we tried to hold it, but we had got into a sort of a whirlpool that was over our heads, and the box body just turned round and round and over and under, and sometimes we were on top and sometimes the buggy was on top, and we see-sawed that way and thingemajigged down the creek for a hundred and fifty yards, and had finally to let go and swim for the bank. If you ever saw drowned rats we were them, and we were so tired and so surprised we just set there on the bank and looked at one another and smiled, but the smiles were faint and sickly. I followed on down the creek and found my overcoat hung on a haw bush, and had to swim in to get it, but my best shoes were gone for good, and my shawl and some other things that were upon the seat and under it. Well, now, you see, the body got broke aloose and went off, and the wheels and running gear are down in Bishop's mill pond. But we got the horse home, and no lives lost or limbs broken, and are thankful. Alf and I walked home bare headed, and we went a half mile out of the way to keep anybody from seeing us. Our clothes weighed mighty nigh a hundred pounds, besides the overcoat, and we left a wet track behind us. Alf smiled again on the way, and says he: 'Oliver, I tell you what's a fact, folks oughtent to be expecting too much good luck in this sin-struck world nohow, but there is always something good mixed up with the bad.'

'Well, I should like to know what good there is about this?' said I. 'Why, said he, 'we got such a good washing; I reckon we are about the cleanest folks in the settlement.' After while he smiled again, and looked at me and said: 'Well, the cyclone struck us and tore us up, and our fall oats are all killed, and now the high waters have overflowed us. I wonder what is to be the next dispensation of Providence. I reckon it's a good time to sing:

'How firm a foundation, ye saints of the Lord.'"

What a good thing it is to have on hand at all times a stock of resignation. How comforting is adversity. An old Latin poet tries to describe a perfect man, and says, among other things, that he must never get out of temper, nor live above or below a certain line of calm serenity. That will do pretty well for a man, I reckon, but it wouldent suit a woman at all. I heard a smart old man say once that a woman who didn't have temper, and show it now and then, was no account, for while a man ought to be a philosopher and go according to reason, a woman wasent made that way. She is full of emotions, and is bound to show them. She is up and down—now calm and now excited—according to circumstances. Her love is stronger, and her dislike more intense. She has more wonder and curiosity, more tenderness and tears, more sympathy and reverence and hope. In fact, she is a purer, better creation, and was made so because she was to be a mother and the nurse of children.

"Her prentice hand she tried on man
And then she made the lasses."

I was talking to a nice lady one day about woman's rights, and she said that men and women both had too many rights now, and indulged themselves in some that dident belong to them. "For instance," said she, a "man has no right to be a fool, and no woman a right to be homely." "But how can she help it?" said I. "If a woman is born 'ugly,' as we call it, it surely is not her fault." "Of course not," said she, "but if she is born that way, she mussent stay that way. She can be good if she wants to be, and she can be kind and entertaining, and that will make any woman pretty on intimate acquaintance. The homeliest woman I ever knew was the most fascinating and attractive. And just so the biggest dunce of a man can keep from being a fool if he tries to; at least he can be a silent one, and then folks wouldent find out he was a fool."

CHAPTER LXIII.

Doctors Turned Loose.

Over 200 new doctors turned loose upon the country—200 from Atlanta alone, and a big lot from Augusta, besides. I went down on Monday to see our boy graduate. His mother went, too, for she believes he is a natural-born doctor and can cure anybody of anything, whether he has got it or not. When he comes home she will get sick just for him to have a patient. Old Uncle Sam was complaining, and she told him to wait until her doctor came. She has confidence in his technical words, all mixed up with Latin and Greek and other foreign languages. And then, there is his diploma that is in Latin, and it was presented by Col. Hammond in a Latin speech. I suppose this dead language is used as a symbol of the doctor's work. Col. Hammond spoke in a grave tone of voice. He said that the prophet Jeremiah exclaimed, "Is there no balm in Gilead—is there no physician there!" If he had lived in our day and witnessed the scene before us, he would not have asked that question concerning Atlanta. Here are eighty-six just made from one college. And he advised them all to emulate St. Luke, whom Paul called the beloved physician. Col. Hammond knows a power of Scripture, but he didn't mention King Asa, "who was diseased in his feet, and his disease was exceding great, yet he sought not the Lord, but sought physicians, and he slept with his fathers." Nor did he mention that "certain woman which had an issue of blood for twelve years, and had suffered many things of many physicians, and had spent all that she had, and was nothing better, but rather grew worse." Col. Hammond is an optimist, and looks on the bright side, and encouraged the young doctors. He looked at the beautiful bouquets that were sent upon the stage, and said: "Young gentlemen, these flowers are very beautiful and very appropriate for the occasion, but they are before you. Let your zeal, your study, your skill so inspire your professional life that you can look back and see flowers behind you. Flowers of praise and confidence from your patients and your patrons."

He then presented the doctors with their sheepskins and called each one by his Latin name, and some of them were so peculiar and unique they brought down the house, for John was Johannes, and William was Gulielmus, and Ralph was Radulphus. It reminded me of a lawsuit in a justice's court that happened a long time ago when Mark Blandford, who recently resigned from the bench of the Supreme Court, was a devilish young lawyer. A doctor sued a man for his medical bill of $15, and the man employed Mark to fight the case, for he said the doctor was no account and he discharged him. The doctor swore to his account, and Mark called for his license, or his diploma, and made the point that no doctor had a right to practice without one, and he read the law to the 'squire. And so the old 'squire told the doctor to show his sheepskin. He said he had one at home, and asked for leave to go after it. It was just six miles to town, and he rode in a hurry, and returned all in a sweat of perspiration. With an air of triumph he handed it over to Mark and said: "Now, what have you got to say?" Mark unrolled it and saw that it was in Latin. The doctor's name was John Williamson Head, but the Latin made it Johannes Gulielmus, filius, Caput. That was enough for Mark. He made the point that it was not a diploma, but was an old land grant that was issued in old colony times to a man by the name of Caput. He said he had read about the Caputs, and one of their ancestors whose name was John Sebastian Caput, discovered America, and this land grant was a bounty from the king of Spain. The doctor raved furiously, but Mark stuck to it that there was no mention in the document of John William Head—that it was issued to one Johannes Gulielmus, filius, Caput—a very different person—and he asked the doctor to please to read the thing to the court. Of course the doctor couldn't do it and he lost his case. The old 'squire said that he didn't know whether it was a land grant or a diploma or a patent for some machine, and if the doctor couldn't read it, he wasent fitten to use it. And so I think those eighty-six doctors had better get Col. Hammond to translate their diplomas, and then learn the English by heart.

Professor Lane gave the large audience a rare treat—a combination of wit and wisdom that only Charley Lane can make up. He rested his manuscript on an hour glass about four feet high, and all his serious, scholarly thoughts were there, but ever and anon he stepped to the front and illustrated his wisdom with humorous anecdotes that kept his hearers' eyes open, and their mouths too. He was hard down upon patent medicines, and told how Yacob Straus got up a nostrum and hired a fellow to certify: "This is to certify that I lost one of my eyes and two of my legs in the late war, and after using six bottles of Yacob Straus's medicine, my blind eye come again, and so did my legs." Openheimer had a drug store, too, and a patent medicine, and when he saw the certificate that Straus had gotten up, he hired a fellow to certify some, too: "I certify that I was unfortunately born without a liver or lights, and suffered untold miseries until I took four bottles of Openheimer's medicine, and now I have as good a liver as anybody and electric lights."

Professor Lane advised the doctors to use common sense in their practice, and said it was not called common sense because it was common, but because it was commonly needed.

Then we had a beautiful valedictory by Dr. Park, and the presentation of medals by Rev. Dr. Anderson, and last of all the boys caned Dr. Johnston, and then the benediction closed the entertaining exercises. I was ruminating about these doctors—how many would succeed and how many wouldn't; how many would take to drink and go to the bad; how many would drift away from parental moorings and become agnostics, or skeptics, or infidels. I thought how much depended on their skill and kindness, and how the loves and hopes of fathers and mothers were centered in what the doctor could do for the child or some loved member of the family. They say that doctors get hardened to suffering. Maybe they do, but they ought not to. If I was a doctor, I would make a show of tenderness and sympathy whether I felt it or not. It goes a long ways with the sick and the suffering, and with the family.

How much depends upon the doctor's skill in saving life can never be known, but a friend of mine in New York told me that a very eminent surgeon said to him some years ago: "I am responsible for Grover Cleveland's election. If it had not been for me he would have been defeated. That man Burchard who made the speech about 'Rum, Romanism and Rebellion,' was about to die from kidney disease. He sent for me as a last resort. I cut him open in the back and took his old republican kidney out and cleaned it and put it back again and sewed him up, and he got well and made that speech that drove the

Roman Catholics away from Blaine and elected Cleveland. Don't you see that if I had made a mistake in my diagnosis, or a mis-cut with my knife, Burchard would have died and Grover would have got left? Eh?"

And there was that poor man Garfield, the President, whom the doctors killed. An eminent surgeon told me that he was probed to death. They hunted for the ball for three days, and bored new holes with their probes until he was lacerated all through, and for no good. He said that pistol balls did no harm to stay in a man; that they became incysted, and it was better to let them alone than probe for them, and that the present practice in London and Paris was never to probe, but let nature go to work at once to heal the wound. Garfield would probably have lived if they hadn't probed him, and if he had lived Harrison wouldent have been president, don't you see? But we can't get along without the doctors. They are our comfort and our security by day and by night. They are our hope and our trust in times of affliction and peril. Then, hurrah for the new doctors! May they live long and prosper! It is a long ways to the goal of their ambition, but they must have patience if they would have patients.

CHAPTER LXIV.

On Hailstorms, Etc.

When all goes well humanity is mightily inclined to be stuck up and consequential. Folks strut around and put on airs as though they had created something, and were the lords of the land, and dident ask favors of anything or anybody. I've seen rich folks sailing about in phaetons and looking serene and complacent and self-satisfied, and they seemed to have an idea that they made the gold and the silver and the bonds and the stocks, when the truth was they got it all by gouging and fudging and taking underholt; not all of them, but a good many. I've noticed that the rich men who made their money honestly are not the proudest folks in the world. It is generally the men who inherit riches who are the proudest; folks who never earned an honest dollar in their lives.

But I was thinking how brave and independent we all feel when there is nothing to scare us. Most anybody will talk big about ghosts and graveyards in the day time, or even at night when sitting by the family fireside. Most men are brave according to circumstances; they are brave when they have a chance for life, and they are brave when they have good backers. They are brave when they have time enough to see the danger beforehand and prepare for it. But they are all cowards when taken by surprise or overwhelmed all of a sudden by some terrible unusual thing, especially some power of nature that no man can contend with—cyclones and storms and earthquakes and thunder and lightning subdues a poor mortal quick and takes all the stiffning out of him. It was only yesterday when the elements were on a rampage at my house, and the thunder pealed and the lightning played around, and black and angry clouds gathered over us, and darkness came before its time, and the children all huddled up around us and looked wild, and the dogs came running from the field, and the first thing we knew somebody threw a white rock on the roof of the house and I saw it bounce and roll off in the front yard, and while we were all wondering who did it a shower of them came down with a crashing noise, and we saw they were hail stones—stones sure enough—none of your coriander seed, but stones as large as walnuts, and some as large as guinea eggs, and they fell as thick and fast as rain drops on a mill pond. It wasent two minutes before the ground was as white as snow and the hail was banked up in piles in all the corners and low places. The sheep came running and bleating from the meadow, the horses made tracks for the stable, the chickens and ducks run under the house. Down, down it came stripping the fruit trees of their blooms and tearing the leaves off the euonimous bushes and mashing down the peas and onions and last, but not least, smashing through every pane of glass on the flower pit. The flowers were about half killed before, and now the wreck is all complete, and I've got work to do before Mrs. Arp comes home, so as to keep domestic affairs all calm and serene. The glass may go until next fall, for the plants needed ventilation anyhow, but I must get some more flowers and fill up the pots anew.

Just about the time when the storm subsided and the children had begun to run about and gather the big round hail, I observed a wayfaring man driving slowly down the hill and stop at my gate. He was humped over nearly double and had a long grizzly grey beard that looked demoralized, and his big broad-brimmed hat was all in a flop and hung down in wet scollops over his face and ears and the back of his neck. He stopped, but never said anything and looked like he didn't know where he come from nor whither he was going. After a minute, he ventured to raise one flop of his hat brim and looked up at me as I stood wondering on the piazza. He never called nor said good morning, but raised one arm and in a beseeching manner motioned me to come. I hurried down to his relief, and found it was my old friend, Col. Hutchinson, and as he looked piteously at me from under the flops, said: "Major, I'm a ruined man, I'm beat all into doll rags, and there's a thousand bumps on my poor head as big as turkey eggs. My back and my neck have been through a threshing machine. I'm as humble as a dead nigger. I'm the rise of sixty years old, and never was whipped before. Major, I want somebody to pray for me. I prayed for myself awhile ago. I prayed more in two minutes than I ever did in all my life, and I prayed harder, and if the good Lord spares me, I'm going to be a better man."

"Why, Colonel," said I, "where were you? Did your horse cut up? Have you been in all that hail?"

"I have, Major," said he, and the tears came in his eyes. "It took me all unawares and my horse got to raring and pitching, and I couldn't get out of the buggy, and so I run him up against your nabor Freeman's fence, and he danced and he pranced and squatted and trembled, and I held him and honied him and prayed all the time as hard as I could pray, and the hail-stones popped me until they mashed my hat down over my ears, and then my skull cotch it hot and heavy, and my head is swelled up so big now I can't get my hat off."

"Mighty bad, Colonel," said I, "awful bad for an old man like you."

"Yes," said he, "and it seemed to me that every time a big old sockdolager struck me I could hear somebody say, 'Oh, you old sinner, you time honored sinner, I'll maul the grace into your unbelieving soul.'"

I tried to get the injured man to get out and come in, but he mournfully said "no," for he must get out o' town and see a doctor and a preacher.

But how long the colonel will remain humble I don't know, for as a general thing a man's repentance and humility passes away with his trouble and his danger.

"The devil was sick, the devil a saint would be.
The devil got well, the devil a saint was he."

Well, the equinox has come and gone, and maybe the spring will open now and let us farm in earnest; all we could do the last two months was to repair damages after the freshets and stay in the house and read. I took a notion the other day to thin out my shade trees in the grove, for they were too thick and were so crowded the limbs of some of them were dying. I've been wanting to do it for a long time, but my wife, Mrs. Arp, thinks nearly as much of a tree as she does of me, and whenever I mentioned the subject there was a veto, and I couldn't pass the bill over it by the proper majority. So while she was away looking after her new grand children, I cut two of the trees down and made firewood of them, and cleaned up every chip and fragment, and put old dirt where the stumps were, and the children have all agreed to make no sign, and they have got up a bet or two as to whether their maternal ancestor will miss the tree or not, and little Jessie has bet her doll against a nickel that her ma will say something about the trees before she gets out of the buggy. But she will get reconciled after awhile, especially if I get some more flowers. And besides, there is a surprise for her in the house, for the girls have painted the dining-room floor and the doors and windows and mantlepiece, and whitewashed the walls a pretty straw color, and painted the ceiling overhead a lovely brown to hide fly specks, and now they are at work on another room; and we boys are building a new front fence and making another terrace, and so, take it all in all, I reckon we will all harmonize and everything be calm and serene.

CHAPTER LXV.

RUNAWAY NEGROES, GHOSTS AND OLD-TIME DARKIES.

"Papa, please tell us a story. Tell us something about runaway niggers."

I had almost forgotten that there ever was a runaway nigger. Good gracious! What a long time ago it was. Here is a whole generation of people under thirty years of age who know nothing about slavery. It is seldom that we old folks talk about it to our children. We tell them frequently of our frolics with the little darkies, and how good old Aunt Peggy was to us, and how we used to hunt with Big Ben and Virgil and Uncle Sam, and we repeat some of the ghost stories they used to tell us and all that, but the idea of slavery hardly ever comes in. These darkies all belonged to the family and just lived with us. That is all. We were all bunched together, and it was understood that when one of the boys got married and set up for himself he was to have little Dave and Buck and black Dan and Aunt Sally, for he had always claimed these and they had always claimed him. And Miss Tavy had picked out her vassals in her early childhood and nobody need lay any claim or expectation to Tip or Sinda or Beck, for they were to be hers and they knew it and were proud of it, and took a peculiar interest in the young man who "come flying around Miss Tavy." They even dared to venture their counsel and were loud in their praise of their favorite. This was right, and it was natural, for while she was choosing her lord they were choosing a master, and a harmonious choice was a good thing all around. Old Aunt Peggy was an oracle in her way. She was little and old and wrinkled, and smoked her pipe in the chimney corner, and never talked much. But she sat and swayed backward and forward and listened to the children—the black and the white. She called them all children if they were under fifty. But ever and anon she would give a grunt or shake her head and say "dat won't do, my child. Better mine how you talk, now; better mine. I hear de screech owl last night and he talk to me, he did," and she would make up some mysterious words that the screech owl said. Aunt Peggy believed in frogs and lizzards and owls and bats and cats and snakes and jack o'lanterns and charms and cunjuring. There were secret mysteries about them all, and they had to be propitiated and kept amiable or some great harm would come upon the household. Where the old negroes got all this superstitious lore nobody knows exactly, but it is not confined to them. There have been just such superstitions in all ages and countries. Macbeth consulted the witches and they made their charms by seething that horrible gruel made of frogs and lizzards and owls and bats and and adders' tongues and goats' gall and a Turk's nose and a Tartar's lips and other unpalatable things, and then cooled it down and settled it with a baboon's blood. Those old-time negroes would have made splendid witches if there had been any witch school to go to. It suited their nature, and it suits it yet. As a race, they delight in the marvelous when it is mixed up with the horrible. Old Uncle Sam was a good old darkey and the children loved him. He was familiar with spirits and graveyards, and had shook hands with Rawhead and Bloodybones, and when freedom came he gave full play to his fancies and got him a little long-eared donkey and a pair of spectacles and rode from cabin to cabin by day and by night, calling himself "Doctor Sam," and professing to cure all diseases of his race by the mysterious art of cunjuring. He carried his professional outfit in an old greasy sack before him, and he was the most ludicrous burlesque upon the medical profession ever seen, I reckon. I would give five dollars for a photograph of the whole concern as it used to slowly perambulate the Chattahoochee region of old Gwinnett some twenty years ago. I prevailed on the old gentleman once to let me see the inside of that bag and take an inventory. Besides nearly everything that Shakespeare named, he had every curious bug he could find. Betty bugs and June bugs and tumble bugs, and the devil's riding horse, and the devil's darning needle, and a green snake, and a thousandleg, and a lot of herbs, such as hemlock and jimpson weed and snake root. He assured me that he had to use all these things in the very bad cases he came across in his extensive practice.

But the children wanted a story about runaway niggers. Well, I never saw a runaway nigger. That is, while he was a runaway. I have seen them after they were caught or come in of their own accord. We boys and girls used to be awfully afraid of them. They were classed among our very worst boogers, such as bears and panthers and Indians and ghosts. Children were always on the lookout for one when they were going through lonely woods. Sometimes we found a hogbed where an old sow had littered her pigs, and we pronounced it a runaway's bed, and got away from there with celerity. They were very scarce in that region. I do not remember but one and he was suddenly cured of his propensity, for when he came back home his master run him off again and made him stay in the woods until he was properly humbled and begged to stay at home. I never thought that I should have a runaway nigger, but I did. Our colored household were, as I thought, devoted to us, and I knew that we were devoted to them. Our maid-servant, Mary, had nursed all our first children, and they loved her. A neighboring gentleman owned her husband, and as he was a high-strung darkey, they did not get along harmoniously. One night he took to the woods, or somewhere else unknown, and he stayed there. In course of time his master got tired of this and offered a reward, but the reward did not seem to catch him. The police frequented my premises by night, for they suspected that Mary harbored him, and so did I, but still Anderson could not be found. I didn't like the darkey, but Mary was faithful and kind, and she begged me with tears to buy Anderson. So I interviewed his master and bought him—bought him in the woods, and that night when I went home and told Mary that Anderson was mine she clapped her hands with joy, and went out hurridly and in ten minutes came back with Anderson, who was smiling and fat with his long rest under the fodder in my stable loft.

It was about two months after this that the foul invaders run us out of Rome. It was about midnight when I aroused the servants and told them that I was going, and their mistress was going, and the children were going, and they could all do as they pleased. With one accord they declared they would follow us to the end of the earth, and so we fled together and camped out together, and Mary had our baby in her arms, and when we reached Atlanta our teams and servants camped on the suburbs while we went into the city to more friendly quarters. Next morning Mary and Anderson were gone. They had run away in the night and returned to Rome. Well, I couldn't blame them, for Anderson was not attached to me, and he longed for freedom, and he persuaded Mary to go. That was all of it—no, not all, for when we got back to Rome, in 1865, they were there, and Mary was repentant and came to us for protection again. Her husband had joined the army, and when the army left he ran away from them and lost his pension and his bounty, and later on he ran away from Mary and I don't know where he is now. But Tip, the faithful Tippecanoe, would not leave me. I did not own his family, but he left them on that dark, unhappy night and followed us to Atlanta, and in a few days I made him go back to take care of things and see after the welfare of his wife and children. To keep from being suspected as a spy he, too, joined the colored regiment as a cook and stayed a few days, and one dark night he swam the Oustanaula river and went down the western bank of the Coosa about ten miles and swam that river, and by a circuitous route reached Atlanta in safety and followed our fortunes until the war was over. Well, those were the only runaways I ever had. Two ran away from me to the yankees, and one ran away from the yankees to get to me. Mr. Lincoln's proclamation was nothing to Tip. Tip was with me in Virginia. Tip was always faithful and affectionate. Tip deserves a pension from somebody, and I wish I was able to give him one. But Tip knows there is a home for him at my house whenever he is homeless. There are thousands of white men whose chances for heaven are not so good as Tip's.

"Run, nigger, run, de 'pat-roller' catch you;
Run, nigger, run, you better get away."

They used to sing that song and pick the music on the banjo. They used to dodge and flank the patrol like the smugglers or the moonshiners dodge the revenue laws. They enjoyed the peril of it, and sometimes would go on a night excursion without a pass rather than ask for one. If they planned to rob a hen-roost or an orchard or a watermelon patch, it was better to have no pass, so as to prove an alibi. "Let Dick pass to his wife's house at Jim Dunlap's and stay till Monday morning." That was Dick's passport and protection, but Dick must keep in the road, and not go skylarking over the settlement. Nevertheless, the petty stealing would happen, and so a law was passed making it a crime for a white man to buy chickens or produce from a negro without an order from his master. My uncle bought ten chickens from a darkey one Saturday night and they happened to be stolen, and the fellow who lost them reported it to the grand jury, and those chickens cost my uncle twenty-five dollars. If they had not been stolen it would have been all right and no harm done. The negroes stole little things then just like they do now. They enjoyed it. It was their nature. They were not hungry. I have known them to rob an orchard and give the fruit away. The best negro would carry something contraband to his wife's house Saturday night if he could get it. But the clever, industrious negroes had no fear of the patrol. The patrol knew all in their beat and never asked a good negro for his pass. The patrol was made up of the best citizens in the naborhood, and they took it time about in doing night duty in their own vicinity. When thieving got bad they went out frequently and raised a big racket and the mean darkies caught it bad. But when everything was quiet they would not go out once a month. Sometimes the darkies made narrow escapes and would jump the back window when they spied the patrol coming, and then the race was to the swift, sure enough, and the old song came in:

"Run, nigger, run, de 'pat-roller' catch you!"

Many a good story have they told us boys how they fooled the patrol and got away. It was more of a frolic than a fear, and one success made them bold and ready for another. Such was negro life in our young days; and it wasn't so bad, so very bad, after all.

CHAPTER LXVI.

The Candy-Pulling.

"What's all this rumpus about?" I came home to dinner and found the house full and yard full of children, grandchildren and other children. "Oh, nothing much," said Mrs. Arp. "I promised them a little party and they have come over to spend the day, and brought some little friends with them."

"Well, but these door-knobs are all stuck up with candy." "Yes, they had a candy pulling, and, I expect, have messed up things just like children will. I will wipe off the door-knobs."

"Well, but here I've gone and set down on a lump of it in this chair."

Mrs. Arp smiled and said: "Well, there's the washbowl and a rag."

I meandered out in the piazza and found candy knee deep in everything. The chaps were in the back yard cooking dinner on a little brick furnace they had built. Some were toting water and some bringing wood, and they had potatoes and rice and eggs and butter and pepper and everything they could beg from the cook. The waterspout was running all over everything. I stopped that part of it and surrendered to the rest, and retired to my accustomed seat at my desk.

"Who has been here projecting with my pens and letter pads, and turned over my inkstand and messed up my papers?"

"Oh, I don't reckon they have hurt anything. Rosa wanted to show me how she was learning to write. There was very little ink in the stand. I wiped off all she spilt."

I got up and walked in the garden, as King Ahasuerus did, to let my choler down, and I found where they had been picking peas and broke the twine that held the vines up, (I always stick my peas with twine), and so I came out of the garden to let my choler down somewhere else. I looked all round for the children to give them a blessing, but they had become alarmed, for Mrs. Arp had told them to run and hide. "I'll wear them out," said I. "I'll wear them out, big and little, old and young. I'm awful mad. I'm as mad as a mad bull. Broke down my pea vines!" And I mocked a bull and pawed dirt. The chaps had run up the ladder and got on the shed roof of the house, and as I pranced and bellowed around they smothered their laughter until I was out of sight, and then they turned loose in full chorus. I found the buggy pulled out of the shed and the whip gone, and the calf was tied up in the back lot with a saddle on, so I took my seat in the front piazza and put my feet on the railing and ruminated. My thoughts carried me away back to my childhood when I took delight in such things, and the whole picture came before me like the turning of a kaleidoscope. What a pity that folks can't be as happy as when they are children. About this time Mrs. Arp came out with a bundle of stuff and remarked that she brought home some pinks and chrysanthemums that must be planted out. "Are you doing anything?" said she. "I am ruminating," said I, solemnly. "Well, you had better ruminate around for the garden hoe, and I'll help you put them out—your back needs exercise."

I was picking peas the other morning, and as they were of the low kind, I had to bend over smartly, and by and by when I tried to straighten up, I couldn't straighten. There was a hitch and a pain in my veins—the same old trouble I had once before when I worked in the water half a day damming up the branch to make a wash hole for the children—so I hurried from the garden to the house half bent and made my usual fuss for help and sympathy. I was down for two days, and took medicine and chicken soup, and they put a bellydona plaster on my back as big as a letter pad, and it is there yet, and I'm not well, by a long shot but my folks seem to think I am. If I get up and creep to town, they put me to work as soon as I get back. I used to have boys of all sorts and sizes to wait upon me and do my bidding, but they have all grown up and left me but one, and he is at school, and when he isn't, he is off somewhere at baseball or tennis or picnicing around. I am the boy now—the waiting boy.

I was ruminating, but I found the hoe and dug around according to orders. Last night at the supper table Mrs. Arp remarked, as she was making the coffee, that to-day was another anniversary. I thought she meant a birthday, for they seem to come about once a week in the family, and she always wants to make a little present of some sort—a spoon, or napkin ring, or sleeve buttons, or something. I tell you what is a fact—where there are ten or a dozen children in a family to start on and they grow up and get married and multiply and replenish, and the posterity keeps on getting "more thicker, more denser," as Cobe says, and the maternal ancestor is a large-hearted woman, these birthday gifts and wedding presents will keep the old man's surplus down as effectually as the Republican party keeps it down in the United States Treasury. It is the easiest thing in the world. I never saw a mother with a numerous flock of lovely offspring but what she wanted a big house and a bushel of money. My wife is always scratching around hunting up something for the children. She reminds me of an old hen with a brood of young chickens, always a-clucking and scratching—and she says that I remind her of the old rooster who every now and then finds a bug or a worm and makes a big fuss and calls up the little chicks, and just before they get there he gobbles it up himself.

No, she didn't mean a birthday. She said that twenty-seven years ago to-day we were running from the foul invader as fast as our good horse and a rockaway could carry us. "Just about this time," said she, "we were hurrying across Euharlee bridge and I trembled all over for fear it would break in two, for it vibrated up and down to old Buckner's heavy trot, but you never slackened up a bit, and we fairly flew through old Van Wert, and took the mountain road until we got to Mr. Whitehead's, about dark."

"Yes," said I, "and we stayed all night there, and they did the best they could for all the runnagees, but they dident have room for the men folks, and we slept out doors under the wagon shed, and the fleas kept us so lively that we got up in the night and run through the bushes to brush them off, just like cattle do when the flies are after them."

"And the next morning about daylight," said she, "the news came that the yankees were coming, and we started up that long mountain, and it did seem to me that we never would get to the top. It must have been three or four miles up, and we felt pretty safe then and stopped awhile to rest, and then we scooted away to Dallas and rested there for dinner, and that night we camped out somewhere near Powder Springs. The wagon and our tent and baggage kept up pretty well, but we found out we dident have anything to cook in except a coffee pot."

"Yes, I remember," said I, "and we sent Tip off to a little farm house to borrow a skillet, and he came back without it and said the old woman told him the old man was washin' his feet in it, and we would have to wait until he got through. She said his feet had sores on 'em, and the dishwater was powerful good for sores. Tip tried another place and got a skillet that wasn't so popular."

"And next morning," said Mrs. Arp, "we stopped to get some water at a house, and the well was in the front yard, and it was locked with a chain and a padlock, and they wouldn't let us have a drop, and you gave the woman 10 cents for a cupful for the baby. Oh, it was just awful."

"I believe," said I, "that we had about seven children then."

"Yes," said she, with a sigh, "poor little half-starved things."

"Why, they enjoyed it," said I. "They thought it was a big frolic, and that we were running a race with Joe Johnston, trying to see who would beat to Atlanta."

"Stella was the baby then," said my wife, looking at her earnestly, "a little fretful, black-eyed baby, and now she is sitting here, a mother, with a child of her own that is so much like what she was then that sometimes I imagine the child is mine, and I am getting ready to make a new run from the yankees."

"May the foul invaders live long, when the devil gets them," said I. "They kept you trotting, and you bore it like a heroine; you have seen a good deal of troublous life, and I'm thankful that now your days are calm and serene."

CHAPTER LXVII.

FAMILY REFORM.

Nature can beat art sometimes. I've been to the theatre afore now, and the players acted the play so natural and sympathetic that I got all tangled up and excited, and would cry or laugh just as they did; but nature can beat art sometimes. Just about sundown, the other evening, while we were all sitting in the piazza, calm and serene, there was a wild shriek down at the corner of the garden, and it was Carl calling, and he said: "Run here to Linton! Linton is killed! Run, papa; run, somebody;" and we did run, and Mrs. Arp and the girls cried, "Oh, mercy! Oh, good Lord!" and all sorts of interjections and conjunctions at every step, and there was a wild and fearful panic when we got to the boy, and he was lying pale and senseless on the rocky ground, with a big limb across his breast. He had fallen about twelve feet from the top of a venerable apple tree that they say was planted by the Indians about sixty years ago. I heaved the old broken limb off of the boy and took him in my arms, and then up the hill to the house, and my escort, oh, my escort! with their cries and screams, demoralized me fearfully. He was a stout lad of thirteen, this grandson of ours, and as tough as a pine-knot, and I knew he was hurt, badly hurt, but I can always keep calm and serene on such occasions, if the women will let me. Laying him gently on the bed, Mrs. Arp ripped his garments with trembling hands and motherly sobbings to find the flowing blood and the gaping wounds and the broken limbs, but they were not there. He was shocked and senseless, and breathed hard and gurgled in his throat, and groaned and sighed, but I had seen those signs before with the other boys, and had faith. And sure enough, in about an hour he came to himself, and looking around upon the excited family, asked what was the matter, and said: "Grandma, I dreamed I was falling from the apple tree." The doctor came about that time and found his arm and shoulder badly bruised and one rib hurt, perhaps fractured, and said he would be awful sore for a day or two, and then get well and be ready for the next skirmish. But Mrs. Arp was not satisfied, and watched him all night, and as he slept she listened to his breathing and felt his pulse and imagined that something was internally wrong. The boy carries his arm in a handkerchief now, and can't go in a washing nor shoot a sling nor climb a tree, and he and Carl have to stay in the house and read story books and look at the pictures. But the like of this has to happen. It is part of a boy's raising. I wasent much account until I fell down a ladder head foremost and was picked up for dead. I told my wife I wouldent give a cent for a boy who had never fell out of an apple, tree or got his arm broke, or his head gashed, or something of the kind. If a man has never had any narrow escapes, or any wounds, or any broken bones, or been thrown from a horse and picked up for dead, what kind of a father will he be? What has he got to tell his little boy, and excite his wonder and admiration? I had lots of mishaps myself, and as I grow older Mrs. Arp says they grow bigger and more numerous. Well, of course! Nobody wants to tell the same old thing the same old way a thousand times. Amplification is a sign of genius. Being knocked down and addled is a big thing; but to be picked up for dead is heroic.

I've got these children to watch now. Mrs. Arp has gone to visit her old home in Gwinnett, and she gave me a whole catalogue of admonitions and ordinations and recapitulations, which I've forgotten already. She has gone to see her brothers and their wives and children, and the dear old home where her father and mother used to wear the parental crown, and had more love and more power than a king. What a sacred temple was that old family room. It was the court where she brought all her childish troubles and got comfort. She remembers every nail in the floor, every brick in the hearth, every knot in the ceiling overhead. She wanted to see the big old oaks in the back yard, under whose shades she played and swung and had her playhouse of broken china. The cooing pigeons made love upon their spreading limbs by day, and the noisy katydids by night. She wanted to see the big old spring at the foot of the hill, for she knew there was no change, no decay, no mortality there. The water is still running, and though the frog and the craw-fish and the spring-lizzard that used to excite her youthful fears, have departed this life intestate, they left children to inherit and enjoy that peaceful, shady spring. The little branch still flows on over its gravelly bed and down into the little fish pond below, and the ripple of its waters still sings that same old song—

"For men may come and men may go,
But I go on forever."

I know that her memory will linger there sweetly, for she used to wade in that branch, and she would like to wade in it again if nobody was looking, but I reckon she won't. There is a 'simmon tree on the hill close by that she used to climb in the fall of the year, for she was as fond of 'simmons as a 'possum, but she will never climb it any more; I reckon she won't. The grape vine swing at the back of the garden and the saplings she used to bend down and ride are gone—all gone; but she doesn't want to ride saplings now. Old Aunt Peggy has gone, too; gone where the good darkies go. She was always old and wrinkled and dried up, but she was faithful unto death, and the children loved her. Nobody knew how old she was. For forty consecutive years she said she was a hundred—no more, no less—always a hundred. But, dearest of all, is the old grave-yard, where "the rude forefathers of the hamlet sleep." I know she will linger there with sweet and sad emotions, for there sleep her nearest and dearest ones—father and mother and brothers and an only sister, and, sweetest of all, a dear little babe of her own. How surely does life and love repeat the scenes of our youth. Hers were fond parents, and there was a flock of children, fair children, all hopeful and happy and loving, and they were ten—just ten. She and I have succeeded them, and we have ten—just ten. We, too, have a cottage home and a spring at the foot of the hill, and a branch for the children to play in, and a fish pond, and big oaks with pigeons cooing on the limbs. Just as they had, we have pea-fowls to scream, and ducks and chickens, and sheep, and cattle, and dogs' bark and cats' purr, and our children and grandchildren come and go; and by and by we will go to sleep and leave them all alone, just as we were left.

And this is right—all right. When we have served our day and generation, then let us go. Let us marshal them the way of life, and give good counsel, and retire in peace and Christian hope of a reunion. Not a reunion like the soldiers have—that comes every year, with diminished numbers—but a reunion in a better land that grows and grows to countless legions, and every year brings new recruits from kindred and from friends. How often do I sit in reverie when I hear of a good parent's, death and dream I hear the glad voices of those who have gone before, as they bring tidings of each other and say, "Our father has come," "Our mother has come at last." What a welcome to the orphan when the angel mother gives the warm embrace and says, "My child, my child! God bless my child!" Some folks don't believe in this, but I do.

I'm going to wallop these boys if they don't mind. I've humored and indulged them until they think there is no willipus wallipus on the plantation. They slipped off and went in a-washing this evening about four o'clock, when the sun was as hot as blazes. I had promised them they might go in late, when the shadows of the willows had covered the pond, and now they say they misunderstood me. Their backs are nearly blistered, and I've a good mind to blister them a little lower down. I would have done it, but Linton has a lame arm and Carl was running at the nose. I see a lame guinea hopping around, and it hops very like a slingshot struck it. They killed a pigeon not long ago, and said they didn't mean to hit it, but was just trying to see how close they could miss it. I found my first and biggest melon plugged in the patch, and, though I didn't believe they would do me that mean, I held a courtmartial and took testimony and looked as fierce and majestic as possible. They declared their innocence and showed a heap of wounded feelings and told how they found our little darkey's knife in the melon patch, and so the little darkey surrendered and confessed, which never was done by a darkey before, and his mother whipped him from Dan to Beersheba, and my boys were discharged with honor and the commendation of the court. Carl is a very good boy by himself, and Linton is good by himself. Each of them work well in single harness, but hitch them together to a wagon and they are bound to break something. I'm going for these chaps while Mrs. Arp is away. I'm for civil service reform now. Their mothers are afar off and I'm the autocrat. I'll teach them how to grabble the goobers before they are ripe.

No, I won't, either, and they know I won't. These boys are mighty good to me. They bring me fresh water from the spring without being told. They black my shoes when I am going to town. They follow me around the farm and help me get roasting ears. They listen to my marvelous stories with an affectionate wonder that flatters my vanity. They borrow my pocket-knife. They find my hat and my walking-stick, and help me dig the potatoes for dinner. They are good company, these boys, now that Jessie has gone. I miss "Jessie, the flower of Dumblane." She is my special comfort when I am ailing or have the blues. She rubs my head and brushes my back hair and talks so loving and kind, and always kisses me good-night after she has said her prayers.

Mrs. Arp will go to meeting Sunday. The same old church is there close by her old home—the church she was raised in and where she went to class-meeting, and heard old Fathers Murphey and Ivy and Norton talk. The church where Judge Longstreet used to preach at quarterly meetings—Judge Longstreet who used to distress old Uncle Allan Turner, a good old man, because the judge would play on the fiddle and flute, and wrote some unheavenly stories in the *Georgia Scenes*. Both of these notable men always found welcome at her father's house, and while the judge was discoursing sweet music in the parlor, old father Turner was walking the piazza, interceding in silent prayer for his forgiveness and reform. There were never two Christian men more unlike than they, but they are both in heaven now, and maybe Uncle Allan has got reconciled to music. We are all a bundle of prejudices, as well as habits, and I am glad to know that the age in which we live to-day is more tolerant that the last.

CHAPTER LXVIII.

Music.

Music is the only employment that is innocent and refining, and that cannot be indulged in to excess. It stands by itself as the peculiar gift of God. It is the only art that is alike common to angels and to men. It has a wonderful compass and variety, and yet from the grandest to the simplest, it is all pleasing and all innocent. Every other pleasure can be carried to dissipation, but not music.

The highest order of music is that which we never hear, but only read about and wonder. It is called the music of the spheres—the grand symphony that is made by the planets and other heavenly bodies coursing around the sun, and which Milton says is heard only by God and the angels. I don't suppose that such creatures as we are, afflicted and limited with original sin, could bear that kind of music. The child that is charmed with a lullaby or soothed to sleep with "Hush, my dear, lie still and slumber," would be frightened at an oratorio from Handel. But musical taste is progressive, like every other good thing.

The time was when I thought "Billy in the low grounds," and "Bonaparte crossing the Rhine," perfectly splendid, but I don't now. I have advanced to a higher grade. By degrees the children have educated me, and as they climb up, I climb a little, too. Time was when I thought "Kathleen Mavourneen" the sweetest song, and my wife, whom I was courting, the sweetest singer in the world. But I don't now—that is, I mean the song. There are sweeter songs. I don't wish to be misunderstood about the singer. No doubt her voice has the same alluring, ensnaring, angelic, elysian sweetness it had forty years ago, more or less, but the fault is in me, for when a man has once been allured, and ensnared, and is getting old and deaf, he loses some of his gushing appreciation. Nevertheless, when her eldest daughter touches the ivory keys and sings Longfellow's beautiful hymn of

"The day is done, and the darkness
Falls from the wings of night,"

my appreciation seems to come back, and it makes me calm and serene

There is nothing in all nature that so proves the goodness of God to his creatures as in giving to them the love of music and the faculty to make it. It is the cheapest and the most universal pleasure. Much of it costs nothing, for we hear it in the winds and waves, the trees, the waterfalls, and from the birds and insects. It is of many kinds, from the pealing anthem that swells the note of praise in Westminster Abbey, down to the plantation harmonies of the old-time darkies around the corn-pile. Between these extremes we have the music of the drama, the concert, the nursery, and the drawing-room.

I was having these thoughts because Mrs. Arp and the children were practicing some church music in the parlor, preparing for Sunday. Some of the family belong to the choir, and it is a good thing to belong to. Choirs have their little musical fusses sometimes, and get in the pouts; but, nevertheless, it is a good place to raise children. It makes them go to church and to Sunday-school, and go early, and if they are facing the congregation they have to keep awake and behave decently, and they do their best to look pretty and sing sweetly. I used to belong to the choir, and it was there Mrs. Arp saw me, and ever and anon heard the sweet strains of my melodious tenor voice. But, alas! that voice has changed to a bass at one end and a falsetto at the other, and "there's a melancholly crack in my laugh."

Young man, young woman, if you have any gifts for music, you had better join the church choir, but if you haven't, don't.

Sacred music is very much varied according to denominations. The Roman Catholic church is the oldest and the richest and has the most passionate music and the finest organs, and embraces a rendering of such intense words as are found in the "Agnus Dei," and "Gloria in Excelsis," and the litany and chants of the old masters. The Protestant church has rejected the dramatic style and confined its music to hymns and psalms of sober temper, and in the main, has done away with the fugue and galloping style of one part chasing another through the vocal harmonies.

I remember when it was the fashion, in fashionable choirs, to give one part several feet the start in the race, and the others would start later and overtake it before they all got to the end of the line. There is a hymn beginning, "I love to steal awhile away," and the tenor would start out with "I love to steal"— and then the alto would prance up with "I love to steal," and then the bass confessed the unfortunate frailty, "I love to steal," and hurried on for fear the first man would steal it all before he got there.

Sacred music is of very ancient origin. Indeed, it is older than the church or the temple, for we find that Moses sang a song when he had crossed the Red Sea, and he said, "I will sing a song unto the Lord, for he is my strength and my salvation," and when he finished his song, Miriam took it up, and she and her maidens sang and made music on timbrels. King David sang all through his psalms, and Isaiah not only sang, but wanted everything to sing, for he says: "Sing, oh ye heavens, for the Lord hath done it. Break forth into singing, oh ye mountains, and every tree, for the Lord hath redeemed Israel."

I was looking over this book that we are now using in our church, a new and beautiful book containing 1,200 hymns, and a tune with written music to every hymn. Here are 360 authors of all Christian denominations. Of these, sixty-one are women, seventy are English Episcopalians, twenty are Scotch Presbyterians, and only eight are American Presbyterians. Eight are Methodists, ten are Baptists, fourteen are Congregationalists, and five are Roman Catholics. The rest are Dissenters, Lutherans, Unitarians, Moravians, Quakers and Independents. Only fifty-four are Americans. Leaving out Isaac Watts and Charles Wesley, most of these hymns were composed by English Episcopalians. Isaac Watts was the founder of hymnology. One hundred and twenty-six of his hymns are in this book. He has been dead 142 years, but we are still singing: "Welcome, Sweet Day of Rest," "How Beauteous Are Their Feet," "When I Can Read My Title Clear," "Before Jehovah's Awful Throne," "Am I a Soldier of the Cross?" and many more of his composing.

He was a very small man with a very large soul. He was only five feet high and weighed less than a hundred pounds, and never married. His hymns are sung all over the Christian world. Our grand-parents and parents, ourselves and our children, have all treasured them and become familiar with them.

Charles Wesley, a Methodist, has thirty-six hymns in this book— most of them inspired from his intense, absorbing love of the Savior —such as "Blow Ye the Trumpet, Blow," and "Jesus, Lover of My

Soul." He was a brother of John Wesley, the founder of Methodism, and came to Georgia with him in 1735.

Rev. John Newton has twenty-six hymns in this collection. What a strange, eventful life was his. Seized and impressed for a seaman on board a man-of-war when he was only nineteen years of age—deserted—was caught, and flogged, and degraded—deserted again, and hired himself to a slave-trading vessel. Four years afterwards he went back to England and married Mary Catlett, the girl he had been loving for years. He then equipped a slaver of his own, and shipped negroes from Africa to the West Indies, and made a fortune.

In a few years he became disgusted with the business, and studied mathematics, Latin, Greek and Hebrew without a teacher. About that time Wesley and Whitfield began their great religious uprising, and he was converted and joined them and went to preaching. When eighty years old he preached three times a week, and when urged to stop on account of his feeble health, he replied: "What! Shall the old African negro trader and blasphemer stop while he can speak? No!" No wonder that the great change inspired him to write those beautiful hymns: "Amazing Grace! How Sweet the Sound;" "One There is Above All Others;" "Glorious Things of Thee Are Spoken;" "Savior, Visit Thy Plantation."

And next comes Cowper—the amiable, lovable, miserable Cowper—whose life was spent in alternating between hope and despair, and who was sent several times to the insane asylum. In his lucid intervals of hope he composed such hymns as "Sometimes a Light Surprises," "There is a Fountain Filled With Blood;" "Oh, For a Closer Walk With God," and many others.

James Montgomery, a Moravian, has twenty-three hymns in this book. His early life was full of trouble. He was indicted, tried and imprisoned for writing a ballad on the fall of the bastile. Soon after his release he wrote an account of the riot at Sheffield, and was again imprisoned. The press had but little freedom in his day, but his gentle, earnest, Christian character finally won for him the regard of his enemies, and he was granted a pension by the crown. There are no hymns in this book sweeter than his. Such, for instance, as "Oh, Where Shall Rest Be Found?" "Prayer is The Soul's Sincere Desire;" "People of The Living God," etc.

Addison, too, that stately, polished writer of essays, found time and inclination to pay poetic tribute to his Maker. There is no poetry more majestic than the hymns beginning, "When All Thy Mercies, Oh, My God," and "The Spacious Firmament On High." And next we have Heber, the gifted bishop of Calcutta, the Christian gentleman, who never knew a want, but, nevertheless, spent his life in charity and missionary work. His world-renowned hymn would have immortalized him, if he had written nothing else.

"From Greenland's Icy Mountains" still stands as the chief of all missionary hymns. He wrote others of exquisite beauty, such as "Brightest and Best of the Sons of the Morning" and "By Cool Siloam's Shady Rill."

Then there were many other composers who did not write much, but wrote exceeding well. There is:

"How Firm a Foundation," by George Keith; "Come Ye Disconsolate," by Thomas Moore, the poet laureate of England; "Awake My Soul," by Medley; "Come Thy Fount of Every Blessing," by Robert Robinson.

Rev. Augustus Toplady has several beautiful hymns, but none compare with his "Rock of Ages Cleft For Me." Sir William Gladstone, the great premier of England, was so much impressed with this hymn that he has translated it into Latin and other languages. Of a later date we find, "Nearer My God to Thee," by Mrs. Adams, an English lady.

The oldest hymn in the book was written by Thomas Sternhold, in 1549. He was groom to Henry VIII. The next oldest is well worth remembrance, for it was written in 1680 by Thomas Ken, and has but one verse, and that verse is sung oftener than any other verse in the world. Its first line is, "Praise God From Whom All Blessings Flow." If Thomas Ken is in the heavenly choir (and we believe he is), what serene comfort does his translated soul enjoy as it listens every Sabbath to his own doxology as it goes up from a million voices and swells heavenward from thousands of organs all over Christendom!

Then we have hymns from Richard Baxter, who was chaplain to Charles II, and resisted the usurpation of Cromwell.

And here we have hymns from Mrs. Charles, the gifted authoress of the Schonberg Cotta stories, and from William Cullen Bryant, our own poet laureate, and Francis S. Key, the author of the "Star Spangled Banner," and from Mrs. Sigourney and John Dryden, another poet laureate of England, and Henry Kirk White, who died in his twenty-first year, but left as his monument "The Star of Bethlehem." Here, too, is the litany by Sir Robert Grant. And here are many hymns from Dr. Muhlenberg, who wrote " I Would Not Live Always."

And now, let me pause to remember that all these men and women are dead. Some have been dead three hundred years, some two hundred and very many one hundred, and some far less, but all are dead. But poetry outlives prose, and a song outlives a sermon. It is a comforting fact that most all of the famous poets have been Christian men and women, and have given to the church some of their sweetest and holiest thoughts in song.

Dr. Oliver W. Holmes and John G. Whittier are both represented in this collection.

But hymns without music lose half their beauty. They are like birds without wings—they cannot fly heavenward.

And now if the choir and congregation will enter into the spirit of these beautiful hymns and sing them with pure religious feeling, it will be acceptable praise. A song without inspiration is music, but it is not praise. Professional choirs who sing for pay, seem to be singing for men and not for God. Such singing is like the funerals that have hired mourners. When the tune fits the sentiment of the hymn, like it was all one creation of genius, it greatly enhances the beauty of both. The Coronation Hymn would not be half so popular if the coronation music were not set to it. And this is one reason why the oratorios of the great masters, such as Handel and Mozart, have never been excelled. They composed both the sentiment and the song.

CHAPTER LXIX.

The Sorrel Hair.

Benson was his name—Tom Benson. He moved to our county and purchased a snug little farm in the valley, about eight miles from town. He had a wife and three children, and a negro man named Dick. When Benson came into the settlement, there was a little cloud came with him—a cloud over his reputation for honesty. It was whispered around that his nabors, who lived near his old home, were willing for him to go, for they said that his hogs and his sheep increased faster than was natural, and theirs decreased in some mysterious manner.

But still, Benson was a member of the church, and, being gifted with language, would sometimes talk and exhort in meeting, and lead in prayer. He was emotional and fervent, and soon made friends in his new home, and the cloud, for a time, dispersed. Mrs. Benson was a woman of good family; she was well mannered and industrious, but had a kind of pleading, pitiful expression, as though she was living under apprehension of trouble. Benson had family prayer night and morning, and always prayed loud, and a good long time; his negro man, Dick, came regularly to prayer, and said amen and amen in good Methodist fashion, but Dick soon got under a cloud, and it got larger and blacker as time rolled on, for the nabors said there was a rogue in the settlement. Chickens were missing, and the mill had been broken open, and Dick had carried chickens to town to sell one Saturday night. The relations between Dick and his master were very confiding—much more so than was usual between master and slave. They were companions, and consulted with each other, and this was after awhile talked about, to Benson's prejudice. If Dick stole chickens and sold them, who had the money? That was the question. Some little debts had followed Benson from his old home, and he had been sued in the Magistrate's Court, and had paid them little by little, and it was a mystery where he got the money, for his crop was not harvested, and he had nothing to sell. But still Benson got along, and met the brethren on the Sabbath with a cheerful face, and prayed and exhorted as usual. There is one other fact—an important fact—that must be mentioned. Benson owed a balance of five hundred dollars of purchase money upon his place, and had been sued for it in the Circuit Court.

Three miles below him, further down in the valley, lived a respectable old gentleman whose name was Montague. He had raised a numerous family, but five of his sons, and as many daughters, were all married, and most of them had settled in the naborhood and were established and comfortable upon farms the old gentleman had given them, for he was quite wealthy. He was a solid man, of primitive habits, a member of the Presbyterian Church, and exemplary in all his conduct, saving the suspicion that he was a little too fond of gold, and when he loaned it exacted too high a rate of interest. He lived off of his "intrust," as he called it, and he firmly believed that his gold was his. His loans were generally made to thrifty, prosperous men, but the poor and the distressed were turned away with the assertion that he did not have a cent in the world. He called his pocket the world, but his money was kept in an old hair trunk.

The weight of many years had dimmed the old man's sight, and almost stopped up his ears. His aged wife was also deaf, but otherwise they were in good health; and almost every Sunday there was a gathering there of children and grandchildren, and the old couple were going down to the grave most happily, considering their wants and their ambition. Sometimes they had one or more of their numerous posterity to stay over night with them, but most generally they were alone in the great big house, and the old man's gold was in the old hair trunk under his bed. His numerous slaves and domestic servants occupied the cabins close by. They were faithful and obedient, for most of them had been born in his household, and knew no king but "master," and no queen but "old mistis," and they were proud of his wealth and his dignity.

One rainy morning in the spring of the year there was a wild alarm in the Montague household. The old hair trunk was gone. Mr. Montague never failed to give a glance that way when he arose. It was his habit as fixed as putting on his garments. He thought at first that his old eyes deceived him, and he stooped down and felt for it with outstretched hand. Hastily dressing himself he looked around the room again and discovered a window up—a back window that looked upon the garden. It had not been raised for months. His wife had noticed his unusual manner and got up hastily and heard his excited voice and saw his misery as he exclaimed, "Gone—it's gone—the trunk—look at the window!" and he sank down in pitiful despair. The old lady hurried to the open window and looked upon the ground and saw nothing but a box—an old box that the robber had stood upon. Tottering to the door, she screamed to the servants and they came and they screamed, too, and sounded the alarm; then came the negroes generally from out their cabins, for it was not yet sunrise, and the wild panic began. The ball was opened. "Fore God deys stole old master's trunk, fore God dey is—tuck it outen de winder—fore God dey did!" "Run Bob, run Jesse, run Jake, run children, run for Mas John and Mas Tom and Mas George—run for everybody and tell 'em come quick—run, honey, don't stop nary minit!" And they did run. In less than an hour the children and many nabors came in hot haste; some on foot and some on horseback, and all wild with desperate energy to catch the robbers. It did not take long to track them through the garden and over the garden fence and through the corn patch to the woods that bordered the clearing. And there in the undergrowth of oak and pine bushes was the trunk—the old hair trunk. It was wide open, and there was no more money in it than there was in the old man's "world." His seven thousand dollars in gold was gone. He had counted it all the day before, and the week before, and knew the amount. The old man tottered feebly to the scene and cried. The shock was too much for him. His daughters led him back sorrowfully to the house, and as he bowed along he shook his head and exclaimed, "Benson! Tom Benson did it!" and he kept up the refrain, and as the crowd passed to and fro, Benson was on every tongue, and the darkies took it up and cried "Benson," on the run.

Old Mr. Montague had a reason for suspecting Benson. About two weeks before the robbery Benson called one morning and requested a loan of five hundred dollars, wherewith to lift that mortgage off his land and save it from sale under the sheriff's hammer. He pleaded his great necessity in touching language, and when the old man declared he did not have a cent in the "world," he grew desperate with disappointment, and as he rose to go he pointed his finger at him and said: "I know you have got it, and ten times over, and God Almighty will curse you with it yet before you die," and he left him greatly irritated.

The old man had known somewhat of Benson long years before when they both lived in the same county, and he did not like him. Benson had served on a jury once when the old man had a case in court, and the jury found against him on a plea of usury, and the old man lost his "intrust." He did not like his methods nor his Methodism. He could not think of any other man in all his acquaintance who was mean enough and smart enough to commit the robbery, and outside of this acquaintance it was not possible for any one to know he had any money, or where the trunk was kept. And Dick, the black rascal! Dick had visited Mr. Montague's premises more than once on Sundays, and had come up to the old lady's door and saluted her, and he could have seen the trunk under the bed, and told his master where it was.

Thus the account stood, and while the more thoughtful nabors were looking around the trunk in the woods, they suddenly discovered tracks—tracks of a horse and a mule. They found where the animals had been hitched while the robbers went after the trunk, and very near by where the mule was tied, there was a small hickory sapling cut off about knee high with a slanting stroke of the axe. It had been long done and the top edge was hard and dry and sharp, and there on the point of it was a little patch of sorrel hair. The mule had skinned his leg and left the mark behind. This discovery settled it and removed all doubts, for Benson had a bay horse and a sorrel mule. Benson and Dick were the robbers.

With hurried haste and fierce determination the male members of the Montague household and their resolute nabors mounted their steeds and went galloping up the valley road to Benson's house. Without ceremony or invitation they entered his stable lot and brought out the sorrel mule, and on close inspection found a skinned place on his knee, and the sorrel hair was all of a color. Benson and Dick were there and looked on with amazement, either feigned or real. Poor Mrs. Benson stood in her door with clasped hands, and looked the picture of alarm and despair. The children stood by their mother and clung to her garments as they looked in her face and then at the crowd of desperate men, who had invaded the sacred precincts of their home.

The leader of the crowd made a motion to his companions and uttered between his teeth, "Take them." Benson and Dick were seized and tied and carried hastily away. They were mounted upon the mule and the bay, and the party were soon far beyond the cries and shrieks of mother and children. An hour's ride found them in a lonely dell back of the Montague farm, and there they dismounted and prepared their victims for confession and restitution, or otherwise for the scourge. It was in vain that Benson and Dick protested their innocence and plead for mercy. They were stripped and pinioned to two trees not far from each other, and as stroke after stroke brought the warm blood spurting from their veins, they called upon God for mercy, for man had none. "Oh, my God," groaned Benson, as the tears ran down his face. "Oh, Mas Tom, dey is killin' of me," screamed Dick. "Be a man, Dick, for Jesus' sake," replied Benson; and so the scourge went on until the avengers began to fear for the lives of their victims and held a whispered consultation. One of the more considerate walked away quietly, and carelessly took another look at the scar on the mule. Returning to Benson he told him how much better it would be for him to give up the gold, and promised that he should not be prosecuted if he would do so; but Benson maintained his innocence with prayers and tears, and the avengers were outdone. Salt water had been brought to garnish their wounds, and half dead with pain the victims were remounted and allowed to go home. It was a sad return to a sadder hearthstone. During the next few weeks, while Benson and Dick were being tenderly nursed and were slowly recovering, this bold and daring robbery was the all absorbing topic of the country and the town. There were not a few who doubted Benson's guilt, and who openly denounced the brutal whipping, but the Montague family were influential in church and State, and Benson's naborhood was almost solid against him. They believed in his guilt. As soon as he was able to ride in a buggy he went to town with his wife and there sent for the sheriff and paid off that mortgage with five hundred dollars in gold. This capped the climax. This made the Montagues desperate. The night afterwards fifteen masked and mounted men visited his house again, and seizing Benson and Dick, gagged and tied and blindfolded them and took them away to parts unknown. They were kept hidden for a week, and were alternately whipped and starved, and every day brought new horrors. Benson endured it all with heroism, but Dick gave up repeatedly, and when under the excrutiating lash would promise to tell it all if they would stop. Then he would confess his guilt and declare that "Mas Tom made him go, and Mas Tom had de money, but he didn't know whar he hid it." "Now Dick—now Dick," Benson would say, "speak the truth if they kill you—you know that ain't so, is it, Dick? Would you tell a lie on your best friend, Dick?" And Dick would reply: "Oh, Mas Tom, dey will kill me if I don't tell somefin." As a last resort they built up a brush-heap and laid their victims on it and set it on fire. The flames leaped quickly through the dry fagots and licked their clothes, and next their skin, and they were hastily pulled off the heap and their burning garments drenched with water, and still they gave no sign. This was the last, and the victims were still alive. They were kept two more days to recover the life that was nearly gone, and then during the darkness of the following night were returned again to their home.

Some two months after this the Circuit Court convened in the county town, and certain members of the Montague family attended and went before the Grand Jury. They exhibited the patch of sorrel hair and recited the other evidences of guilt, and procured a true bill for robbery and burglary in the night-time. Benson and Dick were arrested, and for lack of friends were put in jail. In due time Benson was put on trial. An able counselor and eloquent advocate was employed by him—a lawyer who had doubts of his guilt and sympathized with his misfortune. The prosecution was vigorously urged and as vigorously defended, and resulted in a verdict of guilty, for the patch of sorrel hair was in the way, and proved fatal to liberty. The case was carried to the Supreme Court of the State, and the verdict affirmed, and Benson was sentenced to the penitentiary for twenty years. Alas for the broken-hearted wife and weeping children! The little farm was seized and sold for costs of the prosecution. The father went off in chains one way and his wife and children another. They removed to Mississippi where Mrs. Benson had kindred, who though they were poor, gave her a kind and welcome home.

Benson had served three years of his term. He was growing old, and prematurely gray, and was known among the convicts as Jeremiah, for his lamentations were sad and frequent. He grieved most of all because of the taint that his conviction entailed upon his children, and never failed to assert his innocence to visitors. One day, about this time, his counsel received a letter—a very remarkable letter—written and signed by a man whose name is Robinson. It was written in a dungeon—the dungeon of a jail in a distant county in this State. It was well written, and was scholarly in language, and said, in substance, that the writer was charged with robbery and burglary, and the evidence was conclusive, and he was only waiting the setting of the court to plead guilty and begin the term of his service of twenty years in the penitentiary. But there was a man there by the name of Benson whom he did not want to meet, for Benson was serving and suffering for a crime he did not commit, and if his counsel would visit the writer, sufficient evidence would be furnished to establish his innocence. The letter was of such a character as to merit confidence and demand immediate attention. The counsel lost no time in making the journey. When he arrived and was admitted to the prisoner's cell, he found a gentleman of culture and impressive manner—a man who looked more like a poet than a felon. He was surrounded by many evidences of refinement. Shakspeare and Byron, and various novels were upon his table. His clothing was of fine quality, and sat well upon his well formed person. The counsel was not long in receiving his confession, for it was a confession of his own guilt in committing the Montague robbery. He was educated as a physician, he said, and received his diploma from a Virginia college. In his youth he had become fascinated with the romances that portrayed a brigand's life, and after removing to St. Louis he was induced by some fellows of kindred minds to join in a series of adventures, whereby the rich and miserly could be made to disgorge, and the poor and needy be lifted up. "We have," said he, "distributed thousands and thousands of dollars in this way and saved but little for ourselves, for we enjoyed the excitement and peril of our calling more than we enjoyed the booty. A few years ago our line of service was from St. Louis to Pensacola, and the old man Montague was directly on the route. We learned that he was a miser and that he hoarded his gold. The week before he was robbed my pal and I stayed over night with him, for he was accustomed to entertain travelers. I was riding a blooded Kentucky mare and my companion was well mounted on a fine large sorrel mule. That night we made observations of the plan of the house and the surroundings. The next morning after breakfast I gave the old man a twenty-dollar gold piece to pay our bill, and I saw he was pleased to handle it. I saw him go to his bedroom and unlock the old hair trunk and get the change, and he had to untie a bag of coin to get it; then he produced a small old leather-bound book which he said was his travelers' book. Indeed it had his name rudely written upon the cover. He asked our names, and I gave him mine as William Thompson, of Kentucky. He wrote it down with a pencil at the top of a page, and spelled my name without an "h" or a "p" and marked it "paid" and left out the "i" in that word. I remember these things distinctly. We traveled on to a little village a few miles away and remained there until the dark of the moon. We left one evening under pretense of visiting some friends in the country and then continuing our journey southward, but by the time it was dark we reversed our course, and by ten o'clock had passed old Montague's house, and secreted ourselves in the woods a quarter of a mile back. There we waited until the hour when deep sleep falleth upon man. With our dark lantern it was easy to find our way to the house and the window, and still easier in our stockings to take the trunk from under the bed where two old deaf persons were sleeping. Now, in that trunk we found the seven thousand dollars in gold, and we found the two left-hand halves of two one hundred dollar bills on the Bank of the State of Georgia. These two halves I have kept and they will be sent you in a few days. They are marked letter A, and one is numbered 2,096, and the other 2,097. I have here the Supreme Court reports of this State that contains the sworn testimony of old man Montague, and he does not mention these bills. He says he lost nothing but gold; but he did, and he knew he did, and no doubt put the officers of the bank upon notice. I suppose he had sent off the other halves in a letter and was waiting to hear from them before he sent these. Now, my dear sir, what more no you want? Is this not enough to release Benson?"

It surely is, said the counsel. He sent the jailer for a magistrate and had Dr. Robinson sworn to his confession, and was preparing to leave when the doctor arose and said: "One more thing, my dear sir. I have been here long enough to review my life and consider my great mistake. I have not done bodily harm to any one in pursuing my unlawful avocation, but I have brought dishonor upon my only child. She has no mother and is living with her grandmother, and they know nothing of my manner of life. It has been two years since I saw them, but they have not suffered for anything. My gold watch and chain are very valuable, and I will have them sent you so that you may send them to her. I shall never see her again," and his voice trembled and fell as he uttered the last sentence.

The counsel learned that Robinson had lately robbed an old man in that neighborhood of four thousand dollars, and had blundered in his boldness, for he was pursued, surrounded and caught with the money on his person. The twenty years' sentence would about wind up his life, and he knew it and was resigned to his fate. He had taken his chances and lost.

In a few days after the attorney had returned to his home, he received a letter enclosing the half bills. The letter was mailed in Louisville, Ky., and said this only: "By direction of my friend, I enclose you these half bills." There was no signature. He immediately interviewed Montague's attorneys and submitted evidence to them. They began the perusal of the long confession with a careless incredulity, but as they read along a change came over them—a change from doubt to conviction—and when the half bills were exhibited, the elder attorney said with emotion: "He is innocent. No man knew of those half bills but Mr. Montague and myself. I charged him to keep it a secret, for I thought the robber would seek to collect them from the bank, and it would give us a clue to the gold." Let it be mentioned here that on the trial of Benson he was unable to prove the fact that Mrs. Benson's father had sent her the five hundred dollars that saved the farm from sale. He was old and bedridden, and could not attend court, for he lived a hundred miles away and the friend who brought the money was on his way to the West, and could not be heard from in time. So the gold that he paid the sheriff remained unaccounted for and was a weight in the scale of evidence—a weight not as heavy as the little patch of sorrel hair, but with both together, his conviction was sealed.

Next morning, which was Sunday, the counsel on both sides went down to Montague's. Sons and sons-in-law had gathered there as usual to spend the day and comfort the aged ancestors. In due time the lawyers made known their mission and exhibited all their proofs.

The traveler's book was called for, and there at the top of a page was Wm. Thompson's name, and the spelling was just as it was sworn to, and the date was correct, and the half bills were identified, for the old man had made a cross mark upon the corner of each. The children were all reluctantly convinced, but the old man shook his head solemnly and declared it all a lawyer's trick. "If the travelers took my money," said he, "Benson told them where it was, and Benson helped them." He refused utterly to sign a petition to the governor for Benson's release, but the sons and sons-in-law all signed it after an assurance that Benson's counsel would not advise or take a fee to sue or prosecute them for damages, for by this time it was pretty well known who the masked men were.

Benson's attorney proceeded next day to Milledgeville, which was then the State capital. Howell Cobb was the Governor—a man of great tenderness of heart—and when the whole case was made fully known to him, he said with much feeling: "The poor old man; what sufferings of mind and body he has endured. I have noticed him every time I have visited the convicts, and wondered if there was not possibly some mistake. He had a pleading and heart-broken look. Let us go there at once and release him."

When the warden called Benson to them, it was with a choking utterance that the governor made known their mission. It came upon the poor man with a shock of surprise and joy that sunk him to his knees, and he wept like a child. "The Lord be praised!" he exclaimed. "I said that though He slay me, yet would I trust in Him. Oh, my wife and my children! Thank God, thank God, for His mercy endureth forever!" His rhapsody knew no bounds, and his fellow-prisoners stopped their work to listen and to wonder. Benson's striped garments were soon discarded and he was clothed in a decent citizen's dress. With glad emotion he bade good-bye to all, taking each by the hand and telling them to trust in God and do right. On arriving at his county town where he was tried and convicted, he spent a day in meeting the few friends he had there, and then with the means furnished by the Governor and his counsel, continued his journey to Mississippi in search of his family.

Some six months afterwards his counsel were surprised by an unexpected visit from him. He looked once more like a man, and was clean shaved and well dressed and had less stoop in his broad shoulders than when they saw him last. It did not take him long to disclose his business. He had a letter from an eminent lawyer of Mississippi, advising a suit to be brought in the United States Court against his lynchers, the Montagues and their clan, for damages. His former counsel, of course, declined his case which was no more than he expected, and he went to Marietta, where the Federal Court was held, and there procured the services of an able jurist who at once filed fifteen separate actions against fifteen men, and in each action had the other fourteen summoned as witnesses by the United States Marshal. Each man was sued for ten thousand dollars damages for his arrest and imprisonment and maltreatment while their prisoner.

What a consternation there was in the Montague settlement when the Marshal served those writs! What a shaking and quaking of dry bones! With what haste and alarm did they hurry to town and seek conference with their lawyers. But they found little comfort. The lawyers seemed helpless, for they knew the power and the rigor of the Federal Court. They knew the inflexible integrity and the stern justice of the old judge who presided, and they knew the ability and vigor of Benson's counsel. After much consultation it was agreed that the Montague lawyers should visit Marietta and, if possible, effect a compromise and take the cases out of court.

In this they succeeded. Fifteen thousand dollars was paid over to Benson's counsel without delay. He took one third of it for his fee and Benson returned to his family with ten thousand dollars in his pocket. With this sum he purchased another farm and was living happily with his wife and children when last heard from. And Dick was there—Dick who was released without trial, had followed his mistress and was her faithful and trusty friend during his master's imprisonment. We do not know, but can only imagine, how he rejoiced with her and her children when Benson surprised the long bereaved household with his presence.

But what of Dr. Robinson, the bold and dashing brigand—the dupe of such romances as Jack Sheppherd and the Robber Clifton and the Italian bandit? In due time he was sent to the penitentiary for twenty years. His culture and his bearing and good conduct soon gave him prominence and favor with the warden. He gave the convicts good advice and set them a good example. He organized a Sabbath-school and became fond of the Scriptures. He sought to make amends for his past conduct by reclaiming the bad men within the prison walls. Time and again he had opportunities to escape, but he would not use them. He was urged to ask for a pardon from the Governor, but he refused, and even intimated that he would not accept it if offered to him, for he declared he had a mission to accomplish and there was work for him to do that nobody else would do.

Time rolled on—Robinson had been in service about three years. He had ministered, like a good Samaritan, among his fellow-prisoners. He nursed them when sick, and though there was a nominal physician who was paid by the Government, Dr. Robinson was the real one who used his professional skill and knowledge among them.

About this time the war broke out between the States, and when a few years after, Sherman made his march to the sea and was fast approaching Milledgeville, Governor Brown went down to the penitentiary and made the convicts a speech. He told them of the wrongs our people had suffered, and of the invasion of our State by armed forces who were burning and destroying everything in their path. He pictured to them the utter desolation of those whom Sherman left behind him, and how helpless women and children were fleeing for their lives to escape the brutality of foreign hirelings. He told them he was going to discharge them all and turn them out, and that it did not follow that they were not patriots because they were convicts. And he hoped and believed they would stand up, fight for and defend their State and their people and kindred.

With a wild hurrah, Dr. Robinson threw up his hat and shouted: "To arms, to arms, ye brave!" He had the kettle-drum beat for volunteers, and organized a company of 160 men, and was unanimously elected captain. Their stripes were discarded and soldiers' clothes were furnished and guns placed in their hands, and they marched forth freemen and patriots, and joined the State troops and fought manfully and well, but their efforts were all in vain to arrest the onward march of the foe. When Governor Brown resumed the occupation of the State capital, and the war was over, Dr. Robinson returned singly and alone to serve out his sentence, but was refused admittance. "No, sir," said the Governor, with much feeling. "No, sir, you have no business there, doctor, for your patients are all gone."

A few years ago the writer of this reminiscence had a letter from a friend in St. Louis. "My office," said he, "is next door to that of Dr. Robinson, well known to you as Montague's robber. He is practicing his profession with success in the city. His daughter is happily married, and he lives with her, and is highly esteemed."

www.ingramcontent.com/pod-product-compliance
Lightning Source LLC
Chambersburg PA
CBHW030310240426
43673CB00040B/1123